David Bird

52 BRIDGE MISTAKES TO AVOID

AN HONORS BOOK FROM MASTER POINT PRESS

Honors Books is an imprint of Master Point Press. All contents, editing and design (excluding cover design) are the sole responsibility of the author.

Master Point Press
331 Douglas Ave.
Toronto, Ontario, Canada
M5M 1H2
(416) 781-0351

Email: info@masterpointpress.com

Websites: www.masterpointpress.com
www.bridgeblogging.com
www.teachbridge.com
www.ebooksbridge.com

ISBN: 978-1-77140-151-7

Layout and Editing: David Bird
Cover Design: Olena S. Sullivan/New Mediatrix

2 3 4 5 6   18 17 16 15

CONTENTS

Introduction

Why are the world's top players so successful? They spend a long time building and remembering their complex bidding systems. They acquire a host of cardplay and defensive techniques. They have also played many thousands of deals and feel they have 'been there before' when facing some tricky situation.

There is another reason for their success. They make many fewer basic mistakes! Players at a less exalted level tend to make the same mistakes over and over again throughout their bridge careers. In this book we will see many of the most frequently made mistakes – in the bidding, play and defense. Each type of mistake will be illustrated by several deals where the original player went wrong. Every chapter will end with some Tips, to help you to avoid making such errors yourself.

In the first section, Mistakes in the Bidding, I have used deals from high-level tournament play, including world championships. I watch a lot of top-class bridge, commentating on Bridge Base Online. The cardplay and the defense are usually excellent but it's amazing how often the players surprise the kibitzers with a bid or call that seems to be a clear mistake. Experts make such errors less often than the rest of us but I think you will find it instructive to look at these wayward decisions. Try to analyze why the bid was wrong before reading my own thoughts on the matter. I do not name the famous players involved because this would add nothing to the instructive value. However, I will specify the match or tournament to add authenticity. When it comes to declarer play and defense, expert mistakes are rarer. Most of the time I will illustrate the various mistakes with constructed deals, or deals from a lower level of play.

The more of these 52 common mistakes you can remove from your game, the better your results will be. Mind you, it's just possible that someone out there will finish the book and think: 'Well, I'd never make any of those mistakes'. If so, I look forward to watching you in the next Bermuda Bowl!

David Bird

This book is dedicated to my fabulous
and ever-tolerant wife for 40 years,
the great Thelma.

PART I

Mistakes in the bidding

Board	Contract	By	Tricks	Score	IMPs
3	5♣X	S	6	¦ 1100	¦ 15

Mistake 1

Unsound penalty doubles

Judging whether to make a penalty double is not as easy as you may think. In this chapter we will look at some unsuccessful penalty doubles and try to analyze why the player should have known that it was not the right moment for such an action.

We'll begin with a type of double that you will see countless times, particularly in the less experienced reaches of the game:

N-S Vul. Dealer North

	North	
	♠ 7 3 2 ♡ 5 ◇ A K J 10 7 3 2 ♣ A 6	
West ♠ 8 5 ♡ A 10 6 4 ◇ Q 9 6 ♣ K Q 4 3	N W E S	**East** ♠ K Q 10 9 6 ♡ Q 9 8 3 ◇ — ♣ 10 8 5 2
	♠ A J 4 ♡ K J 7 2 ◇ 8 5 4 ♣ J 9 7	

West	North	East	South
—	1◇	1♠	1NT
pass	3NT	pass	pass
dbl	all pass		

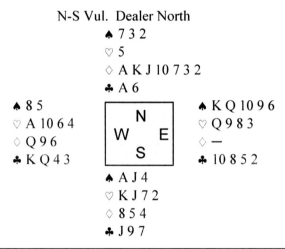

West, who had resisted doubling 1NT, was very happy to double 3NT on the next round. He led the ♠8 to East's ♠Q, ducked by declarer.

At Trick 2, East switched to the ♡Q in the hope that the defenders might enjoy four tricks there. (This was optimistic after declarer's spade duck at Trick 1.) The queen was covered by the king and ace and West returned a heart, declarer winning with the ♡J. A diamond to the ace revealed the 3-0 break. Declarer finessed the ♠J and took the marked finesse of the ◇J to bring in that suit. Seven diamonds, two spades, one heart and one club gave him two overtricks and a score of +1150.

'I had to double after your overcall,' West exclaimed. 'I held 11 points!'

We cannot condemn West's double merely on account of an adverse entry on the score-sheet. We must try to write down a few reasons why he should not have doubled. Think of some yourself before reading my own suggestions.

- North obviously held strong diamonds and West's ♢Q96 sat under them
- Nothing had forced North-South to bid 3NT. They obviously thought they could make it and West had no surprise for them
- If 3NT went down, it would be a good score for East-West anyway
- South's spade honors would sit over East's holding
- An overcall by partner does not promise any defensive strength. West should have paid more attention to the opponents' bidding.

The next deal comes from the semi-finals of a USA2 under-21 trials.

N-S Vul. Dealer North

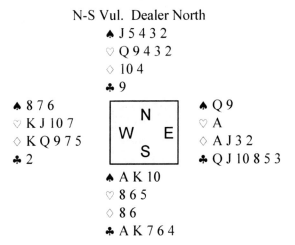

	♠ J 5 4 3 2 ♡ Q 9 4 3 2 ♢ 10 4 ♣ 9	
♠ 8 7 6 ♡ K J 10 7 ♢ K Q 9 7 5 ♣ 2	N / W E / S	♠ Q 9 ♡ A ♢ A J 3 2 ♣ Q J 10 8 5 3
	♠ A K 10 ♡ 8 6 5 ♢ 8 6 ♣ A K 7 6 4	

West	North	East	South
—	pass	1♣	pass
1♡	pass	2♣	pass
pass	2♠	3♣	dbl
3♢	pass	pass	dbl
all pass			

North led the ♣9 against 3♢ doubled. South won with the ♣K and returned the ♣7. Declarer ruffed with the ◇K and was not pressed thereafter to record three doubled overtricks for +770. What did you make of South's two penalty doubles?

The double of 3♣ would appeal to some, although the risk of a red-suit removal was evident. The subsequent double of 3◇ was… well, I mustn't be rude, particularly as they were juniors. Let's just say that it was poorly judged. North had not been able to overcall 1♠, yet he subsequently contested the part-score with 2♠. What should South make of that? North was likely to hold a shapely hand with very few points. Consequently, there was every chance that one of the opponents would have a singleton spade (not so, in fact). How many clubs did South think were going to stand up against 3◇, when West had pulled the double of 3♣ to 3◇? At most one. So, South was doubling 3◇ with a probable two tricks in his hand, opposite a partner who might have no defense whatsoever.

This was the auction at the other table:

West	North	East	South
	pass	1♣	1NT
dbl	2♣	pass	2◇
dbl	2♡	dbl	2♠
dbl	all pass		

West made a slightly risky double of 1NT. The defenders were then caught in a 'doubling rhythm'. I can't see why East should double 2♡ (which can be made). I certainly don't understand for a moment why West thought he should double 2♠. Had he not already shown his hand to the full? Eight tricks were easily made, for another 670 in the minus column, and the total cost was 16 IMPs.

Let's look at something different, a spectacularly unsuccessful double of a Stayman bid. It comes from a match between England and the Netherlands.

N-S Vul. Dealer West

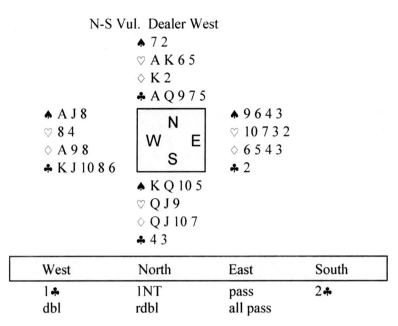

	♠ 7 2 ♡ A K 6 5 ◇ K 2 ♣ A Q 9 7 5	
♠ A J 8 ♡ 8 4 ◇ A 9 8 ♣ K J 10 8 6	N W E S	♠ 9 6 4 3 ♡ 10 7 3 2 ◇ 6 5 4 3 ♣ 2
	♠ K Q 10 5 ♡ Q J 9 ◇ Q J 10 7 ♣ 4 3	

West	North	East	South
1♣	1NT	pass	2♣
dbl	rdbl	all pass	

The England West decided he was worth a lead-directing double of South's Stayman bid. North promptly redoubled, to show interest in playing in that contract. Look at the diagram. How many tricks do you think the Netherlands South made?

The ♡8 lead went to the ten and queen. Declarer led a trump, West inserting the ♣10 and dummy's ♣Q winning. When the ◇K was led, West captured immediately and returned his remaining heart. Declarer won with the nine and played two more diamond winners, throwing a spade from dummy. West ruffed the next diamond with the ♣6, overruffed with the ♣7.

These cards remained in play:

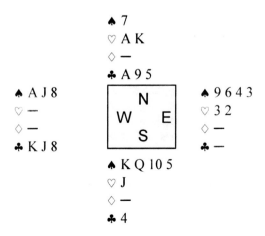

	♠ 7 ♡ A K ◇ – ♣ A 9 5	
♠ A J 8 ♡ – ◇ – ♣ K J 8	N W E S	♠ 9 6 4 3 ♡ 3 2 ◇ – ♣ –
	♠ K Q 10 5 ♡ J ◇ – ♣ 4	

A spade went to the king and ace. When West returned the ♣K, declarer played the ♣5 from dummy. West could not make another trick, whichever card he returned! He eventually scored the ♢A, the ♠A and only one trump trick from his ♣KJ1086. Declarer made two redoubled overtricks, entering +1560 on his score-card. That was 14 IMPs compared with +630.

It's an amusing story but our purpose here is to examine the penalty double of the Stayman 2♣. Was it simply unlucky or was it a bad double? This is how I see it:

- There was limited value in asking for a club lead, particularly if the opponents ended in a suit contract. West had already bid clubs and his holding was not particularly wonderful.
- The 1NT overcall warned West that good clubs sat over him.
- There was no little chance that partner could contest in clubs
- Doubling a Stayman bid gives the next player extra options.

The next deal is from a round-of-16 match in the 2014 Spingold:

N-S Vul. Dealer South

	North	
	♠ 3 ♡ J 10 9 7 6 3 ♢ 8 5 3 ♣ K J 6	
West ♠ K Q 10 7 ♡ 4 ♢ K J 10 9 7 ♣ A Q 8	N / W E / S	**East** ♠ 9 8 6 4 2 ♡ A 5 ♢ A Q 4 2 ♣ 9 3
	♠ A J 5 ♡ K Q 8 2 ♢ 6 ♣ 10 7 5 4 2	

West	North	East	South
—	—	—	pass
1♢	pass	1♠	dbl
4♠	5♡	5♠	dbl
all pass			

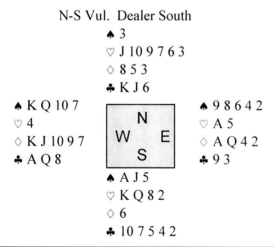

South led the ♢6 to declarer's ace and a trump was played to the king. A heart back to the ace and a second trump saw South rising with the ace. When he switched to a club, declarer rose with the ♣A, drew the last trump and claimed an overtrick for +1050. That was 9 IMPs away compared with

4♠+2 for +680 at the other table.

To avoid making such doubles ourselves, we must sit back and consider exactly why South's final double was a clear-cut mistake. Ponder on the matter before looking at my reasons.

This is how I see it:

- North held long hearts but insufficient strength to overcall 1♡ (or 2♡). It was clear that he had very few points.
- The longer North's hearts were, the less defensive trick potential there was in South's ♡KQ82.
- South's defensive values were no more than his ♠AJ5, which could well be worth only one trick
- North's 5♡ was surely going down, so East's 5♠ was bid to make.
- If East had misjudged and 5♠ was going one down, this would be a good board for North-South anyway.

The next deal arose during an NTU semi-final in China:

Both Vul. Dealer East

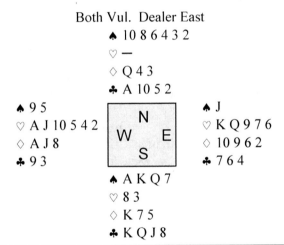

	♠ 10 8 6 4 3 2 ♡ — ♢ Q 4 3 ♣ A 10 5 2	
♠ 9 5 ♡ A J 10 5 4 2 ♢ A J 8 ♣ 9 3	N W E S	♠ J ♡ K Q 9 7 6 ♢ 10 9 6 2 ♣ 7 6 4
	♠ A K Q 7 ♡ 8 3 ♢ K 7 5 ♣ K Q J 8	

West	North	East	South
—	—	pass	1NT
2♡	2♠	3♡	3♠
pass	4♠	pass	pass
dbl	all pass		

An overtrick was easily made, for +990. It was a poor double because the game was freely bid, albeit after an apparent sign-off by North on the first round. The defenders' hearts would be worth little, since an early ruff was likely. West's main defense lay in diamonds and her partner's single heart raise did not promise anything much in addition. West had no 'surprise' for declarer and could expect a good board anyway if 4♠ went down.

The last penalty double to receive our inspection arose in a European Championship match, a good while ago, between England and Finland:

N-S Vul. Dealer South

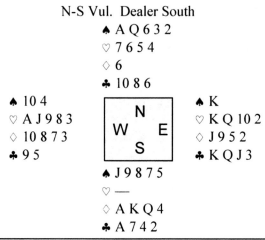

North:
♠ A Q 6 3 2
♡ 7 6 5 4
◇ 6
♣ 10 8 6

West:
♠ 10 4
♡ A J 9 8 3
◇ 10 8 7 3
♣ 9 5

East:
♠ K
♡ K Q 10 2
◇ J 9 5 2
♣ K Q J 3

South:
♠ J 9 8 7 5
♡ —
◇ A K Q 4
♣ A 7 4 2

West	North	East	South
—	—	—	1♠
pass	3♠	dbl	pass
4♡	pass	pass	4♠
pass	pass	dbl	all pass

Tony Forrester (South) ruffed the ♡A lead and played a trump to the ace, felling East's king. He then made the remaining tricks on a cross-ruff. That was three doubled overtricks and an unusual route to the score of +1390.

Why did the Finland East double 4♠? He may have thought it was a sacrifice because Forrester had not bid 4♠ on the previous round. Even on a good hand such as South held, though, there was no need to bid 4♠ immediately when 3♠ had been doubled. If anything, East held less defense than his partner would expect for the original take-out double at quite a high-level. If West did have the hoped-for two defensive tricks, he would have doubled himself. Finally, East's ♠K was likely to lie under the ace in the South hand (it did not, in fact).

The various penalty doubles we have seen were very poor examples, each with several arguments against them. Most unwise penalty doubles have only one or two pointers against them. If you look back and fix in your mind the sort of reasons why these penalty doubles were unproductive, there is every chance that you won't make similar doubles yourself. A few of my partners will think I should do the same!

Tips to avoid Mistake 1

(Making unsound penalty doubles)

- Do not double a freely bid game simply because you have a lot of points. The opponents will have distribution to justify their auction.
- Be more inclined to double when you have an unexpected surprise for declarer, such as a bad trump break.
- Do not double on the basis that your partner has overcalled. An overcall does not promise anything much in defense.
- Do not double when you will get a good result anyway if they have overbid and are going one off.

Mistake 2

Unwarranted Gambling

Many points are thrown away by entering the auction at a dangerous time, in the hope that partner will have a fit for you. We are about to see some examples of this from top-level play. As in the previous chapter, there will be no profit from this exercise unless we try to analyze why the bids were wrong.

The first deal comes from the final stages of the 2014 European Championship, with England facing Norway:

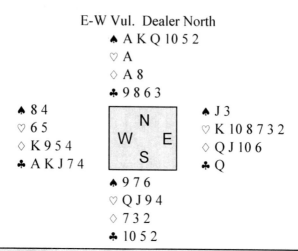

E-W Vul. Dealer North

	North	
	♠ A K Q 10 5 2 ♡ A ◇ A 8 ♣ 9 8 6 3	
West ♠ 8 4 ♡ 6 5 ◇ K 9 5 4 ♣ A K J 7 4	N / W E / S	**East** ♠ J 3 ♡ K 10 8 7 3 2 ◇ Q J 10 6 ♣ Q
	South ♠ 9 7 6 ♡ Q J 9 4 ◇ 7 3 2 ♣ 10 5 2	

West	North	East	South
–	1♠	pass	pass
2♣	3♠	4♡	pass
pass	dbl	all pass	

The England East went 800 down, losing 14 IMPs against 4♠ two down at the other table. Why was East's 4♡ a mistake? This is how I see it:

- East's suit is weak, with no guarantee of support opposite. The bid is a huge gamble and may be very expensive when vulnerable.
- He has only one card in partner's suit.
- The bid will cause no problems for the opponents.
- If he wanted to bid his hearts, he should have overcalled 2♡ on the first round rather than entering at a high-level.

The next dubious intervention comes from a quarter-final of the 2013 Bermuda Bowl, with Canada sitting East-West against USA1:

N-S Vul. Dealer West

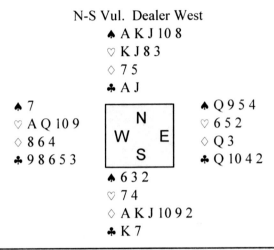

	♠ A K J 10 8 ♡ K J 8 3 ◇ 7 5 ♣ A J	
♠ 7 ♡ A Q 10 9 ◇ 8 6 4 ♣ 9 8 6 5 3	N W E S	♠ Q 9 5 4 ♡ 6 5 2 ◇ Q 3 ♣ Q 10 4 2
	♠ 6 3 2 ♡ 7 4 ◇ A K J 10 9 2 ♣ K 7	

West	North	East	South
pass	1♠	pass	2◇
2♡	dbl	all pass	

What do you make of West's 2♡ overcall? The vulnerability was favorable and he was a passed hand. Yes, but such a risky lead-directing overcall should be considered only at matchpoints, where a heart lead might save an expensive overtrick. As I see it, bidding 2♡ on that hand is a wild gamble at IMPs. The bid may help the opposing declarer to place the cards. It might also lead to an unwarranted sacrifice from your partner if he places you with a more shapely hand, albeit weak in values.

North was able to double for penalties and the contract went five down for 1100. At the other table, North-South bid ambitiously to 6♠ and went three down for a loss of 16 IMPs. They say it is good luck when you have two bad results on the same board. That's because it would have cost more if they had come on separate boards. Wise words, perhaps, but it's the sort of good luck we can all do without.

How often do you hear players say: 'I was only a point or two light? If I'd had another queen, we'd still have gone 800 down and you wouldn't have complained about my bid.' This was one such deal, from a semi-final of the 2014 Grand National Teams in the USA:

N-S Vul. Dealer South

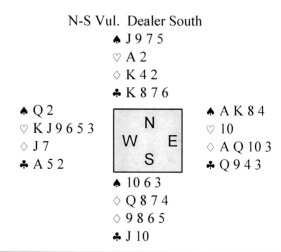

	♠ J 9 7 5 ♡ A 2 ◇ K 4 2 ♣ K 8 7 6	
♠ Q 2 ♡ K J 9 6 5 3 ◇ J 7 ♣ A 5 2	N W E S	♠ A K 8 4 ♡ 10 ◇ A Q 10 3 ♣ Q 9 4 3
	♠ 10 6 3 ◇ Q 8 7 4 ◇ 9 8 6 5 ♣ J 10	

West	North	East	South
—	—	—	pass
1♡	dbl	rdbl	1♠
pass	pass	dbl	2◇
pass	pass	dbl	all pass

What do you make of North's take-out double, vulnerable against not and facing a passed hand? It was risky, with little to gain and possibly a huge penalty to lose. To make matters worse, North was facing two of game's most vicious tigers – Jeff Meckstroth and Eric Rodwell!

South tried his luck in 1♠. When Rodwell doubled this in the East seat, South jumped from the frying pan into the fire, correcting to 2◇. This was also doubled and Meckstroth led the ♠Q, the defenders taking three tricks in the suit. Declarer discarded the ♣10 on a fourth round of spades and West ruffed with the ◇7.

West's ◇J switch was covered by the king and ace. East drew further rounds of trumps with the 10 and queen. He then switched to the ♡10, won with the ace. When declarer called for a low club, East rose with the queen and exited with a low club. Declarer discarded a heart and West won with the ace. He cashed the ♡K and gave East a heart ruff with the ◇3. Declarer scored the ◇9 at Trick 13. With only two tricks before him, he then had to enter -1700 in his scorecard. This cost 15 IMPs compared with 3NT+1 at the other table, where North did not make a take-out double over 1♡.

North's loss on the board is our gain – a valuable warning not to make sub-minimum bids when the possible losses outweigh the potential gains.

We will end with an unwarranted gamble of a different sort. The deal comes from a quarter-final of the 2014 Spingold.

Both Vul. Dealer East

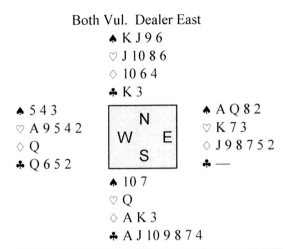

	North	
	♠ K J 9 6 ♡ J 10 8 6 ◇ 10 6 4 ♣ K 3	
West ♠ 5 4 3 ♡ A 9 5 4 2 ◇ Q ♣ Q 6 5 2	N / W E / S	**East** ♠ A Q 8 2 ♡ K 7 3 ◇ J 9 8 7 5 2 ♣ —
	♠ 10 7 ♡ Q ◇ A K 3 ♣ A J 10 9 8 7 4	

West	North	East	South
—	—	1◇	2♣
dbl	3♣	3♠	5♣
dbl	all pass		

At the other table South's 2♣ was passed out and eight tricks were made. Here West contested with a negative double and North raised the clubs, expecting at least six clubs opposite. What should South do over East's 3♠?

Bidding 5♣ is too much. Partner didn't bid 2◇ to show a sound raise to 3♣. There are likely to be three quick losers in the majors and a fair chance that you will lose a diamond too. Even if you think 4♡ or 4♠ will be a make, you won't cause any awkward decision for West by leaping to 5♣. He is a passed hand and can hardly be thinking of going to the five-level.

Declarer lost two spades, one heart, one diamond and a club, conceding 800 for 13 IMPs away. Of course it was unlucky to lose so much but when you make an unwarranted gamble, the cards will often let you down.

Tips to avoid mistake 2

(Unwarranted gambling)

- Entering the auction at an unsafe level, on a hand that is not worth very much, may be a thrilling experience. Like climbing an icy peak, it can also be dangerous.
- Bridge is meant to be a game of skill, not a rival attraction to roulette. When some flight of fancy goes wrong, this can be upsetting for your partner and your teammates.
- By all means try to make life difficult for the opponents, but draw a sensible limit in this regard.

Mistake 3

Rushing into the Wrong Contract

A common mistake is to leap to what seems a likely contract when there is plenty of bidding space available for investigation. We will start with an example from a semi-final of the 2014 Grand National Teams in the USA.

Neither Vul. Dealer North

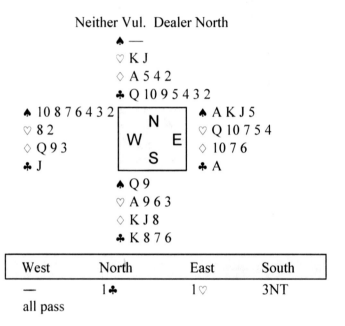

		♠ — ♡ K J ♢ A 5 4 2 ♣ Q 10 9 5 4 3 2		
♠ 10 8 7 6 4 3 2 ♡ 8 2 ♢ Q 9 3 ♣ J		N W E S		♠ A K J 5 ♡ Q 10 7 5 4 ♢ 10 7 6 ♣ A
		♠ Q 9 ♡ A 9 6 3 ♢ K J 8 ♣ K 8 7 6		

West	North	East	South
—	1♣	1♡	3NT
all pass			

West did not even need to lead a spade. He started with the ♡8, won with dummy's king. Declarer played on clubs and East was not pressed to find the spade switch, putting 3NT four down. At the other table, North opened a Precision-style 2♣ and East doubled. West bid spades over South's redouble and it was not difficult for North-South to reach the club game.

Right, let's go back to the auction at the first table. What action should South take after East's overcall? 3NT may be the right contract, but is there any reason to bid this straight away? As I see it, South does better to bid 2♡, showing a sound raise (at least) in clubs. No matter if the 1♣ opening does not guarantee four cards; in that case the final contract will be in notrump. Once North hears of club support, he will not contemplate a contract of 3NT. (Add the ♢Q to North's hand and 3NT would go down with a cold 6♣ available.)

The next deal comes from the 2011 Italy Cup with both sides vulnerable. How would you bid the West hand?

WEST
♠ A
♡ A J 6 4
♢ A Q 10 9 8 4
♣ 4 3

West	North	East	South
–	pass	3♣	pass
?			

This was the full deal:

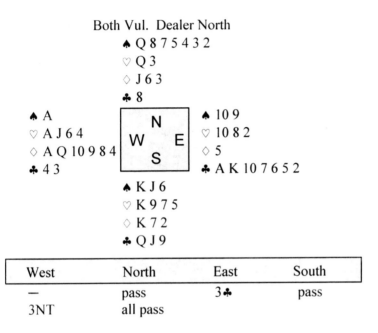

Both Vul. Dealer North

North:
♠ Q 8 7 5 4 3 2
♡ Q 3
♢ J 6 3
♣ 8

West:
♠ A
♡ A J 6 4
♢ A Q 10 9 8 4
♣ 4 3

East:
♠ 10 9
♡ 10 8 2
♢ 5
♣ A K 10 7 6 5 2

South:
♠ K J 6
♡ K 9 7 5
♢ K 7 2
♣ Q J 9

West	North	East	South
–	pass	3♣	pass
3NT	all pass		

West rushed into 3NT, no doubt hoping that the clubs would run or the diamonds would otherwise come to his rescue. North was not embarrassed to lead a spade from his weak hand. When the clubs failed to yield seven tricks, declarer went three down.

At the other table 5♣ was made with an overtrick. Declarer won the spade lead, cashed the ♢A and ruffed a diamond. After a spade ruff and a second diamond ruff, the suit breaking 3-3, declarer played ace, king and another club. He could then claim the remainder.

Let's go back to the bidding at the first table. If East's clubs were solid enough to run in 3NT, then 5♣ would surely be made too. If the clubs were not running, West's spade stopper would probably not allow 3NT to survive a spade lead. Suppose East's clubs were ♣KQJ10652. There would be every chance of making 5♣ but 3NT would be hopeless on a spade lead.

If West was forced to guess immediately which contract to play in, he should bid 5♣. Since no-one was pressing him to make such a decision, he could have marked time with 3♢, still expecting that the hand would be played in clubs eventually.

On the next deal, from the USA2 final of the 2013 under-21 USBC, it is the opponents who open 3♣. How would you have bid this West hand?

WEST	EAST
♠ A Q 9 8 7	♠ J 10 4 3
♡ K 10 3	♡ Q J 8 2
♢ A Q 10	♢ K 6 5 4
♣ A 2	♣ 7

Both Vul. Dealer North

West	**North**	**East**	**South**
	3♣	pass	pass
?			

One West simply bid 3NT. Clubs were led and the game went four down when the spade finesse lost (North had discarded one club.)

The other West saw that little could be lost by starting with a take-out double. When East responded 3♡, West bid 3♠ (showing a strong hand). East raised to 4♠ and eleven tricks were made for a 14-IMP swing.

On the next deal, from a semi-final of the 2014 Norwegian Championships, both North players rushed to name an ambitious final contract before they had any real idea of what partner held.

Neither Vul. Dealer West

	North	
	♠ Q J 6	
	♡ K 3	
	♢ Q 8 5	
	♣ K J 8 6 2	
West		**East**
♠ A 7	N	♠ K 10 9 4 3 2
♡ 6 4	W E	♡ J 5 2
♢ J 9 7 6 2	S	♢ A K 3
♣ A Q 9 3		♣ 7
	South	
	♠ 8 5	
	♡ A Q 10 9 8 7	
	♢ 10 4	
	♣ 10 5 4	

West	North	East	South
1♢	pass	1♠	2♡
pass	3NT	dbl	all pass

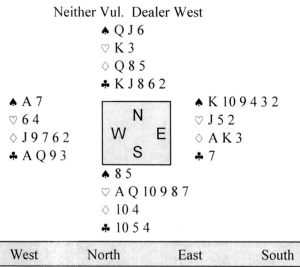

East led the ♢A, receiving a discouraging ♢2 from his partner. When he switched to the ♠2, West won with the ♠A and returned the ♢J, pinning dummy's ◇10. Declarer retained his ◇Q on this trick and a further round of diamonds went to East's ◇K. After cashing the ♠K, East switched to a club. His partner won with the ♣A and cashed two more diamond tricks. That was four down for an 800 penalty.

If we want to draw instructive value from this deal, we must think exactly why it was wrong to rush into 3NT on the North hand. What reasons come to your mind?

This is how I see it:

- Both the opponents had bid and North had little idea what type of hand his partner held.
- Although the ♡K suggested that the heart suit might be running, North had no quick tricks outside to bring the total to nine.
- North had at most one stopper in both spades and diamonds, so it might be hard work to 'win the race' (making nine tricks before they made five).

North-South did a little better at the other table:

West	North	East	South
1◇	pass	1♠	2♡
pass	3NT	dbl	4♡
pass	pass	dbl	all pass

If East scores two club ruffs this contract can go four down too. Not surprisingly West led the ♠A and the contract then went three down for 500 and a swing of 7 IMPs.

In summary, the North hand (with its uninspiring collection of secondary honors) is not worth very much in support of hearts. Few players would pass 2♡, it's true, but if you get to 3♡ (or perhaps 2NT) there is less chance that the defenders will double. Also, you will go down one trick fewer.

North was faced with a 'bash or bid slowly' decision on this deal from the 2009 Seniors Bowl in Sao Paulo, with USA2 facing Poland:

N-S Vul. Dealer East

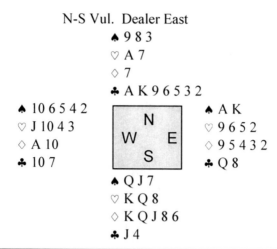

	North	
	♠ 9 8 3 ♡ A 7 ◇ 7 ♣ A K 9 6 5 3 2	
West ♠ 10 6 5 4 2 ♡ J 10 4 3 ◇ A 10 ♣ 10 7	N W E S	**East** ♠ A K ♡ 9 6 5 2 ◇ 9 5 4 3 2 ♣ Q 8
	♠ Q J 7 ♡ K Q 8 ◇ K Q J 8 6 ♣ J 4	

West	North	East	South
–	–	pass	1NT (15-17)
pass	2♠	pass	2NT
pass	6♣	all pass	

North showed his clubs with a transfer bid and South's rebid of 2NT indicated that he did not have a particularly good fit for clubs. What should North bid next?

North can see five losing cards in the side suits, even if he assumes the trumps are good. It's possible that four of these losers may be covered by a strong notrump hand; it's equally possible that the slam may be a poor one, perhaps with two top spade losers. The Poland North leapt straight to 6♣. No doubt he took into account that further bidding might assist the opening lead. If the slam was poor, a helpful lead might let it through.

You can make up your own mind whether North's gamble was a good one. It certainly wasn't a winning one. East cashed the king and ace of spades, receiving the ♠2 and ♠4 to suggest which red suit to switch to. A diamond to the ace resulted in a spade ruff for East and that was three down.

This was the auction at the other table:

West	North	East	South
–	–	pass	1NT (15-17)
pass	2♠	pass	2NT
pass	3◇	pass	3NT
all pass			

By agreement, North's 3◇ showed a shortage and invited a high club contract. South's hand could hardly be worse after this start to the auction. He applied the brakes in 3NT and nine tricks were made for a swing of 14

IMPs. If South did hold the cards necessary for a club slam, there was every chance it would have been reached after the 3♢ continuation.

I will end the chapter with a pet hate of mine — players who like to save five seconds by not bidding Blackwood on their way to a slam. 'I was sure you would hold the ace of trumps, partner!' No bonus is awarded for such acts of bravery. Let's see a typical example, from the final of the 2012 Italy Cup:

E-W Vul. Dealer North

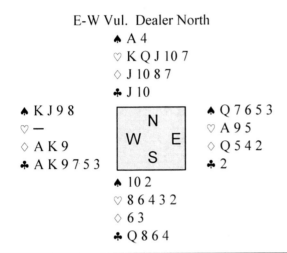

	North	
	♠ A 4 ♡ K Q J 10 7 ♢ J 10 8 7 ♣ J 10	
West ♠ K J 9 8 ♡ — ♢ A K 9 ♣ A K 9 7 5 3	N / W E / S	**East** ♠ Q 7 6 5 3 ♡ A 9 5 ♢ Q 5 4 2 ♣ 2
	♠ 10 2 ♡ 8 6 4 3 2 ♢ 6 3 ♣ Q 8 6 4	

West	North	East	South
—	1♡	1♠	3♡
4♡	pass	4♠	pass
5♣	pass	5♡	pass
7♠	dbl	all pass	

West showed a powerful spade raise with his 4♡ bid. Over partner's sign-off he made a further slam try with a cue-bid of 5♣. East had only overcalled at the one-level and was surely entitled to cue-bid the ♡A when this did not increase the level of the bidding. His partner then leapt to 7♠, assuming that partner held the ♠A (and that there was no club loser).

West had more than one opportunity to ask for the ♠A. Instead of bidding 4♡, when he was almost certain to hear 4♠ in return, he could have bid 5♡ — Exclusion Blackwood. This would show a heart void and ask for key-cards outside the heart suit.

Over 4♠, there was little purpose in 5♣, since West was willing to take the minor-suit situation as read. He could have bid 5NT instead to ask what trump honors partner held. (When spades are trumps, there is room for a sophisticated set of responses.) Even over 5♡, a bid of 5NT might well be used to ask for trump honors, since spades have been agreed as trumps.

At the other table East did not overcall and the partnership stopped in 5♠. By reaching 7♠ rather than 6♠ at the first table, East-West lost 13 IMPs instead of gaining 13 IMPs.

Tips to avoid mistake 3

(Rushing into the wrong contract)

- In general, it is better to exchange information when judging how high to go. You may help the defenders a bit, but it is worth it to reach the best contract.
- Bypassing Blackwood to save 5 seconds (or to prove how macho you are!) is a pointless risk.

Mistake 4

Misjudging sacrifices

When I commentate on top-level bridge shown by Bridge Base Online, I always enjoy seeing how the experts tackle high-level competitive bidding decisions. It's a difficult aspect of the game and on a particular deal you cannot simply say: 'Well, East made a mistake there. Look, he went for 800!' If you think a player's high-level decision was clearly wrong, you must try to analyze the reasons why, not merely rely on how many IMPs it happened to cost on one particular lay-out.

In this chapter we will look at some high-level decisions where I reckon that the player involved should have had enough information to avoid his losing action. You should make your own analysis at the same time and by comparing notes we may be able to improve our own competitive bidding! The first deal comes from a 2014 Interstate Teams in Australia:

E-W Vul. Dealer West

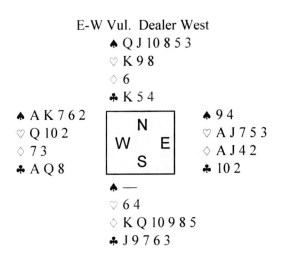

	North	
	♠ Q J 10 8 5 3 ♡ K 9 8 ♢ 6 ♣ K 5 4	
West ♠ A K 7 6 2 ♡ Q 10 2 ♢ 7 3 ♣ A Q 8	N / W E / S	**East** ♠ 9 4 ♡ A J 7 5 3 ♢ A J 4 2 ♣ 10 2
	♠ — ♡ 6 4 ♢ K Q 10 9 8 5 ♣ J 9 7 6 3	

West	North	East	South
1♠	pass	2♡	4NT
dbl	5♣	dbl	all pass

South's 4NT, showed the minors. Probably these thoughts were in the player's mind:

- The vulnerability is favorable
- The opponents will surely have a fit in one of the majors
- By taking away bidding space, I will force them to guess

North went three down in 5♣ doubled for 500, which should have been 800. At the other table East went one down in 4♡. (The contract can be made only by obscure double-dummy play, eventually endplaying North in spades.) So, South's 4NT lost 12 IMPs. What reasons come to your mind why 4NT was a poor bid? Think for a while before I tell you what I think.

These were the reasons that occurred to me:

- With the very bad spade break, East-West may go down in their chosen contract
- By entering the auction, warning East-West of bad breaks, South may deter them from getting too high
- If North held equal length in the minors, he would choose clubs and end in the wrong suit.
- By bidding 2NT instead of 4NT, South could have involved partner in the eventual decision of whether to sacrifice

To sum up, I would say: 'Don't offer the opponents a sizeable penalty when they may be in trouble themselves.'

The next deal comes from the 2014 European Championship, with Italy facing Sweden. (I'm sure you agree that it's more interesting looking at deals played at an expert level, rather than in a local club. The fact that top-class internationals misjudge such situations shows how difficult a topic this is.)

E-W Vul. Dealer North

North:
♠ Q
♡ A Q 10 4 2
◇ A 10
♣ A J 8 7 3

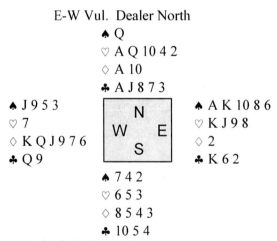

West:
♠ J 9 5 3
♡ 7
◇ K Q J 9 7 6
♣ Q 9

East:
♠ A K 10 8 6
♡ K J 9 8
◇ 2
♣ K 6 2

South:
♠ 7 4 2
♡ 6 5 3
◇ 8 5 4 3
♣ 10 5 4

West	North	East	South
—	1♡	1♠	pass
3◇	dbl	4♠	pass
pass	5♣	dbl	5♡
dbl	all pass		

West's 3♢ was a fit-jump, showing diamonds and spades. The Italian North doubled this to show a good hand. What action should he take when East's 4♠ runs to him?

He chose to bid 5♣ and the eventual contract of 5♡ doubled went 1100 down, costing 10 IMPs against the making 4♠ at the other table. Although North is a truly world-class player, it seems that his 5♣ was poorly judged. Once again, think what the reasons are for not bidding 5♣ before I give my own list. This is how I see it:

- North has no guarantee that there will be a fit for either of his suits
- He has promising defense against 4♠ but might go for a big number, playing at the five-level
- He has already described his hand well (with 1♡ and the double)

Let's look at the other auction from this match:

West	North	East	South
—	1♡	1♠	pass
4♠	all pass		

This time North had not been given the chance to show his strength with a double at the three-level. Many players (including myself, I think) would have doubled at their second turn. South would surely pass and that would be 790 away. Sweden's Johan Sylvan judged well to pass as North and conceded only 620. Perhaps he had in mind that he could not tolerate a take-out into diamonds.

Our next deal is again from the 2014 European Championships, this time with Sweden facing Austria:

N-S Vul. Dealer West

	♠ K Q 8 ♡ 10 7 3 ◇ 10 6 ♣ A K 8 5 4	
♠ 7 ♡ J 9 8 5 2 ◇ A Q J 9 5 4 ♣ 2	N W E S	♠ J 10 5 3 2 ♡ K 6 4 ◇ 8 2 ♣ J 9 6
	♠ A 9 6 4 ♡ A Q ◇ K 7 3 ♣ Q 10 7 3	

West	North	East	South
pass	1♣	pass	1♠
2◇	2♠	pass	4♠
4NT	pass	5♣	dbl
5◇	dbl	all pass	

With the vulnerability in his favor, the Austrian West competed with 4NT to show a second suit alongside his diamonds. East bid 5♣, his preference opposite a minor two-suiter, and the removal to 5◇ showed the red suits. Since West had not made a two-suited call originally, East decided to leave it in diamonds. West went 1100 down and the spade game would not have been made (unless West leads a diamond.) If you think that the 4NT bid was clearly wrong, try to think of the reasons why.

This is my list:

- West had singletons in both of the opponents' suits. The bad breaks might defeat 4♠.
- East had not found a raise to 3◇. West was banking everything on a heart fit, which might not materialize.
- West's second suit (hearts) was flimsy, so the penalty at the five-level might be substantial.

Perhaps the most common type of high-level competitive deal arises when one side holds the spades and the other has the hearts. It's not possible to judge such matters precisely. Suppose you bid 5♡ over 4♠ and go one down, finding that 4♠ would have gone one down too. This is no great cause for concern. You may lose a few IMPs on the deal, but you can console yourself that if you move a card or two your decision would have been right.

When your decision proves to be wrong by a full four tricks (for example, two down when they would have gone two down), you can be almost certain that there was a mistake somewhere in your side's auction. The same is usually true when the decision is wrong by three tricks. Look at this deal from a match between England and Ireland:

N-S Vul. Dealer West

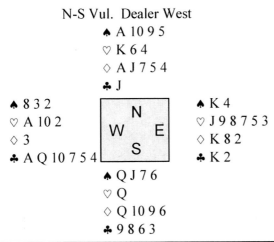

North:
♠ A 10 9 5
♡ K 6 4
◇ A J 7 5 4
♣ J

West:
♠ 8 3 2
♡ A 10 2
◇ 3
♣ A Q 10 7 5 4

East:
♠ K 4
♡ J 9 8 7 5 3
◇ K 8 2
♣ K 2

South:
♠ Q J 7 6
♡ Q
◇ Q 10 9 6
♣ 9 8 6 3

West	North	East	South
1♣	1◇	dbl	1♠
2♣	2♠	3♣	3◇
3♡	4♠	5♡	pass
pass	dbl	all pass	

East's first-round double was part of a transfer system of responses and showed at least four hearts. As the cards lay, East's 5♡ was wrong by three tricks. It was doubled for 100 away whereas at the other table 4♠ was doubled and two down for 500. That was a nett swing of 600. The decision to bid 5♡ rather than double 4♠ cost 12 IMPs. Big stuff.

Try to put into words why you think that East's 5♡ was wrong. Only then, take a look at the reasons that occur to me:

- East held good defense against 4♠ (three kings in short suits) and his partner had opened the bidding.
- The North-South bidding to 4♠ was not particularly convincing. They had no more than half the points in the pack.
- West had not raised hearts immediately and might conceivably hold only a doubleton honor in the suit.

The bidding was different at the other table and East judged the situation better:

West	North	East	South
2♣	dbl	2♡	2♠
3♡	3♠	4♡	4♠
pass	pass	dbl	all pass

West's 2♣ showed around 11-15 and long clubs. Again the North-South bidding was not particularly strong. East had roughly the same information available as his counterpart at the other table. He doubled 4♠ and was well rewarded for his choice.

When the final decision is wrong by a full five tricks, you can be sure that both halves of the losing partnership have produced poor bids. This example comes from the 2014 China Bridge Elite championship:

Both Vul. Dealer North

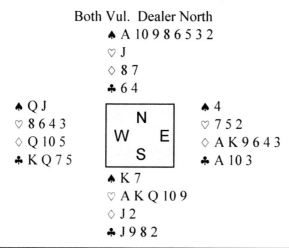

	♠ A 10 9 8 6 5 3 2 ♡ J ◇ 8 7 ♣ 6 4	
♠ Q J ♡ 8 6 4 3 ◇ Q 10 5 ♣ K Q 7 5	N W E S	♠ 4 ♡ 7 5 2 ◇ A K 9 6 4 3 ♣ A 10 3
	♠ K 7 ♡ A K Q 10 9 ◇ J 2 ♣ J 9 8 2	

West	North	East	South
	Zhang LG		*Shen SY*
—	3♠	4◇	4♠
5◇	pass	pass	dbl
all pass			

South cashed three hearts, North discarding two clubs. North ruffed the ♣9 and, reading the spot-card as suit preference, underled the ♠A to receive a second club ruff. That was an 1100 loss for East-West against a spade game that was beaten in top cards at the other table. 15 IMPs away. What do you make of the East-West bidding?

East's hand would not justify an overcall of 4◇, even if non-vulnerable.

The playing strength is low and the defensive strength is high. West's decision to sacrifice at Game All with only 3-card support and no ruffing value is just bad bridge. A good general guideline is this: **do not sacrifice on a balanced hand**.

We will end with a poorly judged advance sacrifice, in other words a high bid made (in the expectation of going down) before the opponents have reached their own contract. It comes from the very top level of play, a semi-final of the 2014 Spingold, with world-class players in every seat.

N-S Vul. Dealer North

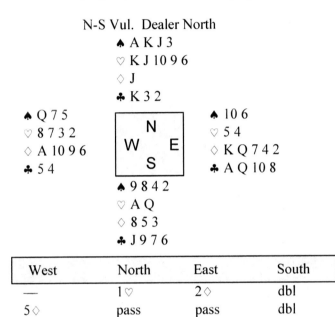

	North	
	♠ A K J 3 ♡ K J 10 9 6 ◇ J ♣ K 3 2	
West ♠ Q 7 5 ♡ 8 7 3 2 ◇ A 10 9 6 ♣ 5 4	N W E S	**East** ♠ 10 6 ♡ 5 4 ◇ K Q 7 4 2 ♣ A Q 10 8
	♠ 9 8 4 2 ♡ A Q ◇ 8 5 3 ♣ J 9 7 6	

West	North	East	South
—	1♡	2◇	dbl
5◇	pass	pass	dbl
all pass			

North's 1♡ promised 14+ points and West opted for an advance sacrifice of 5◇, doubled by South. How many tricks do you think East made after a lead of the ◇3?

To escape for two down, losing 300, requires double-dummy play. You must rise with dummy's ◇A at Trick 1, the ◇J falling from North. You must then finesse the ♣Q, cash the ♣A and ruff a club with the ◇10 or ◇9 (unblocking). When you play a heart, aiming to reach your hand for a second club ruff, South wins with the queen. He exits with a trump, but after your unblocking ruff you can play the ◇6 from dummy and overtake with the ◇7. You can then take a second club ruff.

At Trick 1 declarer called for the ◇10 from dummy, covered by the jack. It seems he should still lose only 500 but the play record merely states that trumps were drawn in three rounds and he went 800 down. At the other table a club was led against 4♠. Two clubs, a club ruff and the ◇A beat the game and that was a swing of 14 IMPs.

Let's look closely at West's advance sacrifice bid of 5◊ and consider why it may have been misjudged:

- West has little idea of his partner's hand. East-West may have enough defense to beat a game by the opponents
- West's hand contains no singleton or void. 5◊ could be expensive.
- North-South may not reach a game anyway.
- If West raises to 3◊ or 4◊, his partner can sacrifice in 5◊ if he has a suitable hand. West should not make the decision on his own when holding such modest values.

Tips to avoid mistake 4

(Misjudging a sacrifice)

- Try to arrange the auction to involve partner in any final decision about a sacrifice.
- Describe your hand accurately early in the auction, so partner has a good basis on which to base his decision.
- Remember that if your hand is very distributional, the bad breaks may cause the opponents' contract to fail.
- Be wary of sacrificing on a balanced hand.

Mistake 5

Overbidding opposite a pre-empt

When partner opens with a pre-empt, either a weak-two or a three-bid, there are two sound reasons to raise. You may have genuine expectations that a game can be made. You may instead hold a weak or moderate hand with a good trump fit. In that case you raise to take away bidding space from the opponents, perhaps causing them to miss an excellent contract their way.

In this chapter we are not concerned with raising partner; we will see that many players overbid opposite a pre-empt when they do not have a trump fit. Either they introduce another suit, hoping to find a fit, or they bid 3NT when the chances of success are much too low. We will start with this deal from the final of the 2013 Grand National Teams in the USA:

E-W Vul. Dealer East

WEST	EAST
♠ K Q J 7 2	♠ 9
♡ 8 7	♡ 6 3
◇ K 7	◇ A Q 10 9 6 4 2
♣ A Q 9 8	♣ K 5 4

West	East
–	3◇
3♠	3NT

It was reasonable for West to hope that the diamond suit was ready to run. What action do you think he should take, if any? He decided to respond 3♠, which is forcing. He may have thought 'three-card spade support will give us good play for 4♠'. Yes, but when you hold five spades and only two hearts, what is the chance of three spades opposite?

Software written by Taf Anthias shows that East's spade length will be:

0 spades	7%
1 spade	32%
2 spades	41%
3 spades	20%

There is only a 20% chance of a 5-3 spade fit. Partner is unlikely to hold two aces for a pre-empt, so you can expect three major-suit losers playing in diamonds and may have a further minor-suit loser. Meckstroth and Rodwell cashed five hearts and the ♠A against 3NT, for two down.

What do players say when they overbid and the contract goes down? They often look for some change to partner's hand that would have made the overbid pay off. On this deal, West might say 'Give yourself the ♡K instead of the ♣K and you would have nine tricks after a heart lead.'

That's true but bidding is all about assessing the expectation of making a contract. It is not enough for partner to have a hand that is 'only one card-change away from the contract becoming a good one'. You don't have to bid game every time a game is vaguely possible! At the other table, Mike Becker very sensibly passed his partner's 3♢ opening and picked up a useful swing.

Our next example of responding to a three-bid comes from the semi-final of a USA Bermuda Bowl trial:

N-S Vul. Dealer East

WEST	EAST
♠ A	♠ 8 7 6 4
♡ K 8 4 3	♡ 10 2
♢ A Q 8 6 4 3 2	♢ —
♣ 7	♣ Q J 6 5 4 3 2

West	North	East	South
–	–	3♣	pass
3♢	pass	3♠	dbl
4♢	dbl	all pass	

West's contract of 4♢ doubled went 1100 down! What on earth was West thinking about, bidding so high with a misfitting hand and a moderate suit? If his excuse was that the opponents might have a vulnerable spade game available, then I don't buy it. South has already passed and 3♢ will not stop North introducing a good spade suit.

At the other table Rodwell also opened 3♣ on the East cards. Meckstroth passed on the West cards and was happy to enter an eventual 14 IMPs into his plus column.

Overbidding opposite a weak-two opening has reached epidemic proportions! I realize that the standards for a weak-two vary considerably from country to country. In particular, the standards in the USA are very much higher than they are in Europe. Even so, you should not try for game on a balanced 12-14 points, just because you can visualize a particular hand opposite that will give you a game.

Here is one of countless examples of such optimistic assessment, taken from the 2011 Bulgarian trials:

N-S Vul. Dealer North

WEST	EAST
♠ A 6 5 4	♠ Q 9 6 3
♡ A 8 2	♡ K J 10 5 4 3
◇ K 10 2	◇ 9
♣ Q 9 8	♣ 7 6

West	North	East	South
–	pass	2♡	pass
2NT	pass	3◇	pass
4♡	all pass		

East, a top-rate international player, opens with a weak 2♡ in second seat. Do you like that action, with a four-card spade suit on the side? I am very happy with it. He has good hearts and the length in spades may give his LHO a difficult call to make.

West's 2NT is a relay bid, asking for further information. East's 3◇ shows a feature in that suit and it was no surprise when the resultant 4♡ went two down.

West holds a weak 1NT. He has some sort of heart fit, yes, but no ruffing value. He should pass! North was a passed hand, so there was no question of West bidding for pre-emptive reasons. In any case, a raise to 3♡ would be the pre-emptive action.

Overbidding opposite weak two-bids is a worldwide phenomenon. The next deal arose in the 2014 Turkish Teams Championship:

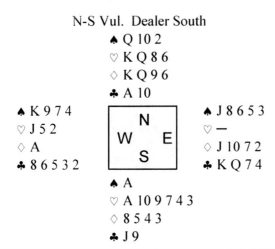

N-S Vul. Dealer South

	North	
	♠ Q 10 2	
	♡ K Q 8 6	
	◇ K Q 9 6	
	♣ A 10	
♠ K 9 7 4	N	♠ J 8 6 5 3
♡ J 5 2	W E	♡ –
◇ A	S	◇ J 10 7 2
♣ 8 6 5 3 2		♣ K Q 7 4
	♠ A	
	♡ A 10 9 7 4 3	
	◇ 8 5 4 3	
	♣ J 9	

West	North	East	South
–	–	–	2♡
pass	2NT	pass	4♡
pass	4NT	pass	5♡
pass	6♡	all pass	

How much more was North expecting from South's weak 2♡?

Declarer won the spade lead with the ace and drew trumps in three rounds. When he led a diamond towards dummy, West won with the ◇A and switched to a club. Declarer rose with the ♣A and ran some trumps. On the penultimate trump, East had to reduce to ♠J ◇J107 ♣K. Declarer crossed to the ◇K and led the ♠Q, pinning East's ♠J and discarding his club loser. The ♠10 was now good for a diamond discard and he escaped for one down.

Had the contract been 4♡, declarer's excellent play would have been rewarded by 1 IMP in the plus column. As it was, he lost 12 IMPs.

Tips to avoid mistake 5

(Overbidding opposite a pre-empt)

- When you have a 5-card major opposite a 3♣ or 3◇ pre-empt, the odds are poor of finding a 5-3 fit.
- Many players overbid opposite weak-two openings. A balanced hand of 12-14 points is unlikely to provide a game, particularly when it is loaded with queens and jacks.

Mistake 6

Not knowing Your System

At all levels of the game, points are frittered away because players have not learnt their bidding system properly. Look at the misadventure suffered by the England open team during the 2002 European Championships:

Both Vul. Dealer West

WEST	EAST
♠ A K J 6	♠ Q 4 2
♡ K 5	♡ Q
♢ 8 6 2	♢ A K 9 7 5 4 3
♣ A Q 6 4	♣ 7 3

West	North	East	South
1♣	pass	1♢	pass
2NT	pass	3♢	pass
3♠	pass	4♢	pass
all pass			

France easily bid and made 6♢ at the other table. Here West took the view that 4♢ was non-forcing. A jump rebid of 2NT shows around 18-19 points and any continuation by the responder is best played as game-forcing.

There are 101 different ways of losing IMPs, matchpoints or money at the bridge table without doing anything much wrong. It's a shame to add eminently avoidable items to this list, such as not knowing your bidding system. It barely matters which England player was at fault on this deal; the problem was that his partner held a different view of the situation.

The next misunderstanding is from the 2014 Australian Interstate Finals:

Both Vul. Dealer South

WEST	EAST
♠ A 9 8	♠ Q 4
♡ 8 7 4	♡ A 3
◇ A J 10 5	◇ K Q 6
♣ A 9 4	♣ K J 10 8 7 2

West	North	East	South
—	—	—	2◇
pass	2♡	3♣	pass
3◇	all pass		

South opens with a multi 2◇ (usually based on a weak-two in one of the majors). North bids 2♡ to say that partner should pass if he has long hearts and bid 2♠ with long spades. East overcalls 3♣ and the question now is: should a change of suit by West (3◇ here) be forcing?

Yes, thought West. No, thought East. Twelve tricks were made in 3◇ and that was a loss of 11 IMPs again 3NT+4 at the other table. What did you make of that?

Most players would say that a change of suit should be forcing, particularly at the three-level. East held 15 points anyway and was worth further action, even if West's change-of-suit were merely invitational. The main fault, however, was that the two halves of the partnership did not have an agreement about a relatively basic situation.

Many misunderstandings arise after an opponent has opened a possibly short 1♣ or 1◇. Is a subsequent bid in that suit by your side natural or a strength-showing cuebid? A partnership including a six-time world champion was uncertain on this deal from a quarter-final of the 2014 USBC:

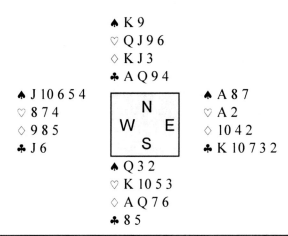

	♠ K 9 ♡ Q J 9 6 ◇ K J 3 ♣ A Q 9 4	
♠ J 10 6 5 4 ♡ 8 7 4 ◇ 9 8 5 ♣ J 6	N W E S	♠ A 8 7 ♡ A 2 ◇ 10 4 2 ♣ K 10 7 3 2
	♠ Q 3 2 ♡ K 10 5 3 ◇ A Q 7 6 ♣ 8 5	

West	North	East	South
—	—	1◇	pass
1♠	dbl	rdbl	2◇
all pass			

East made a Support Redouble to show his 3-card spade support. South intended his 2◇ bid as a strength-showing cuebid. You would expect such an exalted partnership to know their system but North read 2◇ as natural and passed it out. Perhaps he was distracted by the fact that East and West had both bid; since he held 16 points himself, this seemed to leave too few points for South to hold a strength-showing cuebid. South scored +130 for his ten tricks but this was a 10-IMP loss against +620 for 4♡ at the other table.

On the first round, my advice is to treat all 1♣ and 1◇ bids as if they were a normal, natural bid. So, 2♣ over a possibly short 1♣ is Michaels if that is what you normally play. Responses to a takeout double are strength-showing cuebids, not natural.

The next deal is from a USBC semi-final, with Nickell facing Bramley:

N-S Vul. Dealer North

WEST	EAST
♠ K 9 4 2 ♡ A K Q J 7 3 ◇ — ♣ A J 2	♠ Q J 10 7 6 ♡ 8 4 ◇ K Q J 7 ♣ Q 8

West	North	East	South
—	1♣	1♠	pass
5NT	pass	6♠	pass
7♠	dbl	all pass	

West was happy to bid a grand slam if the trump suit was solid. He bid 5NT and heard a response of 6♠. He advanced to the grand slam, explaining at the table that his partner held the ace-queen or king-queen of trumps. Their convention card offers no mention of 5NT, but it's amazing that players at this level should not know their method of checking for top trump honors.

At the other table Meckstroth (West) used Exclusion Blackwood: 5♦ to ask for key-cards excluding diamonds. On discovering that the ♠A was missing, he bid 6♠. Rodwell (East) played in 6♠ and went one down on a club lead (he rose with the ♣A and played three top hearts, hoping that North would have to ruff with a bare ♠A). So, the cost of the 'grand without the ace of trumps' was only 7 IMPs. Cheap at the price!

The next deal is from a semi-final of the 2014 Turkish Teams Championship:

E-W Vul. Dealer East

WEST	EAST
♠ A K 9 3	♠ Q
♡ 10 8 6 4 3	♡ J
◇ 8 4 2	◇ A 7
♣ 8	♣ A K Q 10 7 5 4 3 2

West	North	East	South
–	–	4NT	pass
5♠	pass	7♣	all pass

The generally agreed meaning of an opening 4NT bid is that it asks partner to name any ace that he holds. He should respond 5♣ with no ace, 5◇/5♡/5♠/6♣ with the ace of the bid suit, and 5NT with two aces. That is how West interpreted the bid but East must have had some different set of responses in mind. South led the ♡K from his ♡KQ7 and was agreeably surprised when this won the trick. East opened only 1♣ at the other table and gained 16 IMPs for his admirable 6♣ contract.

(I once opened 4NT when playing with a new partner. He took it as straight Blackwood and the adverse swing cost us the match. It's a great convention, yes, but it arises very rarely and you need to know that you and your partner both play it!)

The next bidding deal arose in the final of the 2011 USA2 trials:

Neither Vul. Dealer South

West	East
♠ 4	♠ Q 6
♡ K 10 7 6	♡ 9 5
◊ Q 5	◊ A K 10 7 4
♣ A 10 9 8 7 3	♣ K 5 4 2

West	North	East	South
—	—	—	1♠
pass	2♠	2NT	3♠
4♡	dbl	all pass	

This went three down for -500, while the opponents made 5♣ for +400. It was a loss of 14 IMPs. At this exalted level of play, can you believe that East thought 2NT showed the minors and West thought it showed hearts and a minor? There may well be some merit in 2NT showing a two-suiter including hearts but don't play such an unusual method (no pun intended) unless you are confident that both of you will remember it.

I hope you don't think this chapter is a bit of a lightweight filler. I don't regard it as such because mistakes due to not knowing your system properly are commonplace and cost a barrow-load of IMPs. Many of them are caused by tinkering with your system after one bad board in some area. When the same situation arises, perhaps six months later, you find yourself thinking: 'Hey, what did we decide on this? Did we think it was a good idea to switch the meaning of the two bids?'

Whatever your level of bridge and however complex your system is, don't adopt more conventions and agreements than you can remember!

Tips to avoid Mistake 6

(Not knowing your system)

- It is risky to keep making small changes to a bidding system. The situation may not arise for a while and it may be hard to remember what you agreed.
- Avoid making exceptions to a general bidding agreement. Although the exception may be a small improvement, the risk of forgetting it is always there.
- Beware of playing different systems in various positions around the table, or at different vulnerabilities. Many bidding misunderstandings arise as a result.
- If you are uncertain how partner will read a particular bid, consider making a more straightforward bid.

Mistake 7

Misreading a double

Most partnerships have some general rule that allows them to determine whether a double is for penalties or take-out. However simple or detailed these rules may be, situations will always arise where the two halves of a partnership disagree. Look at this amazing deal from an under-21 USA2 selection final.

N-S Vul. Dealer West

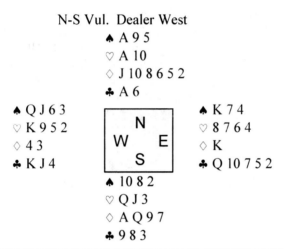

	♠ A 9 5 ♡ A 10 ◇ J 10 8 6 5 2 ♣ A 6	
♠ Q J 6 3 ♡ K 9 5 2 ◇ 4 3 ♣ K J 4	N W E S	♠ K 7 4 ♡ 8 7 6 4 ◇ K ♣ Q 10 7 5 2
	♠ 10 8 2 ♡ Q J 3 ◇ A Q 9 7 ♣ 9 8 3	

West	North	East	South
pass	1◇	pass	1NT
pass	2◇	pass	pass
dbl	all pass		

West could judge that the opponents had some sort of diamond fit. He knew also that they had made no attempt to bid a game. He was entitled to contest the auction with a double rather than let North-South play in a fit at the two-level.

East read this as a penalty double. He passed and declarer racked up three doubled overtricks for +780. You don't find that particularly amazing? Ah yes, but I have not yet told you that it was a flat board with exactly the same bidding and result at the other table!

Why was it wrong for East to read this as a penalty double? What reasons come to mind?

Firstly, is it very unusual to make a penalty double when your trump holding lies under that of the opponent with the long trumps. It's a good general rule that all such doubles should be for take-out. Secondly, the North-South auction strongly suggested a good diamond fit, probably 6-3. South would hold fewer than three diamonds only when he had long clubs and East's club length made this unlikely. A final reason was that West could hardly hold a penalty double of 2♢ when he was a passed hand.

The next deal comes from a quarter-final of the 2007 Venice Cup (the women's world championship), with USA2 facing France.

Neither Vul. Dealer West

	North	
	♠ 10 ♡ K 9 7 ♢ A Q 10 8 ♣ 9 7 4 3 2	
West ♠ A K 3 ♡ Q 2 ♢ K J 9 5 4 2 ♣ K 10	N W E S	**East** ♠ 8 6 4 2 ♡ 10 8 5 4 ♢ 7 6 ♣ A Q 8
	♠ Q J 9 7 5 ♡ A J 6 3 ♢ 3 ♣ J 6 5	

West	North	East	South
1NT	pass	pass	2♣
3♢	dbl	pass	3♠
all pass			

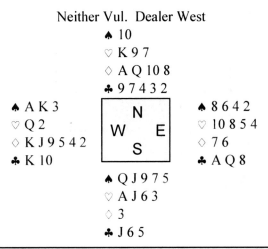

South for France bid 2♣ to show both majors. The American West jumped to 3♢ to show the nature of her hand and North doubled. How do you think South should view this double?

The world championship book says that South thought the double 'showed cards'. In other words that it showed some values but was not specifically a penalty double. She pulled to 3♠ and went three down, mercifully undoubled.

Although the bidding situation was somewhat unusual, it should have been clear that North's double was for penalties. Three suits had already been bid or indicated, so there would be little point in any sort of take-out double. Also, North sat over the player who had shown the long diamonds; with a good trump holding in that seat, a penalty double might well be profitable.

Suppose South had been the dealer and had opened the type of 2♣ opening currently fashionable in some parts of Europe, showing 5-9 points and both majors. If West had overcalled 3♢ and North had doubled, that would again be for penalties.

Misreading the double resulted in losing 6 IMPs instead of gaining 5 IMPs. It would have been more if South's 3♠ had been doubled.

When the meaning of a particular double has not been discussed in a fairly new partnership, you sometimes have to rely on evidence from other quarters. Take a look at this board from a match between Ireland and Northern Ireland:

E-W Vul. Dealer East

West		East
	♠ J 4 ♡ J 9 8 5 ♢ 10 6 ♣ A J 6 5 3	
♠ K 10 9 8 7 6 5 ♡ K 10 3 ♢ 7 3 ♣ 8	N W E S	♠ A 2 ♡ A Q 7 2 ♢ J 9 8 4 ♣ Q 7 4
	♠ Q 3 ♡ 6 4 ♢ A K Q 5 2 ♣ K 10 9 2	

West	North	East	South
–	–	1NT (12-14)	dbl
2♠	dbl	all pass	

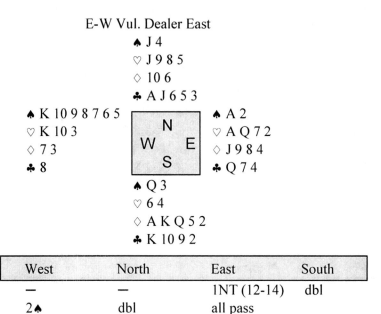

South's double was for penalties and West's 2♠ was non-forcing. You can understand that North was reluctant to let East-West choose trumps when his side held the balance of the points. He might have placed his betting chips on the club suit alone but with two places to play he judged that a take-out double was better.

Over to South now. How should he read the double? In other partnerships (we were told) South played such doubles as 'optional', which is hardly a risk-free method in itself. Suppose he was uncertain how the present North treated such doubles, what other evidence was there to help him?

It was just about possible that West had run from the double of 1NT into a 5-card spade suit and that North held a penalty double with four spades to East's two. Against that, South's doubleton in hearts strongly suggested that North held four hearts – a standard component of a take-out double. If the double was 'optional' (whatever that means in such a situation), it was surely too risky to allow it to stand.

Well, South did pass it out and was soon writing minus 1070 in his scorecard for two doubled overtricks. At the other table East opened 1♢ and South's 1NT was passed out. The defenders took the first seven tricks in spades but East failed to persuade his partner to switch to hearts and 1NT went only one down for gain of 14 IMPs.

The original auction was not such a rare one and the final message from the deal is that you simply have to know your system – in particular, what a double means in such a situation.

Tips to avoid mistake 7

(Misreading a double)

- Since most low-level doubles are for take-out nowadays, the easiest way to agree the meaning of a double is to concentrate on the relatively few occasions when it will be for penalties.
- It is rare to double for penalties when your trumps lie under the opponents' long trumps.
- The higher the opponents' contract the more often you should consider passing a double from your partner. When you hold a shapeless 3-count, it may be easier to take a plus-score in defense.

Mistake 8

Misusing Blackwood

The best of conventions are open to abuse. Perhaps the most commonly ill-treated is Blackwood, or its superior cousin Roman Key-card Blackwood. Inexperienced players tend to treat it as a 'slam try'. It is nothing of the sort. When you ask partner for aces (or key cards) you are really saying: 'I've decided that we have enough power to make a slam. I am going to bid it, provided we don't have two aces (or keycards) missing.'

Blackwood when you will still have to guess afterwards

When you use Blackwood, you should know what to do after you have heard the response. If only one key-card is missing, for example, you should be strong enough to bid a small slam. You should not sit back in your chair wondering whether to play in five or six.

West misused Blackwood in this way on a deal from the 2011 Victor Champion Cup, in Melbourne.

WEST	EAST
♠ A Q 9 6	♠ K J 8 4 3
♡ K 10 8 7 6	♡ A 9
◇ A 10 9	◇ K 7
♣ J	♣ K 10 4 3

West	East
1♡	1♠
3♠	4♣
4◇	4♡
4NT	5♡
5♠	

West decided he was worth a jump raise to 3♠. The next three bids were control-showing cue-bids (showing the ace or king of the bid suit). West was still interested in a slam and continued with RKCB. This was not a good move. He was assuming 'captaincy' of the auction when he had relatively little idea of how strong his partner was. Even though the 5♡ response told him that only one key-card was missing, West still had a guess to make. He guessed to play in 5♠ and the excellent small slam was missed.

What should West do instead? He should bid 4♠ instead of 4NT! He had already bid his hand to the full, with the jump-raise and a diamond cue-bid. His partner would then assume captaincy, bidding 4NT. At the other table it was East who asked for key-cards and the slam was easily reached.

Blackwood with two top losers in a side suit

It is not ideal to ask for aces (or key-cards) when you have two top losers in one of the side suits. Partner's Blackwood response may reassure you that there are not two key-cards missing, but it's still possible that you have the ace and king missing in one of the side suits. That's what happened on this deal from the final of the 2011 Wagar teams, where a European team faced a team from the USA:

WEST	EAST
♠ Q 3 2	♠ 10 4
♡ 9	♡ A Q 10 7 2
◇ Q 10	◇ A J
♣ A K Q 7 6 5 2	♣ J 10 9 4

West	East
—	1♡
2♣	3♣
4♣ (RKCB)	4♠ (2 keycards, no ♣Q)
6♣	

West's 4♣ would be reasonable if it were a prelude to cue-bidding, which would allow the partnership to detect that no spade control was held. In the system being played, 4♣ asked for key-cards with clubs agreed as trumps. (To use 4NT would often carry you too high, when a minor suit is agreed.) East indicated two key-cards, known to be aces, and North promptly defeated the resultant 6♣ by cashing the two top spades.

West had little idea how strong East was because the partnership was playing a 2-over-1 system, where 2♣ was forcing to game and East might bid 3♣ with extra values. Regardless of that, it was not a good idea to ask for key-cards with two top losers not just in one suit but in two suits.

At the other table, Sylvie Willard and Bénédicte Cronier reached a much better spot:

West	East
Cronier	*Willard*
–	1♡
2♣	3♣
3♠	3NT

West's 3♠ showed a spade stopper and East was happy to bid 3NT with ace-jack doubleton in the unbid suit. 10 IMPs was the French stars' reward.

The next deal comes from the 2011 Australian Trials. East and West are world-class players who have participated in several world championships.

WEST	EAST
♠ 9 3	♠ A K 6 2
♡ Q J 7 6	♡ 9 5
◇ A K J 9 6 4	◇ Q 10 8
♣ Q	♣ A K 7 5

West	North	East	South
1◇	1♠	2♣	2♡
3◇	pass	?	

What bid would you make on the East cards now? It's hard to believe that East chose 4NT, despite holding two top losers in one of the suits bid against him. When West responded 5♡ (two keycards: the ◇A and ◇K), East bid 6◇. North doubled and the defenders score two heart tricks. Instead of 4NT, East should have bid 4◇ to agree diamonds as trumps. His partner's failure to cue-bid hearts would then alert him to the fact that no control was held in that suit.

The next example featured a psychic bid in the 1972 World Championship. East was one of the finest cardplayers known to mankind but he fell from grace in the bidding of this deal:

Neither Vul. Dealer South

	North	
	♠ 8 6 ♡ 7 5 ♢ J 10 7 ♣ A 9 5 4 3 2	
West ♠ Q 10 5 2 ♡ Q 8 4 2 ♢ Q 8 3 ♣ K Q	N W E S	**East** ♠ A K 4 ♡ A K J 9 ♢ A K 9 ♣ J 10 7
	♠ J 9 7 3 ♡ 10 6 3 ♢ 6 5 4 2 ♣ 8 6	

West	North	East	South
	Priday		*Rodrigue*
—	—	—	pass
pass	1♣	dbl	pass
2♣	pass	3♡	pass
4♡	pass	4NT	pass
5♣	pass	5♡	all pass

With neither side vulnerable, Tony Priday mischievously opened 1♣ and East doubled, hearing a strength-showing cue-bid from partner. A continuation of 2♡ would presumably not have been forcing, facing a passed hand, so he jumped to 3♡. When this was raised to game, East decided to bid a slam only if West held the ♣A, since if he held the ♣K that card could be led through at Trick 1. When West denied the ♣A, the auction ground to a halt in 5♡.

This was clearly not an exemplary use of Blackwood. West surely held the ♣K, since he would not respond 2♣ with only four queens and a jack or two. If East was worried that the opening lead would give North two club tricks, he might perhaps have arranged the auction so West would become declarer. It was suggested that he should have bid 3♣ at his second turn. If West then bid 3NT, as he might well have done with the 4-card majors already implied by his previous 2♣, East could have raised to 6NT.

North did not open at the other table. Jeremy Flint and Jonathan Cansino then reached 6NT in four bids: 2♢ (multi) - 2♡ – 2NT – 6NT.

The Italians are rightly famed for their slam bidding, ever since their Blue Team ruled the bridge world. It is therefore rather unfair of me to feature an Italian misuse of Blackwood from the Italy-Brazil final of the 1998 Rosenblum Cup. Well, I will risk public disapproval. This was the deal:

WEST	EAST
♠ 9 5	♠ A J
♡ Q 9 8	♡ A K 7 6 5 3
◇ K Q 6	◇ A 10 4
♣ A J 10 5 4	♣ 9 6

West	North	East	South
1♣	1♠	2♡	pass
3♡	pass	3♠	pass
4♣	pass	4◇	pass
4♡	pass	4NT	pass
5◇	pass	6♡	all pass

Hearts were agreed as trumps and three cue-bids followed. What should East say over 4♡? Some would say that he had done enough, after cue-bidding his two side-suit aces, and should pass. If he took the view that he was worth one more try, he could always bid 5♡. This would give the message: 'I have no more side-suit controls to bid but I am too strong to pass'. If West held a hand such as ♠95 ♡Q98 ◇Q85 ♣AKQ54, he would know that it was a good one and raise to 6♡.

What is not justified, as I see it, it to commit to a slam via Blackwood. As you see, West held the missing ace but there was very little play for twelve tricks after a spade lead. Ah well, no-one is perfect!

Tips to avoid mistake 8

(Misusing Blackwood)

- Blackwood is not a slam-try. It is a last-ditch mechanism to avoid a slam when missing two big cards.
- Do not use Blackwood when a particular response will leave you wondering what to do next.
- Do not use Blackwood when the response may carry you too high.
- Although it may occasionally be unavoidable, be wary of bidding Blackwood with two top losers in a side suit.
- Do not use ordinary versions of Blackwood with a void. You may then have to guess whether partner has the ace of your void suit.

Mistake 9

Opening 1♢ on 4-5 shape

Even nowadays, you see players opening 1♢ when they hold four diamonds and five clubs. They might hold this hand, for example:

♠ A 7 ♡ K 6 ♢ K Q 8 4 ♣ J 10 9 6 3

'If I open 1♢, I will have an easy rebid of 2♣,' they explain learnedly. All too often this is what happens:

WEST	EAST	West	East
♠ A 7	♠ K 10 8 2	1♢	1♡
♡ K 6	♡ Q J 7 3	2♣	2♢
♢ K Q 8 4	♢ 10 5		
♣ J 10 9 6 3	♣ Q 7 4		

East cannot pass 2♣ because his partner might hold 17 points or so. He has to give false preference to 2♢ and they end in a 4-2 diamond fit. Meanwhile there was a 5-3 fit available in clubs and 1NT was also a good contract.

The same thing may happen when the responder is 2-2 in the minors:

WEST	EAST	West	East
♠ K 9	♠ Q J 6 3	1♢	1♡
♡ 7 5	♡ A J 8 4 3	2♣	2♢
♢ A J 6 4	♢ 9 2		
♣ K Q 6 5 2	♣ 10 8		

East gives preference to the first-bid suit and again the partnership ends in a 4-2 fit. Once again both 2♣ and 1NT are better contracts.

How can such unacceptable contracts be avoided? It is not rocket science! You should open the longer suit with 5-4 shape. On the two West hands that we have seen, you are not strong enough to open 1♣ and rebid 2♢, since this would show reversing values (17+ points). You can open 1♣ and rebid 1NT, though. When partner is not strong enough to make another bid, this will leave you in a much better contract than a 4-2 fit.

Suppose that you have the same 2-2-4-5 shape and 17 or more points. Now there is no problem whatsoever. You open 1♣, intending to reverse to 2♢. When you hold 15 or 16 points and are not strong enough for a reverse, you have the option of opening 1NT:

WEST	EAST	West	East
♠ A J	♠ K 10 6	1NT	2♢
♡ K 3	♡ Q J 9 7 2	2♡	
♢ A Q 7 3	♢ 10 6		
♣ J 10 8 5 2	♣ 9 4 3		

You might prefer to be in 2♣, but 2♡ is better than 2♢ on a 4-2 fit.

Opening 1♢ on 4-5 shape works poorly when responder is 3-3 in the minors too:

WEST	EAST	West	East
♠ A 3	♠ K 10 6	1♢	1♡
♡ J 7	♡ Q 10 8 3	2♣	2♢
♢ A J 6 2	♢ 9 4 3		
♣ K 10 8 5 2	♣ Q 9 4		

Hopeless! If you bid 1♣ - 1♡ - 1NT, you are much better placed, particularly at matchpoints where 1NT is usually a high-scoring spot.

Let's see what happens when the opener holds a major-suit singleton:

♠ J ♡ K 10 3 ♢ K Q 7 3 ♣ A 9 7 6 2

Opening 1♢ runs the risks that we have already seen. Suppose you open the recommended 1♣ and partner responds 1♡. What is your rebid?

WEST	EAST	West	East
♠ J	♠ A 10 6 2	1♣	1♡
♡ K 10 3	♡ A J 9 4	2♡	
♢ K Q 7 3	♢ 10 6		
♣ A 9 7 6 2	♣ 8 4 3		

You should rebid 2♡, as more and more players do nowadays. Do not be afraid of raising hearts with 3-card support. When partner passes 2♡, ending in a 4-3 fit, he will often be in a great spot. By taking spade ruffs in your hand he may pick up a fine score, particularly at matchpoints. When partner is stronger and makes a move towards game, he will have the space to discover whether you have 3-card or 4-card heart support.

Finally, let's see what happens when you are 4-5 in the minors with a singleton in responder's major suit:

WEST	EAST	West	East
♠ A Q 4	♠ J 9 5 3	1♣	1♡
♡ 6	♡ K 10 8 5 2	1NT	
◇ K Q 10 3	◇ 10 6		
♣ Q 9 7 5 4	♣ K 2		

You rebid 1NT. Yes, with a singleton in your hand! Of course you do. It's the best contract and cannot be reached unless you bid it now. You will find players, even some bridge teachers, protesting: 'Why distort your hand in this way?' Let them play in 2◇ while you rack up your joint top in 1NT.

There is one more hand type to consider. You hold 15-17 points, with 4-5 in the minors and a singleton in one of the majors:

WEST	EAST	West	East
♠ A Q 4	♠ J 9 5 3	1♣	1♡
♡ 6	♡ K 10 8 5 2	?	
◇ K Q 10 3	◇ 7 6		
♣ A 9 7 5 4	♣ K 2		

Now you do have a slight problem, whatever opening bid you make. If you open 1♣ and rebid 1NT, this will show 12-14 points. It would not be so bad, because you're entitled to shave off a point with a singleton in partner's suit. The alternative is to rebid 2♣, which East would pass. At least you would then be in a 5-2 fit rather than a 4-2 diamond fit.

Tips to avoid mistake 9

(Opening 1◇ on 4-5 shape)

- Do not open 1◇ with four diamonds and five clubs. By doing so, you will often end in a 4-2 fit.
- After a start such as 1♣ – 1♡ (or 1♠), be happy to raise partner's major with 3-card support.
- With 12-14 points, it works well to rebid 1NT when you have a singleton in responder's suit. This will win you truckloads of extra matchpoints at duplicate pairs.
- When the bidding starts 1♣ – 1♡ – 1NT, and you allow this rebid on a singleton heart, do not rebid 2♡ as responder with five hearts.

Mistake 10

Talking yourself out of a slam

We have all been in the situation where the bidding has suddenly reached a high level and you have values to spare for your bidding so far. Should you bid a slam or not? It's a common mistake for players to start imagining hands opposite where a slam would be poor or would have no play. They decide not to bid the slam, perhaps forgetting that there are many more possible hands opposite where a slam would be excellent.

Let's see some examples. The first one comes from a 2002 McConnell Cup match between the women's teams of Austria and England. This was the auction of the two world-class Austrian players sitting East-West:

WEST	EAST
♠ 10 8 7 4	♠ A
♡ A 10 8 2	♡ 9
♢ 3	♢ A 10 7 6 2
♣ Q J 10 8	♣ A K 9 7 6 2

Neither Vul. Dealer West

West	**North**	**East**	**South**
pass	1♠	2NT	pass
5♣	all pass		

Do you think that East should have raised to 6♣, holding four of the five key-cards, a singleton heart and a sixth club? The answer is surely: yes! Of course West had stronger routes available to 5♣, but she must still have considerable playing strength to leap to such a high level. Is it too much to ask for ♢Kx of diamonds and four or five clubs?

At the other table, Nicola Smith (West for England) bid only 4♣ at her second turn. Heather Dhondy (East) cue-bid 4♠ on her splendid hand and Smith then jumped to 6♣.

Some players talk themselves out of bidding a slam by constructing possible hands for partner where the slam may fail. If such hands are only a 20% chance and the slam will romp home on the other 80%, there is no excuse for holding back.

The next example is from the 2014 National Open Teams in Canberra. Again, both East and West were respected international players:

E-W Vul. Dealer North

WEST	EAST
♠ Q 10 6 5 3	♠ A
♡ A K 4	♡ 10 8
♢ 3	♢ A K 10 6 4
♣ A Q J 7	♣ K 10 5 4 2

West	**North**	**East**	**South**
–	3♡	4♢	pass
4♠	pass	5♣	all pass

Facing a partner who has bid so strongly when vulnerable, West was surely worth at least a raise to 6♣. Indeed, a cue-bid of 5♡ seems right to me. Although West may be able to create some East hands where there are two losers after this auction, there must be at least five times as many where a slam is worth bidding.

The next action comes from the 2014 European Championship, with England's women facing those of Denmark:

Both Vul. Dealer South

WEST	EAST
♠ —	♠ K 8 5
♡ Q J 9 8 7 2	♡ A 6
♢ K Q 8 7 6 2	♢ A 10 5 3
♣ K	♣ A 7 4 2

West	**North**	**East**	**South**
–	–	–	1♠
2NT	4♠	5♢	all pass

West's 2NT shows specifically the red suits. How strongly should East bid now?

The North-South bidding makes it likely that West is void in spades. With three aces facing a vulnerable two-suited overcall, surely there will be good play for a small slam. At the other table Sally Brock for England bid 6♢ (her partner had overcalled 3♣ to show the red suits). Here the Denmark East must have talked herself out of bidding a slam, picturing some weaker two-suiter where a slam would not be good. It was a clear mistake, as I see it. What about the myriad of West hands where the slam would be cold and another large bundle where it would have good play?

The next deal comes from the 2014 USA Grand National Teams final:

Both Vul. Dealer South

WEST	EAST
♠ J 8 4	♠ A Q 6
♡ J 9	♡ 10
♢ A K J 9 5 2	♢ Q 8 7 6
♣ 10 3	♣ A K J 7 4

West	**North**	**East**	**South**
3♢	pass	4♣	4♡
pass	5♡	dbl	all pass

How do you like that East hand when partner opens with a vulnerable 3♢? If you had to choose the final contract in one bid, would you not raise to 6♢?

East began with 4♣, which was presumably some sort of slam-try, and the bidding took an unexpected turn. South intervened with 4♡ and was raised to 5♡. What should East do next?

The odds still look good to me that you can score seven diamond tricks (assuming partner holds a 7-card suit), three top cards in the black suits, and another two tricks from setting up the clubs and/or taking heart ruffs. On this particular auction there is a fair chance that the opponents will go to 6♡ over 6♢, too. A final reason to bid 6♢ is that the penalty from 5♡ doubled is unlikely to be generous; the opponents are vulnerable too, yes, but East knew that when he bid 5♡. Even if 6♢ requires a finesse this may be a better prospect than accepting only 500 in defense.

East talked himself out of bidding 6♢ and the resultant 500 lost 13 IMPs against a successful 6♢ at the other table. The opponents managed to reach the slam after West opened with a weak 2♢.

Tips to avoid Mistake 10

(Talking yourself out of a slam)

- When a slam seems to be a good prospect, do not talk yourself out of it because you can imagine some situations where it may go down.
- Remember that failing to bid a making slam is just as expensive as bidding one and going down.

Mistake 11

Making Unsound Overcalls

More auctions are contested nowadays than ever before. The potential advantages of overcalling are well known. You can take away bidding space from the opponents, suggest a good opening lead, push the opponents up a level or maybe find a good contract or sacrifice of your own. That's all true but you have to know where to draw the limit. In particular, some players make unsound overcalls at the two-level when they have little to gain and a potential big number to lose.

What do you make of South's effort on this deal:

N-S Vul. Dealer West

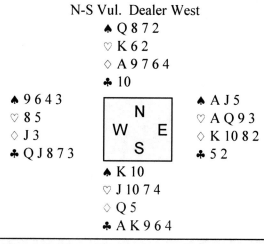

	North	
	♠ Q 8 7 2 ♡ K 6 2 ◇ A 9 7 6 4 ♣ 10	
West ♠ 9 6 4 3 ♡ 8 5 ◇ J 3 ♣ Q J 8 7 3	N W E S	**East** ♠ A J 5 ♡ A Q 9 3 ◇ K 10 8 2 ♣ 5 2
	♠ K 10 ♡ J 10 7 4 ◇ Q 5 ♣ A K 9 6 4	
	South	

West	North	East	South
pass	pass	1◇	2♣
pass	pass	dbl	all pass

The declarer, an English grandmaster who has won several national championships, went 800 down. Meanwhile East would have gone down if 1◇ was passed out. 'My 2♣ overcall was just normal bridge!' he exclaimed.

Of course South was unlucky that West held five clubs, Nevertheless his bid was a poor one. Why is that? South held only 13 points, so it was unlikely that a game could be made opposite a passed hand. If it could, his partner might be able to re-open the bidding when 1♢ ran to him. So, South was risking the occasional big penalty for relatively little gain. If he lost 500, say, it was all too likely because of the defense in his hand that the opponents would not have a game their way.

Suppose East had opened 1♠ instead and South had held this hand:

♠ K 10
♡ A K 9 6 4
♢ Q 5
♣ J 10 7 4

Now there would be some justification for bidding 2♡, despite the fact that he holds only a 5-card suit. That's because there is more chance that his side can make a vulnerable game (in hearts).

Next we will see an example from the 2014 European Championships with Germany facing Russia:

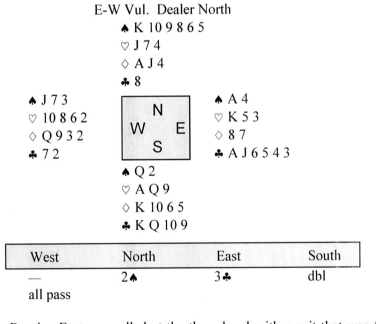

E-W Vul. Dealer North

	♠ K 10 9 8 6 5 ♡ J 7 4 ♢ A J 4 ♣ 8	
♠ J 7 3 ♡ 10 8 6 2 ♢ Q 9 3 2 ♣ 7 2	N W E S	♠ A 4 ♡ K 5 3 ♢ 8 7 ♣ A J 6 5 4 3
	♠ Q 2 ♡ A Q 9 ♢ K 10 6 5 ♣ K Q 10 9	

West	North	East	South
—	2♠	3♣	dbl
all pass			

The Russian East overcalled at the three-level with a suit that was far from robust. He was doubled and went 1400 down, scoring only the ♠A and three trump tricks. Was this mainly a question of bad luck or do you think he was wrong to bid? If you don't like the bid, once again try to think of the reasons why you would not overcall 3♣ yourself.

These are some of the factors that make the bid a mistake, as I see it:

- You are unlikely to miss a game by passing. If South passes, your partner will have the chance to protect.
- You are vulnerable against non-vulnerable.
- Your suit has no solidity. If you are doubled, you may go for a substantial number.
- Facing a weak-two, your LHO will have a penalty double available.

At the other table, this was the bidding:

West	North	East	South
—	1♠	2♣	pass
pass	dbl	all pass	

Many players would bid 2♣ on the East cards, so we can't call it a clear-cut mistake. Still, 2♣ did not consume much bidding space and the lack of solidity in the suit again proved costly. East went 1100 down against non-vulnerable opponents.

I will now beg your indulgence by including a deal that was played in the qualifying rounds of the 1935 Vanderbilt! Even in those early days of the game an unsound overcall could be a costly affair.

Both Vul. Dealer South

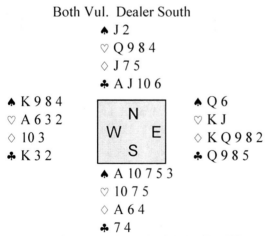

North: ♠ J 2 ♡ Q 9 8 4 ♢ J 7 5 ♣ A J 10 6

West: ♠ K 9 8 4 ♡ A 6 3 2 ♢ 10 3 ♣ K 3 2

East: ♠ Q 6 ♡ K J ♢ K Q 9 8 2 ♣ Q 9 8 5

South: ♠ A 10 7 5 3 ♡ 10 7 5 ♢ A 6 4 ♣ 7 4

West	North	East	South
Schenken		*Gottlieb*	
—	—	—	pass
pass	pass	1♢	1♠
dbl	all pass		

Negative doubles did not rule the convention cards in those days. When South ventured a dubious 1♠ overcall, Howard Schenken doubled for penalties.

Declarer won the ♢10 lead with the ace and led a club. Would you have had any special plans, sitting in the West seat? Schenken defended brilliantly by inserting the ♣K! The wonderful double-dummy analyzer, Deep Finesse, tells me that declarer could have saved a trick by playing low from dummy. Is that so? Well, back in 1935 the declarer won with the ♣A and could not then avoid the loss of three trumps, three hearts, two diamonds and a club. That was a penalty of 800 points and a reminder to look at the vulnerability before you overcall on a flimsy hand. Not that minus 500 would be a good return if you were non-vulnerable.

At the other table Oswald Jacoby was South (what a name-dropper I am). He declined to overcall 1♠ and was rewarded a few moments later by the chance to defend 2♠ played by West. This went one down for a net swing of 900 points. Historians would be able to tell us how many IMPs that was worth in those days.

Right, there will be no more Golden Oldies in this book. I promise you! (Well, not many, anyway.)

One warning note against making a questionable overcall is that you hold three cards in the suit that has been opened against you. This was the case in a deal from the 2010 Festival of Bridge in Australia. Ron Klinger reported a deal from a match involving his own team. The players' names were not given but I think it's safe to assume that Ron was not sitting South...

Both Vul. Dealer East

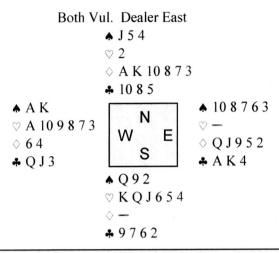

	North	
	♠ J 5 4 ♡ 2 ♢ A K 10 8 7 3 ♣ 10 8 5	
West ♠ A K ♡ A 10 9 8 7 3 ♢ 6 4 ♣ Q J 3	N W E S	**East** ♠ 10 8 7 6 3 ♡ – ♢ Q J 9 5 2 ♣ A K 4
	♠ Q 9 2 ♡ K Q J 6 5 4 ♢ – ♣ 9 7 6 2	

West	North	East	South
—	–	1♠	2♡
pass	pass	dbl	all pass

This was the auction at both tables. West cashed the ♠AK and switched to the ♣Q. Neither declarer could avoid the loss of two spades, three clubs and four trump tricks. Both sides lost 1100 and no IMPs were exchanged.

I cannot improve on Ron's analysis: 'I think you have rocks in your head to overcall 2♡ on these values. South's 2♡ got what it deserved.'

Tips to avoid mistake 11
(Making unsound overcalls)

- There are many good reasons to make an overcall, but you have to draw a sensible limit.
- When you are vulnerable, do not risk going for a large number in a dubious cause. Weigh up the potential advantages of your overcall against the possible cost.
- When your hand is very shapely and you are considering a dubious overcall, remember that bad breaks may cause the opponents to go down, left to their own devices.

Mistake 12

Hoping partner has the perfect hand

Beginners tend to be terrified of bidding slams, in case they go down. More experienced players take a different view — they are terrified of missing a makeable slam! Some of them take too rosy a view of their hand, imagining that partner will hold the perfect cards opposite. It may happen in your dreams (unless you have something better to dream about), but it rarely seems to happen at the bridge table.

Our first example of this type of mistake comes from the 2010 Spingold in New Orleans, with two world-class Polish players sitting East-West:

WEST	EAST
♠ K Q 8 4	♠ A J 9 6 5
♡ A 6 5 4 2	♡ Q 9 8
◇ K 6 2	◇ A Q 5
♣ 10	♣ Q 3

West	East
1♡	1♠
2♠	2NT
4♣	4◇
4♡	4NT
5♠	6♠

When West raised spades, East saw no harm in investigating further with a forcing 2NT relay. His partner now jumped to 4♣, a splinter bid showing a singleton club. After two cue-bids, East took a favorable view of his hand, bidding RKCB. Perhaps he imagined that West might hold: ♠K10xx ♡AKxxx ◇Kxx ♣x, although the slam would be borderline even then.

It's not a winning tactic to hope that partner holds perfect cards. Indeed, it is a persistently losing tactic. Here, West had quite a good hand for his 2♠ raise. He had 4-card trump support, only six losers and four useful honor cards. East could not possibly be accused of underbidding if he bid just 4♠ at his fourth turn, having already suggested a slam with the 4◇ cue-bid.

The next deal comes from the 2010 European Championships in Ostend, with Serbia facing France. This time I will give you just the West cards for the moment:

WEST
♠ K 6 2
♡ K Q
♢ A 10 2
♣ K Q 9 5 4

West	North	East	South
		1♣	1♢
2♢	pass	3♣	pass
4♣	pass	4♠	pass
?			

Your 2♢ shows at least a sound raise to 3♣ and is unlimited. Your partner's 3♣ is a sign-off opposite the sound-raise type. You show slam-try values with 4♣ and partner cue-bids the ♠A. What next?

Encouraged by his partner's cue-bid, the Serbian West leapt to 6♣. This was a hopeless contract:

WEST	EAST
♠ K 6 2	♠ A Q 3
♡ K Q	♡ 8 6 2
♢ A 10 2	♢ 9 3
♣ K Q 9 5 4	♣ A J 10 6 3

Whose fault was it?

East was blameless as the driven snow! He showed his minimum hand and West nevertheless suggested a slam. East's 4♠ cue-bid indicated a spade control (ace, king or shortage). It also meant that he did not have a heart control, otherwise he would have cue-bid 4♡. The focus was on the diamond suit. East could, just possibly, hold the ♢K, since he might be reluctant to cue-bid that card when sitting under the overcaller. He might also hold the ♢QJ, allowing a finesse to be taken. Hoping for the perfect diamond holding opposite, West went for the slam. As is usually the case, his partner did not hold the perfect cards and the slam had no play. West should have signed off in 5♣.

The next donning of the rose-tinted spectacles is from the 2014 European Championships, with Israel (the eventual gold medalists) facing Sweden.

WEST
♠ A K 10 7 6
♡ K
◇ K Q 5
♣ K J 9 5

West	North	East	South
—	—	pass	pass
1♠	2♣	3♣	pass
3◇	pass	4♠	pass
?			

East's 3♣ showed an 'invitational or better' spade raise. What action should you take?

The Israeli West bid 4NT to ask for key-cards. When partner showed only one, he screeched to a halt in 5♠. East held ♠QJ9 ♡AQJ5 ◇9874 ♣102. Even though North led a heart and declarer was able to discard all three diamonds, the contract could not be made. North held ♣AQ8643 over him and South held five trumps (four would have been enough to defeat 5♠, since declarer would be forced each time he gives up a club).

Anyway, we are not concerned particularly with the chances of 5♠. We want to look at the sort of 'perfect hand' that West needed to make 6♠. With the clubs marked over him by the overcall, he would need partner to hold both red aces for a start. He would have to find him with the ♠Q too. That is already asking for quite a lot from a passed hand.

If partner holds two clubs, the ♣A lead and a club ruff might defeat 6♠; even without that lead, declarer would somehow need to dispose of three clubs. If East held the ♠Q, the red aces and a singleton club, he would surely have bid 4♣ over 3◇. Even then, you might not be able to dispose of three club losers with East poised to overruff on the third round.

It was simply too ambitious to hope for a slam, despite West's 19 points. The clue was provided by North's 2♣ overcall.

At the other table, Sweden bid the hand magnificently, gaining 13 IMPs:

West	North	East	South
		pass	pass
1♠	2♣	3♣	pass
3◇	pass	3♡	pass
3NT	all pass		

The next deal comes from the 2013 Bermuda Bowl, with Poland facing USA1.

Both Vul. Dealer East

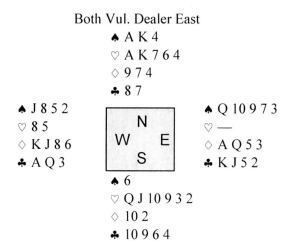

West	North	East	South
	♠ A K 4 ♡ A K 7 6 4 ◇ 9 7 4 ♣ 8 7		
♠ J 8 5 2 ♡ 8 5 ◇ K J 8 6 ♣ A Q 3		♠ Q 10 9 7 3 ♡ — ◇ A Q 5 3 ♣ K J 5 2	
			♠ 6 ♡ Q J 10 9 3 2 ◇ 10 2 ♣ 10 9 6 4

West	North	East	South
–	–	1♠	pass
2NT	pass	4♣	pass
4◇	pass	4♡	dbl
pass	5♡	pass	pass
6♠	dbl	all pass	

The USA West's Jacoby 2NT showed at least 4-card spade support and was forcing to game. This was already a slightly generous assessment of his hand. The 4♣ rebid showed a void heart in the version of Jacoby being played; 4◇ was a cue-bid and 4♡ kept the auction alive. The bidding now took an unexpected turn. South doubled to show good hearts and North bid 5♡. East made a forcing pass and this ran to West. What should he do now?

As I see it, West had already done full justice to his hand. He held a minimum Jacoby response and his trumps were jack-high. Placing his partner with perfect cards (only one trump loser and filling all the minor-suit gaps), West chose to bid 6♠. This was doubled and one down, losing 13 IMPs to Poland's 1♠ – 2NT – 4♠ auction at the other table. Look at it another way. Suppose West bids only 5♠ instead of 6♠. Surely East would advance to 6♠ if he held the ♠K in addition to his actual cards (or the ♠A instead of the ♠Q)?

Both East and West were hoping that partner held the 'perfect hand' on this deal from a quarter-final of the 2014 Spingold:

E-W Vul. Dealer West

	North	
	♠ A K Q 10 5 ♡ A 10 4 ◇ 9 5 3 ♣ 4 2	
West ♠ 4 ♡ Q J 9 8 3 ◇ A 8 7 ♣ Q 10 9 7	N / W E / S	**East** ♠ 9 8 6 2 ♡ 5 ◇ Q J 6 ♣ A J 8 5 3
	♠ J 7 3 ♡ K 7 6 2 ◇ K 10 4 2 ♣ K 6	

West	North	East	South
pass	1♠	pass	2♠
dbl	pass	4♣	pass
5♣	all pass		

East could diagnose a spade shortage opposite, it is true, but 4♣ was too much opposite a passed hand. It was similarly ambitious for West to raise to 5♣. Even though trumps were 2-2 and one of the minor-suit finesses was onside, the contract went two down for a loss of 200.

At the other table 3♠ went two down. (Declarer won the heart lead, drew trumps in four rounds and played a diamond to the king.) If East had bid only 3♣, in the auction shown, he would have saved himself 7 IMPs.

Tips to avoid mistake 12

(Hoping partner holds the perfect hand)

- 'If partner has the ♠K-Q, the ♡Q and the minor-suit suit aces, we'd make a slam.' Yes, but he probably hasn't. Do not risk getting too high when you need perfect cards.
- If you bid strongly in search of a perfect fit, your partner may carry you too high when he has a great hand but not the precise cards that you need.
- Aim to make a slam-try below the game-level and then leave it to your partner to judge if his hand is good enough.

Mistake 13

Bidding the Wrong Slam

Deciding which of two slams to bid can be no easy matter. Nevertheless, you see many big swings where the losing decision appears to have been a clear mistake. As I see it, this was one such deal from the final of the 2011 New South Wales teams.

WEST	EAST
♠ K J 7	♠ A
♡ A	♡ K Q J 10 9 7 2
♢ K Q 7 4 3	♢ A 10 9
♣ K 5 4 2	♣ 7 3

West	East
–	1♡
2♢	3♡
4NT	5♢
?	

West's 4NT is Roman Key-card Blackwood with hearts agreed. East's 5♢ is a 1430 response, showing three key-cards. Put your thumb over the East cards for a moment and decide what you would bid next on the West hand.

At one table West bid 6♡, which was passed out. He looked anxiously at his partner when the ♣Q was led. No reassuring smile was forthcoming and the defenders claimed two club tricks for one down.

West at the other table appreciated the danger of South leading a black suit against 6♡. The missing key-card was likely to be an ace (rather than the ♡K) and might well be a black-suit ace. He therefore bid 6NT, where West would be the declarer. This contract could not be beaten and 13 tricks were made after a spade lead.

The next deal comes from the 2003 Lederer Trophy in London:

WEST	EAST
♠ K J 8 6 5	♠ Q 10 7
♡ A Q	♡ K J 9 8 5 3
♢ K J	♢ A 6 4
♣ A K 6 5	♣ 3

West	East
–	1♡
1♠	2♡
3♣	3♠
4NT	5♣
5♢	5♡
?	

4NT is RKCB and East's 5♣ shows one key-card (using 1430 responses). The 5♢ continuation asks for the ♠Q and East's response shows both the trump queen and the ♡K. What would you bid next on the West cards?

There are two good reasons to bid 6NT. If you choose 6♠ instead and hearts break 4-1, you may suffer a heart ruff after a lead of the heart singleton. If you choose 6♡ and spades break 4-1, you may be defeated by a spade ruff. Two pairs in the event did end in 6♡, going down when a singleton spade was led.

Another reason to avoid 6♠ is that if East holds (say) ♠Q74, there could be two trump losers when trumps break 4-1. In 6NT, meanwhile, you might waltz home with six hearts and two tricks in each of the other suits.

Judging between 6NT and six of a suit is so important that we will take one more example, this time from a 2013 match between England and the Netherlands:

Both Vul. Dealer East

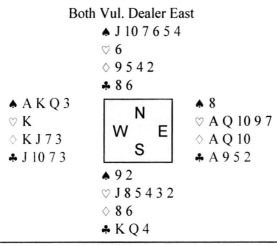

	North	
	♠ J 10 7 6 5 4 ♡ 6 ◇ 9 5 4 2 ♣ 8 6	
West ♠ A K Q 3 ♡ K ◇ K J 7 3 ♣ J 10 7 3	N / W E / S	**East** ♠ 8 ♡ A Q 10 9 7 ◇ A Q 10 ♣ A 9 5 2
	♠ 9 2 ♡ J 8 5 4 3 2 ◇ 8 6 ♣ K Q 4	

West	North	East	South
—	—	1♡	pass
1♠	pass	2♣	pass
2◇	pass	2NT	pass
3♣	pass	4♣	pass
4◇	pass	4NT	pass
5♣	pass	6♣	all pass

East's ♣9 did at least give declarer a fair chance of avoiding two trump losers. It was not to be and the slam went one down. With 33 points between the hands there was likely to be good play for 6NT. Indeed, you can see that there are eleven top tricks and a twelfth can be developed from the heart suit. (If a club is led, this provides a twelfth trick straight away). How would they bid it at the other table?

West	North	East	South
—	—	1♡	pass
1♠	pass	2♣	pass
2◇	pass	3NT	pass
6NT	all pass		

A neat auction to the top spot. West gave no thought to playing in clubs, which was known to be only a 4-4 fit when East declined to bid 3♣ at his third turn.

Let's look once more at the need for the trump suit to be sound. This deal arose in the final of a USA2 under-26 trial:

WEST	EAST
♠ A 4	♠ K Q 9 7 3
♡ K Q J 10 8 2	♡ 9
◇ 8	◇ A J 9
♣ A Q 9 7	♣ K J 6 4

West	East
	1♠
2♡	2NT
3♠	4♠
4NT	5♠
6♡	6♠

It was the style of this pair to rebid 2NT on a hand with no side suit of 5 cards or longer. (At the other table, East rebid 3♣ and 6♣ was easily reached). However, there was no need for the 2NT rebid to cause a problem. The partnership was playing two-over-one, a system where the 2♡ response was forcing to game. West could therefore have continued with 3♡ on the next round. A rebid of 3♣ would have been even better, paving the way for a club slam.

Whatever West's future intentions, it was dangerous to bid 3♠ when the spade fit was almost certain to be 5-2. East decided not to cue-bid the ◇A, presumably because he wanted to limit his hand. West advanced with RKCB, hearing of two key-cards and the ♠Q. He then bid 6♡, hoping to benefit from the solidity of his holding in this suit. It is hard to blame East for reverting to spades, with only a singleton in partner's heart suit. A 4-2 trump break put paid to their chosen slam and that was a loss of 16 IMPs.

A useful gadget to locate the best slam is a 5NT bid (not preceded by a Blackwood 4NT). It is called the 'pick-a-slam' 5NT. Here are some sample auctions:

WEST	EAST	West	East
♠ K 6	♠ A Q 9 8 2	1NT	2♡
♡ A Q 9 2	♡ J 3	2♠	5NT
◇ K J 6 4	◇ A Q 2	6NT	
♣ Q J 4	♣ A 10 3		

East has shown five spades and now wants West to choose between 6♠ and 6NT (or perhaps to offer some 5-card suit of his own).

WEST	EAST	West	East
♠ K 8	♠ A 9 2	1♡	2♣
♡ A Q 7 5 3	♡ K 8	2NT	5NT
◇ Q 7 2	◇ K 10 4	6♣	
♣ Q 10 5	♣ A K J 8 2		

West can now offer 6♣ with 3-card support. On a different hand he might bid 6NT, or perhaps 6♡ with a chunky suit.

Tips to avoid mistake 13

(Bidding the wrong slam)

- It is often better to bid 6NT instead of six of a suit, particularly when you have a high point-count.
- In 6NT you may succeed when the trump suit that you would otherwise have chosen happens to break badly. You will also avoid the risk of an adverse ruff.
- When you have a choice of two trump suits in a small slam, consider which one may protect a king from the opening lead.
- 5NT is no longer used to ask for top trump honors (since the advent of RKCB). Use it to carry a 'pick-a-slam' meaning.

PART II

Mistakes in the play

Board	Contract	By	Tricks	Score	IMPs
7	6♠	S	11	¦ 100	¦ 17

Mistake 14

Drawing Trumps too Soon

The three main situations where you may need to delay drawing trumps are: when you need to ruff losers in dummy, when you need to take immediate discards and when you need to establish a discard or two before your remaining stopper is driven out. If you're nodding your head and muttering: 'Yes, that's all fairly basic,' you'll be happy to hear that we will be considering other situations in this chapter.

Declarer failed to take advantage of a helpful opening lead on this deal:

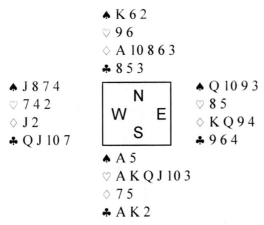

	North	
	♠ K 6 2 ♡ 9 6 ♢ A 10 8 6 3 ♣ 8 5 3	
♠ J 8 7 4 ♡ 7 4 2 ♢ J 2 ♣ Q J 10 7	N W E S	♠ Q 10 9 3 ♡ 8 5 ♢ K Q 9 4 ♣ 9 6 4
	♠ A 5 ♡ A K Q J 10 3 ♢ 7 5 ♣ A K 2	

West	North	East	South
—	—	—	2♣
pass	2♢	pass	2♡
pass	3♢	pass	3♡
pass	3♠	pass	3NT
pass	4♡	pass	6♡
all pass			

How would you play 6♡ when West leads the ♣Q?

The original declarer won the club lead and drew trumps in three rounds. His next move was to duck a round of diamonds, hoping to establish the suit. He won the club return, crossed to the ♢A and ruffed a diamond. A 3-3 break would have rescued the contract but no such luck materialized. The slam went one down.

To make the contract against a 4-2 diamond break, you must use dummy's ♡9 as an extra entry. Only one move is good enough at Trick 2. You must duck a diamond. You win the club return, cross to the ◇A and ruff a diamond high, West showing out. You return to dummy with the ♡9 and ruff a fourth round of diamonds high. You can then draw the outstanding trumps and cross to the ♠K to discard your club loser on the thirteenth diamond. As it happens, a lead in either major suit would have killed the slam. The defenders would have been able to remove dummy's entry in that suit when a round of diamonds was ducked.

The original declarer mistimed the play of the trump suit here too:

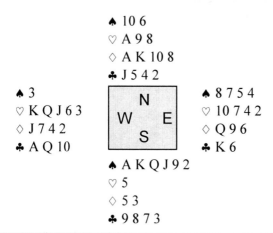

	North	
	♠ 10 6 ♡ A 9 8 ◇ A K 10 8 ♣ J 5 4 2	
West ♠ 3 ♡ K Q J 6 3 ◇ J 7 4 2 ♣ A Q 10	N W E S	**East** ♠ 8 7 5 4 ♡ 10 7 4 2 ◇ Q 9 6 ♣ K 6
	♠ A K Q J 9 2 ♡ 5 ◇ 5 3 ♣ 9 8 7 3	

West	North	East	South
—	—	—	1♠
2♡	dbl	3♡	3♠
pass	4♠	all pass	

You win the ♡K lead and play two rounds of trumps. Do you? If you make that mistake, you will go down. When you drive out the three club stoppers, the defenders will force you in hearts on each occasion. You will lose trump control.

At Trick 2 you should turn immediately to the club suit. West wins and forces you with a heart. When you play on clubs again, they win and force you to ruff once more. You are down to four trumps, with East holding four. However, you are in control! When West wins a third round of clubs, a further heart will be ineffective. You will be able to ruff with dummy's ♠10. On any other return, you will draw trumps and claim.

The next deal is trickier that it may appear. Once again, many players would go down by drawing trumps too soon.

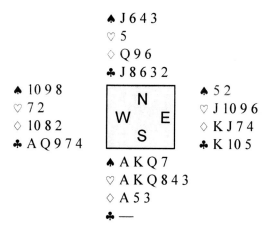

	North	
	♠ J 6 4 3 ♡ 5 ♢ Q 9 6 ♣ J 8 6 3 2	
West ♠ 10 9 8 ♡ 7 2 ♢ 10 8 2 ♣ A Q 9 7 4	N / W E / S	**East** ♠ 5 2 ♡ J 10 9 6 ♢ K J 7 4 ♣ K 10 5
	South ♠ A K Q 7 ♡ A K Q 8 4 3 ♢ A 5 3 ♣ —	

West	North	East	South
—	—	—	2♣
pass	2♢	pass	2♡
pass	2NT	pass	3♠
pass	4♠	pass	6♠
all pass			

How would you play the slam when West leads the ♠10?

If West holds the ♢K and hearts are no worse than 4-2, you can establish the heart suit with one ruff and arrive at twelve tricks fairly easily. Can you see how to make the contract when hearts are 4-2 but the ♢K is offside?

You will need to take two ruffs in the dummy — one in hearts and one in diamonds. In that case it would be a mistake to draw trumps at the start. You win the first trick with the ♠A and play the ace and king of hearts, throwing a diamond from dummy. Next you play a low diamond to the queen. East wins with the ♢K and returns a second round of trumps. You win with the ♠K and the suit breaks 3-2. What now?

You ruff a heart, establishing that suit, return to your hand with the ♢A and ruff a diamond with the ♠J. You can then reach your hand with a club ruff and draw West's last trump with your queen. Twelve tricks are yours.

How will you play 4♠ on the final deal of this chapter? (It is just possible that the winning line may have something to do with the trump suit...) West leads the ♡K and continues with the ♡A.

	♠ A Q 8 ♡ 8 2 ◇ K Q 8 6 3 ♣ 6 5 4		
♠ 10 ♡ A K J 9 5 4 ◇ 7 5 ♣ K Q 10 3	N W E S	♠ K 9 3 ♡ Q 10 6 3 ◇ J 10 4 2 ♣ 8 7	
	♠ J 7 6 5 4 2 ♡ 7 ◇ A 9 ♣ A J 9 2		

West	North	East	South
1♡	pass	2♡	2♠
4♡	4♠	all pass	

You ruff the second heart and play a trump to the queen, losing to the king. Back comes the ♣8. You should win with the ♣A and cash the ♠J, leaving the ♠A as a potential entry to dummy. West discards a heart on this trick. If you make the mistake of drawing East's last trump immediately, you will need the diamond suit to break 3-3. A better idea is to play the ace and king of diamonds and lead a third round of the suit. If diamonds break 3-3, nothing has been lost. You will ruff in the South hand and re-enter dummy with the ♠A to enjoy the rest of the diamond suit.

The benefit of this line is demonstrated when East holds four diamonds. You ruff the third diamond in your hand and West cannot overruff; he has no trumps left. With diamonds established, you cross to the trump ace and claim the remainder.

Tips to avoid mistake 14

(Drawing trumps too soon)

- The three main reasons not to draw trumps immediately are: you need to take ruffs, you need to take discards or establish discards.
- You may need to use the entries provided by dummy's shorter trumps, perhaps to establish a long side suit.
- You may need to keep the last trump in the shorter holding to prevent a force in the long-trump hand.

Mistake 15

Failing to diagnose a blockage

Many a contract survives when the defenders' winners in a suit become blocked. Sometimes you can arrange this yourself, as the declarer. Deals such as the following are commonplace:

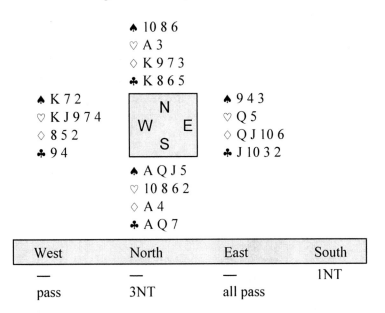

	North	
	♠ 10 8 6 ♡ A 3 ◇ K 9 7 3 ♣ K 8 6 5	
West ♠ K 7 2 ♡ K J 9 7 4 ◇ 8 5 2 ♣ 9 4	N / W E / S	**East** ♠ 9 4 3 ♡ Q 5 ◇ Q J 10 6 ♣ J 10 3 2
	♠ A Q J 5 ♡ 10 8 6 2 ◇ A 4 ♣ A Q 7	

West	North	East	South
—	—	—	1NT
pass	3NT	all pass	

How will you play 3NT when West leads the ♡7?

You start with seven tricks on top. A 3-3 club break would bring you to eight tricks but you will need to develop the spades to make the contract. If the spade finesse was into the East hand, you could simply hold up the ♡A until the second round. East would then have no heart to return in the dangerous case where hearts broke 5-2. Here the spade finesse is into the West hand. What can be done?

It would be a mistake to play the ♡3 at Trick 1. East would win with the ♡Q and clear the suit. When the spade finesse lost, West would cash three more hearts and you would be one down. You must rise with the ♡A at Trick 1. Whether or not East decides to unblock the ♡Q on this trick, you will then make the contract. You run the ♠10 at Trick 2 and West wins the first or second round. If East retained the ♡Q, the defenders' hearts will be blocked. If instead he unblocked that card, your ♡1086 will be a stopper with West on lead.

You could be certain that hearts would be blocked if they were 5-2. West would have led an honor from ♡KQJ75 or ♡KQJ74. The Rule of 11 says that East has one card higher than the ♡7, which is surely an honor.

You would make the same play (rising with dummy's ace) if you held only ♡9652. West would not usually lead the ♡7 from ♡KQJ74, ♡KQ1074, ♡KJ1074 or ♡QJ1074, so East is likely to hold two honors. If you play low from dummy, East will win and clear the hearts. Instead you should rise with the ♡A and block the suit:

(1)	♡ A 3		(2)	♡ A 3	
♡ K Q 8 7 4		♡ J 10	♡ K J 8 7 4		♡ Q 10
	♡ 9 6 5 2			♡ 9 7 5 2	

Rise with the ♡A at Trick 1 and the defenders cannot untangle their four tricks in the suit. The situation would be the same if West had started with ♡K10874, ♡QJ874 or ♡Q10874.

Now try this one:

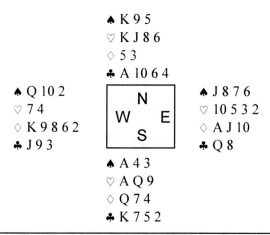

	♠ K 9 5 ♡ K J 8 6 ♢ 5 3 ♣ A 10 6 4	
♠ Q 10 2 ♡ 7 4 ♢ K 9 8 6 2 ♣ J 9 3	N W E S	♠ J 8 7 6 ♡ 10 5 3 2 ♢ A J 10 ♣ Q 8
	♠ A 4 3 ♡ A Q 9 ♢ Q 7 4 ♣ K 7 5 2	

West	North	East	South
—	—	—	1NT
pass	2♣	pass	2♢
pass	3NT	all pass	

West leads the ♢6 to the ace. How will you play when East returns the ♢J?

The original declarer gave the matter insufficient thought and played low on the second round, hoping that East had started with ♢AJ doubleton. East continued with the ♢10 and the defenders scored five tricks in the suit, putting the game one down.

Had declarer looked more carefully at the ♢6 opening lead, he would have noted that only one lower spot-card was out. West therefore had at most five diamonds and East could not hold ♢AJ doubleton. Declarer should have covered the ♢J with the ♢Q, in the hope that East's remaining card in diamonds would block the suit. If West allows the ♢Q to win, declarer will swiftly cash nine top tricks. Suppose instead that West wins and crosses to East's ♢10. Declarer will then win the return and play a club to the ten, ducking a trick into the safe East hand and setting up his ninth trick in clubs.

Let's see something different now. To ring the changes, I will present only two hands:

♠ 9 8 5 2
♡ 8 6 5
♢ 10 7 6
♣ A Q J

N
W E
S

♠ A K
♡ K 10 7
♢ A Q J 9 3 2
♣ K 5

West	North	East	South
1♡	pass	pass	2NT
pass	3NT	all pass	

2NT is not the Unusual Notrump in the pass-out seat. It shows around 18-20 points, often with a long minor. How would you play 3NT when West leads the ♡4 and East plays the ♡J?

Only 12 points are still missing, so West is a huge favorite to hold the ♢K. Two spades, one heart, one diamond and three clubs amount to only seven top tricks. If you had eight you might be able to win the first trick and cash black winners to reduce West to four good hearts and ♢Kx. You could then exit with the ♡10 and wait for two diamond tricks at the end. That's for a different day. What chance do you have on the present lay-out?

You could hope that West has opened on a 9-count and play for the ♢K to be onside. Another possibility is to lay down the ♢A, hoping that West's ♢K is singleton. However, the best chance is to hope that the heart suit is blocked! In other words, you hope that West began with ♡AQ9432 with East holding the bare ♡J. This is not so unlikely when West's 1♡ opening shows at least five hearts – why should he not hold a sixth heart?

You duck the first trick and East switches to a spade. Now it doesn't matter how you play the diamond suit. Five diamonds and five tricks in the black suits will give you an overtrick.

Tips to avoid mistake 15

(Failing to diagnose a defensive blockage)

- The Rule of 11 and a knowledge of standard leads from an honor sequence often allow you to diagnose that winning the first trick will cause a blockage.
- When your RHO holds a doubleton honor in the suit led, he must decide whether to unblock the honor or retain it.
- Unblocking may promote the value of your own cards, perhaps creating a second stopper. Retaining the honor may block the defenders' suit.

Mistake 16

Taking the Wrong Finesse

When entries to dummy are in short supply, you may need to think carefully how to make best use of them. In particular, you may need to judge which finesse to take. Look at this deal:

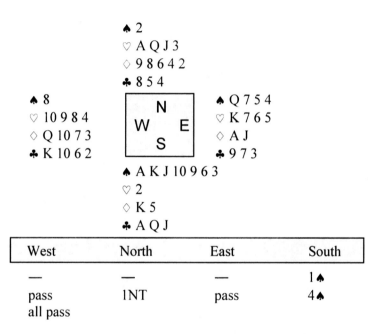

	North	
	♠ 2 ♡ A Q J 3 ♢ 9 8 6 4 2 ♣ 8 5 4	
West ♠ 8 ♡ 10 9 8 4 ♢ Q 10 7 3 ♣ K 10 6 2	N W E S	**East** ♠ Q 7 5 4 ♡ K 7 6 5 ♢ A J ♣ 9 7 3
	♠ A K J 10 9 6 3 ♡ 2 ♢ K 5 ♣ A Q J	

West	North	East	South
—	—	—	1♠
pass	1NT	pass	4♠
all pass			

You win the ♡10 lead with dummy's ace. You will never reach dummy again (not on this deal, anyway...). Which finesse should you take?

Look at the three available finesses in turn, asking yourself: 'If it wins, will I make the contract?' The original declarer made the mistake of finessing the ♠J. It won the trick but he didn't make the contract. East had started with four spades and still had to make his ♠Q. Taking a club finesse would be even worse. You would not gain a trick unless East held ♣Kx. The correct finesse to take is a diamond to the king. If East holds the ♢A, you are almost certain to make the contract.

Another important question to ask yourself as you compare possible finessing chances is this: 'If the finesse loses, what will my fallback chances be?' Suppose you lead a diamond to the king on this deal and it loses to West's ace. You will still have a reasonable second chance that the ♠Q will fall in two rounds. If instead you take a trump finesse and it loses, you will have hardly any chance of avoiding three further losers in the minor suits.

The next deal may look similar but this time declarer has two entries to dummy and can therefore take two finesses. He still needs to consider carefully which suit to play first.

	North	
	♠ 8 6 5 ♡ A 7 4 2 ◇ K 6 4 ♣ 6 5 3	
♠ 2 ♡ Q J 10 9 5 ◇ Q 10 8 3 ♣ 10 9 2	N W E S	♠ K 9 4 3 ♡ K 3 ◇ J 7 5 ♣ K 8 7 4
	♠ A Q J 10 7 ♡ 8 6 ◇ A 9 2 ♣ A Q J	

West	North	East	South
—	—	—	1♠
pass	2♠	pass	4♠
all pass			

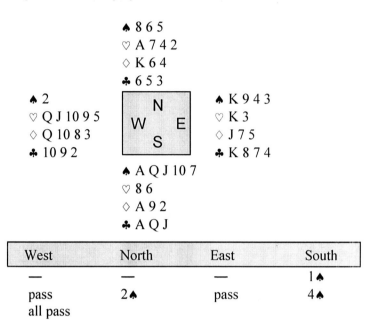

How will you play the spade game when West leads the ♡Q?

Let's see first how the original declarer went down. He won the heart lead with the ace and finessed the ♠Q successfully. He then returned to dummy with the ◇K and finessed the ♠J. The finesse won but, sadly for declarer, West showed out. There was now no way to avoid a loser in each of the four suits and the contract went one down.

As you see, finessing in trumps did not guarantee the contract even if the repeated finesse succeeded. Declarer should therefore have taken the club finesse instead. That finesse would win too, as it happens, and now the contract would be made. Declarer plays the ace and queen of trumps, draws trumps and later crosses to the ◇K to repeat the winning club finesse. The recommended line of play will succeed around 53% of the time, way ahead of the 37% chance when you start with a trump finesse.

A further edge in favor of playing on clubs is this: if the first club finesse loses, you will still have the chance to use the ◇K entry to pick up a possible ♠Kx with East. In theory, West can prevent this with the super-clever play of holding up the ♣K to make you think that the club finesse has worked. That would be a double-dummy defense, though, since he doesn't know that you hold the ♣J.

Right, now try this one:

	North	
	♠ A Q J 9 ♡ K 10 2 ◇ Q J 4 ♣ 8 6 2	
West ♠ 4 3 ♡ 8 7 5 ◇ 10 8 7 5 ♣ Q 10 4 3	N / W E / S	**East** ♠ K 10 8 6 ♡ A Q 3 ◇ 9 2 ♣ J 9 7 5
	♠ 7 5 2 ♡ J 9 6 4 ◇ A K 6 3 ♣ A K	

West	North	East	South
—	—	—	1NT
pass	3NT	all pass	

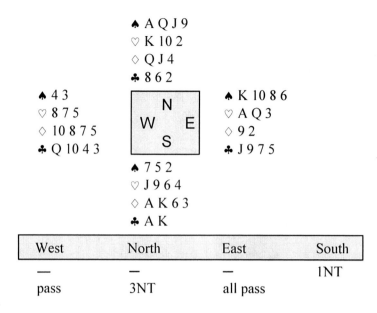

How will you play 3NT when West leads the ♣3 to East's jack and your king?

The original declarer counted seven top tricks and looked to the spade suit for the two extra tricks that he needed. At Trick 2 he finessed the ♠Q, losing to East's king. When he won club return and played the ace and jack of spades, the ♠10 refused to drop. 'It's the story of my life,' he observed as he scribbled the minus score on his score-card.

West's ♣3 lead announced that the club suit was breaking 4-4. Declarer should therefore have finessed the ♡10 at Trick 2. The finesse would lose and the defenders would clear the clubs, but this would not damage the contract. Declarer could knock out the ♡A, establishing two extra tricks in hearts. He would then make the game for the loss of two clubs and two hearts.

The declarer on the next deal had potential finesses in both red suits. He went down by taking the finesses in the wrong order. Would you have made the same mistake?

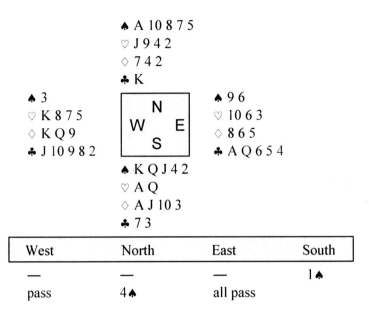

♠ A 10 8 7 5
♡ J 9 4 2
◊ 7 4 2
♣ K

♠ 3	N	♠ 9 6
♡ K 8 7 5	W E	♡ 10 6 3
◊ K Q 9	S	◊ 8 6 5
♣ J 10 9 8 2		♣ A Q 6 5 4

♠ K Q J 4 2
♡ A Q
◊ A J 10 3
♣ 7 3

West	North	East	South
—	—	—	1♠
pass	4♠	all pass	

West led the ♣J, East winning with the ♣A and switching to the ◊8. When declarer finessed the ◊J, West won with the ◊K. (He was hoping to persuade declarer that he did not hold the ◊Q.)

Declarer ruffed the club return in dummy and drew trumps. Fondly imagining that East held the ◊Q, he finessed the ◊10. West won with the ◊Q and exited safely with his last diamond. Declarer now needed the heart finesse to win. Not today! West won with the ♡K and the spade game was one down.

Declarer should have finessed the ♡Q before taking a second diamond finesse. The finesse loses and he wins the heart return. He crosses back to dummy with a trump and plays the established ♡J, discarding a diamond. By good fortune the ♡10 falls and ten tricks are his.

By taking the heart finesse before the second diamond finesse, you give yourself an extra chance. How bridge players love that phrase!

Tips to avoid Mistake 16

(Taking the wrong finesse)

- One question to ask when considering an early finesse is: 'What will the residual chances be if the finesse loses?'
- On many contracts the choice of finesse will be affected by the damage a defender might do if the first finesse loses.
- By finessing into the safe hand, you may have time to take a second finesse (or duck a trick) later.

Mistake 17

Losing to a 4-1 Trump Break

On countless occasions dummy goes down and you think: Well, everything will be fine if trumps break 3-2. Many players proceed to test the trumps, sitting back with a worried look when a defender shows out on the second round. This is not the time to plan how to overcome the bad break! You should do it right at the start.

North-South did well to reach 6♡ here, but declarer mismanaged the play.

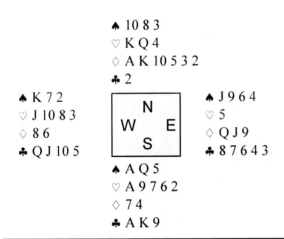

North:
♠ 10 8 3
♡ K Q 4
◇ A K 10 5 3 2
♣ 2

West:
♠ K 7 2
♡ J 10 8 3
◇ 8 6
♣ Q J 10 5

East:
♠ J 9 6 4
♡ 5
◇ Q J 9
♣ 8 7 6 4 3

South:
♠ A Q 5
♡ A 9 7 6 2
◇ 7 4
♣ A K 9

West	North	East	South
—	1◇	pass	1♡
pass	2♡	pass	4NT
pass	5♠	pass	6♡
all pass			

I like North's decision to raise the hearts. If South held only four hearts and passed, this would be a playable contract. If South were stronger and took the bidding higher, there would be space to determine whether North held four-card support. How would you play 6♡ when the ♣Q is led?

The original declarer decided to establish the diamonds, hoping for a 3-2 break. Since he would need to re-enter dummy in the trump suit, to score the long diamonds, he drew only two rounds of trumps with the king and ace. His intention was to establish the diamonds with a ruff and then return to dummy with the ♡Q. Providing both red suits broke 3-2, this plan would succeed even if he was overruffed on the third round of diamonds. Unfortunately, East showed out on the second round of trumps and there was no way to recover the situation.

Do you see how the contract can be made? You should begin by drawing only one round of trumps, with the ♡A. You then turn to the diamond suit, cashing the ace and king and ruffing the third round. If West overruffs, consuming his natural trump trick, you will win his return and draw trumps with the dummy's ♡KQ. You can then discard three black-suit losers on the diamonds.

Suppose instead that West retains his trump length, discarding when you ruff the third round of diamonds. You will cross to the ♡K and lead good diamonds, throwing losers from your hand. Whenever West chooses to ruff, you will be able to win his return and cross to dummy's remaining trump honor to score the remaining diamonds.

Declarer on the next deal blamed the 4-1 trump break for his defeat, continuing the match without even realizing that he could have made the contract. Try it for yourself.

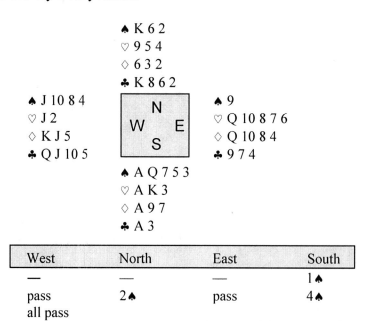

	♠ K 6 2 ♡ 9 5 4 ◇ 6 3 2 ♣ K 8 6 2	
♠ J 10 8 4 ♡ J 2 ◇ K J 5 ♣ Q J 10 5	N W E S	♠ 9 ♡ Q 10 8 7 6 ◇ Q 10 8 4 ♣ 9 7 4
	♠ A Q 7 5 3 ♡ A K 3 ◇ A 9 7 ♣ A 3	

West	North	East	South
—	—	—	1♠
pass	2♠	pass	4♠
all pass			

How will you play 4♠ when West leads the ♣Q? You have ten top tricks if trumps break 3-2, so you should turn your mind to a 4-1 break. You win with the ♣A and play the ace and queen of trumps, East throwing a heart on the second round. You now seem to have two losers in diamonds, one in hearts and one in trumps. What can you do about it?

It's a deal where you do better to think of winners instead of losers. You have five side-suit winners. If you can add five trump tricks to the pile, this will give you the game. You must aim to score three top trumps and two club ruffs in your hand.

You cross to the ♣K and ruff a club with the ♠3. You return to dummy with the ♠K and lead another club. Yes, East shows out! You ruff with the ♠5 and West has to follow suit. Ten tricks are yours. As you see, you needed two entries to dummy to take the club ruffs (the ♣K and the ♠K). That's why you won the club lead in your hand and tested trumps by playing the ♠A and ♠Q.

If you watched a good player making the next contract, you wouldn't think that he had done anything special. Quite right, but many players would find a way to go down. Would you have survived the 4-1 trump break?

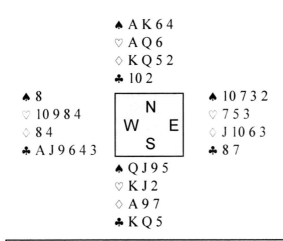

North:
♠ A K 6 4
♡ A Q 6
♢ K Q 5 2
♣ 10 2

West:
♠ 8
♡ 10 9 8 4
♢ 8 4
♣ A J 9 6 4 3

N
W E
S

East:
♠ 10 7 3 2
♡ 7 5 3
♢ J 10 6 3
♣ 8 7

South:
♠ Q J 9 5
♡ K J 2
♢ A 9 7
♣ K Q 5

West	North	East	South
—	—	—	1NT
pass	2♣	pass	2♠
pass	6♠	all pass	

How would you play the slam when West leads the ♡10?

Looking at the losers from the South hand, you can see just two in clubs. These can be reduced to the necessary one if the ♣A is onside. The same is true if trumps break 3-2 and you can ruff the third club with dummy's fourth trump. Finally, the diamond suit may break 3-3 and provide a discard. You have a wealth of chances to make the slam.

After winning with the ♡A, you should play the ♠Q and ♠A. By doing so, you keep your ♠J9 intact in case East holds four trumps including the 10; you also retain a high trump in dummy. West shows out on the second trump and you continue with a club to the king. Let's say that West wins with the ♣A and returns another heart. You win with the ♡Q, cross to the ♣Q and ruff a club. Do you ruff with a low trump? No, because this would allow

East to overruff! You ruff with the ♠K and then pick up East's remaining trumps with a marked finesse of the ♠9, followed by the ♠J.

Tips to avoid Mistake 17

(Losing to a 4-1 trump break)

- Sometimes you can avoid losing control by setting up and running a long side suit.
- To avoid having to ruff in the long-trump hand, discard instead and then ruff in the short-trump hand.
- By discarding once and ruffing the force suit later, you may exhaust a defender of that suit.
- When a defender's trump holding includes a winner (J10xx), you may be able to score all your trumps by ruffing in the long-trump hand.

Mistake 18

Failing to look for a better line

Dummy goes down and straight away you spot a possible way to make the contract: 'If West has the ♢Q, I can make the contract.' How easy it is to head for this line of play without looking any further. If East turns up with the ♢Q you go down and, perhaps only then, wonder if there was a better way of playing the hand. Look at this deal:

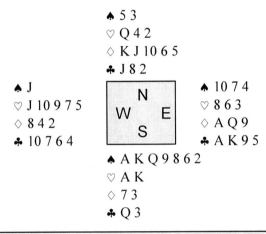

	North	
	♠ 5 3 ♡ Q 4 2 ♢ K J 10 6 5 ♣ J 8 2	
West ♠ J ♡ J 10 9 7 5 ♢ 8 4 2 ♣ 10 7 6 4	N W E S	**East** ♠ 10 7 4 ♡ 8 6 3 ♢ A Q 9 ♣ A K 9 5
	♠ A K Q 9 8 6 2 ♡ A K ♢ 7 3 ♣ Q 3	

West	North	East	South
—	—	—	1♠
pass	1NT	pass	4♠
all pass			

You bid 4♠, expecting it to be easy. West leads the ♡J and a somewhat unhelpful dummy goes down. How will you play the contract?

The original declarer thought that he would need the ♢Q to be onside. He won the heart lead, drew trumps in three rounds and tried a diamond to the jack. East cashed four winners before declarer could blink and that was one down.

Declarer's mistake was to stop planning once he had seen that a successful diamond finesse would give him the contract. Suppose East holds the ♣AK, which is a solid 1-in-3 chance once West has not led a club (and is therefore unlikely to hold both the honors). After drawing trumps, you can cash the other top heart and lead the ♣Q, which East will have to win. If he continues with two more rounds of clubs, you will have one diamond discard on the ♣J and another on the ♡Q. If instead East returns a heart to dummy's queen, you will discard your second club and lose just two diamonds and one club. Finally, a diamond return will ensure that you lose only trick in that suit.

Declarer played carelessly on the next deal. The cards lay adversely, it's true, but that was to be expected from the bidding.

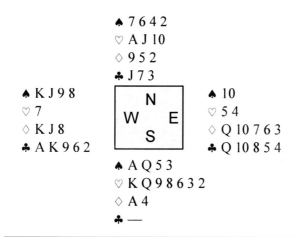

North:
♠ 7 6 4 2
♡ A J 10
♢ 9 5 2
♣ J 7 3

West:
♠ K J 9 8
♡ 7
♢ K J 8
♣ A K 9 6 2

East:
♠ 10
♡ 5 4
♢ Q 10 7 6 3
♣ Q 10 8 5 4

South:
♠ A Q 5 3
♡ K Q 9 8 6 3 2
♢ A 4
♣ —

West	North	East	South
—	—	—	1♡
dbl	2♡	pass	4♡
all pass			

How would you tackle 4♡ when West leads the ♣K?

The original declarer noted that he would go down only if he lost three spade tricks. He would succeed if the ♠K was onside or the suit broke 3-2. Recalling that a 3-2 break was a healthy 68% prospect, he gave no further thought to the play. He ruffed the club lead and drew trumps in two rounds, ending in the dummy. A spade finesse lost (surprise, surprise) and the ensuing 4-1 break put the contract one down.

West's double made it likely that he would hold four spades to the king. Had declarer borne this in mind, he might have looked for a better line. Can you spot it?

The minor suit situation may make an elimination ending seem unlikely but it can be done. After ruffing the club lead, you cross to a trump and ruff another club. You return to dummy with a trump and ruff dummy's last club, eliminating that suit. You then cash the ♠A and exit with ace and another diamond. When spades break 4-1, the defender who wins cannot safely play a spade. Neither can he play a club, which would give a ruff-and-sluff. He must therefore assist you by returning a diamond, eliminating that suit too!

The lead is then in the South hand and these cards remain:

	♠ 7 6 4 ♡ A ♢ — ♣ —	
♠ K J 9 ♡ — ♢ — ♣ K	N W E S	♠ — ♡ — ♢ Q 10 ♣ 10 5
	♠ Q 5 3 ♡ K ♢ — ♣ —	

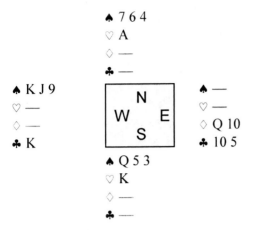

You exit with a spade. West wins and must give you the contract.

Can you see more than one way of playing the next contract? If so, you will have the chance to work out which line will give you the better chance.

	♠ 8 5 4 ♡ 7 5 4 ♢ Q J 10 6 2 ♣ 7 4	
♠ Q J 10 3 ♡ J 10 3 2 ♢ 8 3 ♣ Q J 3	N W E S	♠ 9 6 2 ♡ 9 8 6 ♢ K 9 5 ♣ K 10 8 5
	♠ A K 7 ♢ A K Q ♢ A 7 4 ♣ A 9 6 2	

West	North	East	South
—	—	—	2♣
pass	2♢	pass	2NT
pass	3NT	all pass	

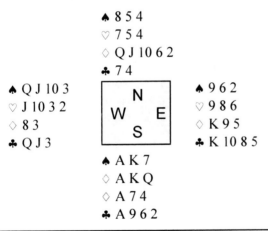

West led the ♠Q against 3NT. Declarer counted seven top tricks and only the diamond suit offered the possibility of establishing the two extra tricks that were needed. What would you have done after winning the spade lead?

Declarer cashed the ♢A and led the ♢7 to the ♢Q. If the ♢K was doubleton, the defenders could not hold it up. If a defender held ♢Kxx, declarer hoped that he would make the mistake of taking his king on the second round, which would allow three more diamond tricks to be scored.

East was a sound performer and made no such mistake. He noted his partner's high-low count signal in diamonds, the ◇8 followed by the ◇3, implying that it was declarer who held the missing ◇4. East duly held up the ◇K on the second round, restricting declarer to just two diamond tricks and the contract went one down.

How could declarer have given himself a better chance? His original line required the ◇K to be doubleton or singleton. This was around a 33% chance. A better chance was to lead the ◇4 to dummy's ◇Q on the first round. When East holds the ◇K, he cannot afford to win on the first round or you will score four diamond tricks. If instead he holds up the ◇K, you can finesse against it on the second round by running the ◇J. It is a 50% chance that East will hold the ◇K. You will also make the contract when West holds a singleton ◇K (or rises with the king from ◇Kx). This makes the recommended line around twice as good as the chosen one. It's amazing that a line of play can be so good and yet declarer fails to spot it!

Tips to avoid mistake 18

(Failing to spot a better line)

- When you spot a promising line of play, spend a while looking for an even better line.
- When a contract seems to be a near certainty, determine which bad lie of the cards can cause a problem and seek a solution before you start to play.

Mistake 19

Taking a no-hope finesse

Many contracts are surrendered by taking a finesse that has little hope of succeeding. Let's see an example:

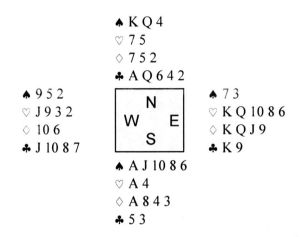

	♠ K Q 4 ♡ 7 5 ◊ 7 5 2 ♣ A Q 6 4 2	
♠ 9 5 2 ♡ J 9 3 2 ◊ 10 6 ♣ J 10 8 7	N W E S	♠ 7 3 ♡ K Q 10 8 6 ◊ K Q J 9 ♣ K 9
	♠ A J 10 8 6 ♡ A 4 ◊ A 8 4 3 ♣ 5 3	

West	North	East	South
—	—	1♡	1♠
pass	2♡	pass	4♠
all pass			

West leads the ♡2 against the spade game. If the club finesse wins, ten tricks can be made by ruffing the fourth round of diamonds (if necessary). How likely is it that the club finesse will win, though? West's ♡2 lead suggests that he holds three or four hearts to an honor. If he held the ♣K in addition, he might have raised to 2♡. Even if you ignore this pointer, it is much more likely that the player who opened the bidding will have any missing high card.

After winning the heart lead you should duck a round of clubs. East wins, cashes a heart trick and switches to the ◊K. You win with the ◊A and cross to the ♣A, dropping East's ♣K. A club ruff in your hand establishes the club suit and you draw trumps in three rounds, ending in the dummy. You discard two of your three diamond losers on the ♣Q6 and the contract is yours.

On the next deal there is no bidding by the opponents. Nevertheless, you may judge that a potential finesse is unlikely to succeed.

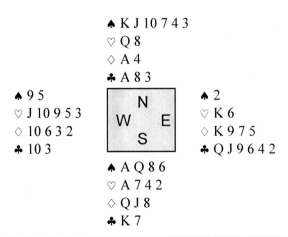

	♠ K J 10 7 4 3 ♡ Q 8 ◇ A 4 ♣ A 8 3	
♠ 9 5 ♡ J 10 9 5 3 ◇ 10 6 3 2 ♣ 10 3	N W E S	♠ 2 ♡ K 6 ◇ K 9 7 5 ♣ Q J 9 6 4 2
	♠ A Q 8 6 ♡ A 7 4 2 ◇ Q J 8 ♣ K 7	

West	North	East	South
—	—	—	1NT
pass	2♡	pass	3♠
pass	4NT	pass	5♠
pass	6♠	all pass	

West leads the ♡J. How will you tackle the play?

The original declarer liked his chances. 'One of two finesses,' he muttered. When the ♡Q was covered by East's king, he won and drew trumps. A subsequent diamond finesse failed and he was one down.

Prospects of dummy's ♡Q winning the first trick were not entirely hopeless, but how many West players would lead from a KJ10 combination into a strong notrump? Very few. It was many times more likely that East held the ♡K. Since West had almost certainly led from a sequence in hearts, so there was a solid chance that East's ♡K was doubleton. In that case the contract could be made when the ◇K was offside!

You should play low from dummy and win the first trick with the ♡A. You then draw trumps and eliminate the club suit by ruffing the third round. When you exit with a heart, East has to win with the bare ♡K. He must either return a diamond, guaranteeing you no loser in the suit, or concede a ruff-and-sluff. You make the slam either way. (If East has a safe heart return when you throw him on lead, you can still take the diamond finesse.)

When the opening lead in a suit contract comes through an AQx combination in the dummy, it is rarely right to play the queen on the first round. Most players hate leading from a king, quite rightly. If nothing good happens during the early play, you can always lead towards the queen later. How would you have played the next deal?

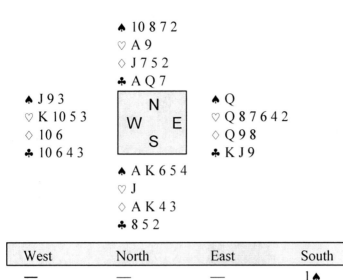

	North	
	♠ 10 8 7 2 ♡ A 9 ◇ J 7 5 2 ♣ A Q 7	
West ♠ J 9 3 ♡ K 10 5 3 ◇ 10 6 ♣ 10 6 4 3	N / W E / S	**East** ♠ Q ♡ Q 8 7 6 4 2 ◇ Q 9 8 ♣ K J 9
	♠ A K 6 5 4 ♡ J ◇ A K 4 3 ♣ 8 5 2	

West	North	East	South
—	—	—	1♠
pass	3♠	pass	4♠
all pass			

West leads the ♣3. The club finesse is close to a no-hoper, the way that most defenders regard leads from a king. You play the ♣7 from dummy and East wins with the jack. He switches to a heart, won with dummy's ace, and you eliminate that suit by ruffing the ♡9 in your hand. Two rounds of trumps reveal that West has a winner in the suit. You continue with the ace and king of diamonds, everyone following but the queen not appearing. What next?

Exiting with a trump is no good because West will win and play another club through the queen. You should exit with a diamond instead, hoping that East wins the trick. This duly comes to pass and East is endplayed. He has to lead into dummy's ♣AQ or give you a ruff-and-sluff in hearts. The game is yours. If it was East who had started with three trumps, you would exit with a trump instead. In that case you would not care who held the ◇Q.

Tips to avoid mistake 19

(Taking a no-hope finesse)

- Particularly at Trick 1, you can often tell from the bidding (or opening lead) that a finesse is likely to fail.
- When dummy goes down with AQx in the suit led, it is rarely right to finesse immediately.
- By rising with the ace from AQx, or ducking to RHO, you may retain other options later in the play.
- Similarly, you should rarely commit the king straight away from Kxx or Kxxx.

Mistake 20

Allowing an overruff

The game of bridge offers various unpleasant experiences and one of them is being overruffed. Sometimes this is the result of a mistake (or missed opportunity) by the declarer, as was the case on this deal:

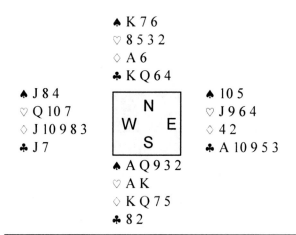

	North	
	♠ K 7 6 ♡ 8 5 3 2 ◇ A 6 ♣ K Q 6 4	
♠ J 8 4 ♡ Q 10 7 ◇ J 10 9 8 3 ♣ J 7	N W E S	♠ 10 5 ♡ J 9 6 4 ◇ 4 2 ♣ A 10 9 5 3
	♠ A Q 9 3 2 ♡ A K ◇ K Q 7 5 ♣ 8 2	

West	North	East	South
—	1♣	pass	1♠
pass	2♠	pass	4NT
pass	5♡	pass	6♠
all pass			

Rough and ready bidding, you may think, but there was nothing wrong with the final contract. Unfortunately the same cannot be said about the way that declarer played it.

He won the ◇J lead with dummy's ◇A, crossed to the ♡A and led a club to the king, hoping to set up a discard for his diamond loser. East won with the ♣A and returned a second round of hearts. With no discard available on the clubs, declarer now needed to ruff his diamond loser. He played the ◇K and ruffed a third round of the suit with the ♠6. It was not an uplifting moment when East overruffed with the ♠10, putting the slam one down. Ruffing with the ♠K would have been no good, of course, since this would promote a trump trick for the defenders. What should declarer have done?

He should have played the ace and king of trumps before taking his diamond ruff in dummy. This would give him an extra chance if East had started with only two diamonds – namely that he would not have a trump left. The chance would have paid off, allowing the slam to be made.

You frequently need to decide whether to ruff with a low trump or a trump honor. The first option may risk of an overruff; the second may promote a trump trick for the defenders. You face such a situation here and must judge which option to take:

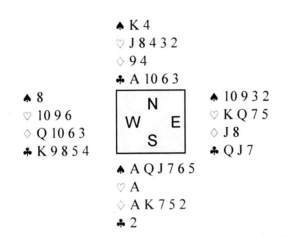

	♠ K 4 ♡ J 8 4 3 2 ♢ 9 4 ♣ A 10 6 3	
♠ 8 ♡ 10 9 6 ♢ Q 10 6 3 ♣ K 9 8 5 4	N W E S	♠ 10 9 3 2 ♡ K Q 7 5 ♢ J 8 ♣ Q J 7
	♠ A Q J 7 6 5 ♡ A ♢ A K 7 5 2 ♣ 2	

West	North	East	South
—	—	—	1♠
pass	1NT	pass	3♢
pass	4♠	pass	4NT
pass	5♡	pass	6♠
all pass			

You win the heart lead and play the ♢AK, everyone following. When you lead a third round of diamonds, you must decide whether to ruff with the ♠K or the ♠4. What choice would you make?

You cannot afford East to overruff and return a trump, so, you should ruff the third diamond with the ♠K, even though this may promote a trump trick for one of the defenders. When East shows out, you play the ♣A and ruff a club to return to your hand. You then ruff a fourth round of diamonds with the ♠4. Whether or not East decides to overruff, you will reach your hand again with a heart ruff and play the ♠AQJ followed by the established card in diamonds. The slam is yours for the loss of just one trump trick.

On the next deal no trump honor is available for your first ruff:

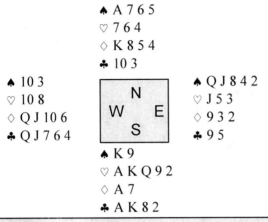

	♠ A 7 6 5	
	♡ 7 6 4	
	◇ K 8 5 4	
	♣ 10 3	
♠ 10 3	N	♠ Q J 8 4 2
♡ 10 8	W E	♡ J 5 3
◇ Q J 10 6	S	◇ 9 3 2
♣ Q J 7 6 4		♣ 9 5
	♠ K 9	
	♡ A K Q 9 2	
	◇ A 7	
	♣ A K 8 2	

West	North	East	South
—	—	—	2♣
pass	2◇	pass	2♡
pass	3♡	pass	3♠
pass	4◇	pass	6♡
all pass			

The original declarer won the ◇Q lead with the ◇K and cashed the two top clubs in his hand. He then led a third round of clubs, ruffing with the ♡4. It was a nasty moment when East overruffed with the ♡5. Declarer won the diamond return with the ◇A and drew a second round of trumps, hoping that East would have no trump left. When he led a fourth round of clubs, East overruffed with the ♡J and the slam was one down. Did you spot the mistake that was made?

Declarer should have ruffed the third round of clubs with the ♡7. East could overruff with the ♡J but would have been unable to overruff the ♡6 on the fourth round of clubs. His last trump would be the ♡5! The deal shows how it can be worthwhile ruffing with dummy's highest trump, even when it is not a master.

The last deal in this chapter requires a completely different technique:

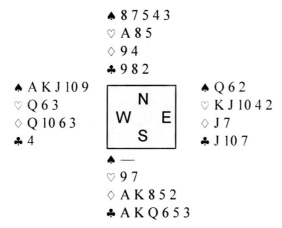

	♠ 8 7 5 4 3 ♡ A 8 5 ♢ 9 4 ♣ 9 8 2	
♠ A K J 10 9 ♡ Q 6 3 ♢ Q 10 6 3 ♣ 4	N W E S	♠ Q 6 2 ♡ K J 10 4 2 ♢ J 7 ♣ J 10 7
	♠ — ♡ 9 7 ♢ A K 8 5 2 ♣ A K Q 6 5 3	

West	North	East	South
—	—	—	1♣
1♠	pass	2♠	3♢
pass	4♣	pass	5♣
all pass			

Declarer ruffed the ♠A lead and played the ♢AK. On the next round West followed with a mildly deceptive ♢Q and declarer ruffed with the ♣9, East overruffing with the ♣10. Declarer ruffed the spade return and played the ♣A. When he ruffed a fourth diamond, East overruffed again for one down.

On the third round of diamonds, declarer should have discarded a heart from dummy. He ruffs the next spade and leads a fourth round of diamonds, discarding yet another heart from dummy. Declarer ruffs the next spade, crosses to the bare ♡A and returns to his hand with a trump. He can then ruff a heart in dummy, which cannot be overruffed. Finally he draws East's two remaining trumps and enjoys the thirteenth card in the diamond suit.

Tips to avoid Mistake 20

(Allowing an overruff)

- One simple way to reduce the risk of an overruff is to draw a round or two of trumps beforehand.
- Ruffing with a high trump can work well even when it is not a master.
- By swapping a dangerous ruff for a safer ruff in a different suit, you can reduce the risk of an overruff.

Mistake 21

Failing to unblock

There are various common situations where declarers fail to unblock a card to their cost. Let's start with a deal or two where an unblock promotes an entry to the opposite hand.

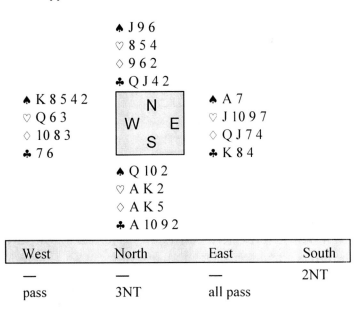

	♠ J 9 6 ♡ 8 5 4 ◊ 9 6 2 ♣ Q J 4 2	
♠ K 8 5 4 2 ♡ Q 6 3 ◊ 10 8 3 ♣ 7 6	N W E S	♠ A 7 ♡ J 10 9 7 ◊ Q J 7 4 ♣ K 8 4
	♠ Q 10 2 ♡ A K 2 ◊ A K 5 ♣ A 10 9 2	

West	North	East	South
—	—	—	2NT
pass	3NT	all pass	

West leads the ♠4 to the ♠A and East returns the ♠7. What is your plan?

The original declarer followed with the ♠2 on the first round ('Mistake!') and the ♠Q on the second round. West knew that declarer had the ♠10 because East would not have returned the ♠7 from ♠107. He therefore allowed the ♠Q to win, preventing declarer from reaching dummy with the ♠J to take a club finesse. It was no longer possible to score the four club tricks that were needed and the contract went down.

To give himself a chance of four club tricks, declarer needs to reach dummy in spades. He must unblock the ♠Q under East's ♠A at Trick 1. When the ♠7 is returned, West cannot prevent declarer from reaching dummy on either the second or third round of the suit. He will then lead the ♣Q to pick up four club tricks and the contract.

(We did not consider which card declarer should play from dummy on the first trick. He should play the ♠9. This will ensure an entry when West had led from the ♠AK. When the cards lie as in the diagram, it will also prevent some inspired East player from covering dummy's ♠6 with the ♠7! A bit double-dummy, yes, but it would defeat the contract by keeping declarer out of the North hand.)

On the next deal the required unblock is simpler in a way because it relates only to the play in the suit led. Nevertheless, many players would put the contract on the floor.

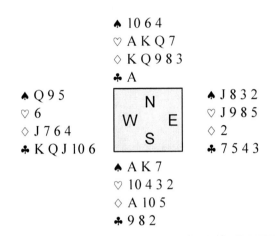

West	North / South	East
	♠ 10 6 4 ♡ A K Q 7 ◇ K Q 9 8 3 ♣ A	
♠ Q 9 5 ♡ 6 ◇ J 7 6 4 ♣ K Q J 10 6	N W E S	♠ J 8 3 2 ♡ J 9 8 5 ◇ 2 ♣ 7 5 4 3
	♠ A K 7 ♡ 10 4 3 2 ◇ A 10 5 ♣ 9 8 2	

West	North	East	South
—	1◇	pass	1♡
pass	4♣	pass	4NT
pass	5♣	pass	6♡
all pass			

Despite his poor trumps, South headed for a slam. He won the ♣K lead in dummy and played the ace and king of trumps, West throwing a club on the second round. How would you continue?

You must aim to ruff one club and to discard your two remaining black-suit losers on dummy's diamond suit. You draw a third round of trumps, with the queen, and play the ◇K. On this trick you make the key play of unblocking the ◇10 from your hand. You then lead the ◇3, playing the ◇A from your hand even if East decides to ruff the trick. Subsequently you can finesse dummy's ◇9 and continue to play diamonds, throwing two losers from your hand. East can score his ♡J whenever he wishes. Twelve tricks are yours.

Suppose you mistakenly follow with the ◇5 on the first round of diamonds. You cross to the ◇A, East showing out, and lead the ◇10. You are praying for West to cover with the ◇J, so you can untangle your diamond winners. No, he meanly retains his jack and you go one down.

Another purpose of unblocking one or more middle spot-cards is to create an extra entry on a later round of a suit. Test yourself on this deal:

North:
♠ J 7 4
♡ A 6
◇ A 6 4 2
♣ 10 9 8 3

West:
♠ Q 5 2
♡ K 10 7 4 3
◇ 10 8
♣ A 5 2

N
W E
S

East:
♠ K 6 3
♡ 8 5 2
◇ Q 9 3
♣ J 7 6 4

South:
♠ A 10 9 8
♡ Q J 9
◇ K J 7 5
♣ K Q

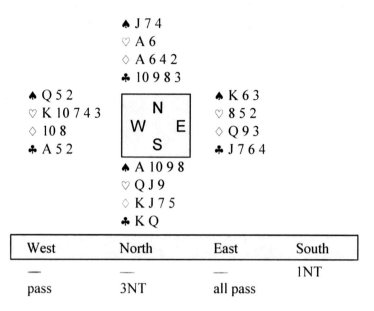

West	North	East	South
—	—	—	1NT
pass	3NT	all pass	

West leads the ♡4 against 3NT and you win in your hand with the ♡9. What now?

If East holds two or three diamonds including the queen, you can cross to the ◇A and finesse the ◇J to pick up four diamond tricks. Two hearts and three spades (you hope) will then bring the total to nine.

Only one play is good enough at Trick 2. You must lead the ◇7 to dummy's ◇A. If the suit breaks 3-2, this will allow you to lead the ◇5 to the ◇6 on the fourth round. At Trick 3 you lead the ◇2 to your ◇J, which wins. You continue with the ◇K and return to dummy with the ◇6, as planned. When you lead a low spade to your ♠10, West wins and clears the hearts. You repeat the spade finesse, leading the ♠J this time, and all is well. You make three spades to go with four diamonds and two hearts. The game is yours and this was possible only because you had the forethought to unblock the ◇7.

Right, let's end the chapter with this one:

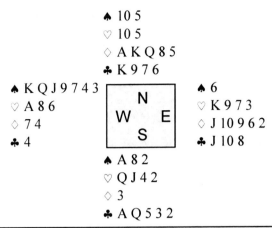

	♠ 10 5 ♡ 10 5 ♢ A K Q 8 5 ♣ K 9 7 6	
♠ K Q J 9 7 4 3 ♡ A 8 6 ♢ 7 4 ♣ 4	N W E S	♠ 6 ♡ K 9 7 3 ♢ J 10 9 6 2 ♣ J 10 8
	♠ A 8 2 ♡ Q J 4 2 ♢ 3 ♣ A Q 5 3 2	

West	North	East	South
1♠	2♢	pass	2NT
pass	3NT	all pass	

You duck the ♠K lead and East discards a heart on the spade continuation. How will you play the contract?

With East out of spades, the original declarer saw no need to hold up the ♠A again. He won with the second round of spades and… 'Mistake!' He had failed to notice the potential blockage in clubs. Unless the defenders' clubs split 2-2, he would have to expend the ace, king and queen on the first three rounds. Dummy's remaining spot-card would then block the suit.

Declarer needed to discard one of dummy's blocking club spot-cards on the ♠A. This could only be done if he held up the ♠A for one more round. He could then ditch a club on the third spade and run five clubs unimpeded.

Tips to avoid mistake 21

(Failing to unblock)

- By playing a higher card than necessary from your hand (whether winning the trick or following suit), you may promote an extra entry to dummy.
- Always check that the spot-cards in a suit where you hold length in both hands (a 5-4 suit, for example) will not cause a blockage.
- Keep a low spot-card in the stronger hand, in case this will give you an extra entry to the weaker hand.

Mistake 22

Winning in the wrong hand

Many a contract is lost by winning the first trick in the wrong hand and you may need to plan the whole contract before deciding how to play at Trick 1. Quite a good player went wrong on this heart game:

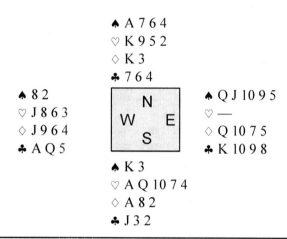

	♠ A 7 6 4 ♡ K 9 5 2 ◇ K 3 ♣ 7 6 4	
♠ 8 2 ♡ J 8 6 3 ◇ J 9 6 4 ♣ A Q 5	N W E S	♠ Q J 10 9 5 ♡ — ◇ Q 10 7 5 ♣ K 10 9 8
	♠ K 3 ♡ A Q 10 7 4 ◇ A 8 2 ♣ J 3 2	

West	North	East	South
—	—	—	1♡
pass	3♡	pass	4♡
all pass			

West led the ♠8 and declarer won with the ♠K. There were three unavoidable club losers, so declarer needed to pick up the trumps without loss. This could be done, against ♡J863 in either hand, by playing the ♡A on the first round. East showed out on this card and declarer's next move was to finesse the ♡9. A diamond ruff was needed to bring the total to ten, so declarer cashed the ◇K and ◇A, proceeding to ruff the third round. He cashed the bare ♡K and then had to return to his hand to draw the last trump. He attempted to do this with a spade ruff but West overruffed to put the game one down.

All would have been easy if declarer had won the first trick with dummy's ♠A. After taking the diamond ruff, he could have returned to his hand with the ♠K to draw the last trump. It was necessary to plan the play (against a 4-0 trump break either way) before playing to the first trick.

With that deal firmly in mind, you will have a good chance of solving the next problem correctly. Don't let me down!

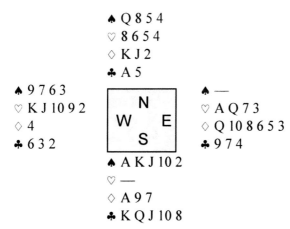

	♠ Q 8 5 4 ♡ 8 6 5 4 ◇ K J 2 ♣ A 5	
♠ 9 7 6 3 ♡ K J 10 9 2 ◇ 4 ♣ 6 3 2	N W E S	♠ — ♡ A Q 7 3 ◇ Q 10 8 6 5 3 ♣ 9 7 4
	♠ A K J 10 2 ♡ — ◇ A 9 7 ♣ K Q J 10 8	

West	North	East	South
—	—	—	1♠
pass	3♠	pass	4♣
pass	4◇	pass	4♡
pass	5♣	pass	7♠
all pass			

How will you play the grand slam when West leads the ◇4?

Your only potential loser is in diamonds. Provided trumps are not 4-0, you will be able to draw trumps and discard one of dummy's diamonds on your clubs. A diamond ruff in dummy will then wrap up the contract.

What if the trumps break 4-0, though? Arranging a diamond ruff in dummy would then require some favorable breaks in the minors. A better idea would be to ruff two hearts in the South hand, planning to discard dummy's remaining two hearts and one diamond on your surplus club winners.

The moment you conclude that this line of play might become necessary, you will see that you need to win the first trick in dummy! You rise with the ◇K, ruff a heart with the ♠10 and play the ♠A, East showing out. You then cross to the ♣A and ruff another heart with the ♠J. After the two ruffs with trump honors, you are left with ♠K2 opposite ♠Q85. You cash the king, finesse the 8 and draw West's last trump with the queen. Tired but happy, you play the four good clubs in your hand, throwing two hearts and a diamond from dummy. The guys in your office will be impressed tomorrow!

Playing in notrumps, without the benefit of ruffing entries, you may have to manage the entry situation more carefully. Test yourself on this deal:

	North	
	♠ K 8 6 2 ♡ A 8 5 ♢ Q J 10 2 ♣ 9 7	
West ♠ Q 10 7 4 ♡ K 4 3 ♢ A 9 8 5 ♣ 4 2	N / W E / S	**East** ♠ J 9 5 ♡ Q 9 7 6 ♢ 6 3 ♣ A 8 5 3
	♠ A 3 ♡ J 10 2 ♢ K 7 4 ♣ K Q J 10 6	

West	North	East	South
—	—	—	1NT
pass	2♣	pass	2♢
pass	3NT	all pass	

West leads the ♠4 against 3NT. What plan will you make?

The original declarer played a low spade from dummy and… the contract could no longer be made! He won with the ♠A and played clubs, East winning the second round. The spades were cleared and declarer led dummy's ♢Q, which was allowed to win. When he tried a diamond to the king, West produced the ♢A and cashed two spades, exiting with the ♢9. After taking one more diamond trick, declarer had to play away from the ♡A. He lost two heart tricks and went two down.

To make the contract, you must win the first trick with the ♠K and clear the clubs. East takes his ace on the second round and plays a spade to your ace. In the right hand now, you run the clubs and play on diamonds. West wins with the ♢A and cashes two spades. The remaining tricks are yours.

Tips to avoid mistake 22

(Winning in the wrong hand)

- An important part of planning a contract is to foresee the entries you need to the weaker hand.
- Do not make the first play from dummy until you are happy with your plan to manage the entries.
- Running the lead to your hand seems natural but sometimes the next play must be made from dummy.

Mistake 23

Failing to false-card

As declarer you can play whatever spot-cards you like at any time. Free from the responsibility of informing partner about your hand, you can do your best to mislead the opponents. Some players reckon this is a waste of time. 'Well, I might have tried that,' they say, 'but I'm sure West would have seen through it.' Maybe he would, maybe he wouldn't. That's no excuse for not trying! Even if only one defender in five falls for your little traps, that will still be a healthy profit.

We will start with a typical 3NT contract where the original declarer did not even consider disguising his holding.

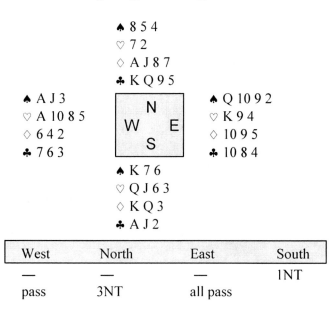

	♠ 8 5 4 ♡ 7 2 ♢ A J 8 7 ♣ K Q 9 5	
♠ A J 3 ♡ A 10 8 5 ♢ 6 4 2 ♣ 7 6 3	N W E S	♠ Q 10 9 2 ♡ K 9 4 ♢ 10 9 5 ♣ 10 8 4
	♠ K 7 6 ♡ Q J 6 3 ♢ K Q 3 ♣ A J 2	

West	North	East	South
—	—	—	1NT
pass	3NT	all pass	

West led the ♡5, East winning with the ♡K and declarer playing the ♡3. Because no spot-card lower than the 5 was missing, East now knew that his partner had led from a four-card suit. Since that suit alone could not provide the tricks to beat 3NT, he switched to the ♠10. Jackpot! The defenders would now score at least three spades to go with the ace and king of hearts.

Declarer should have feared a spade switch at Trick 2 and done what he could to encourage a heart continuation. He should have followed with the ♡6 rather than the ♡3 on the first trick. This would foster the illusion, in

East's eyes, that West had led from a 5-card heart suit. A spade switch would be less attractive when West might have led from ♡AJ853.

The theme is the same on the next deal:

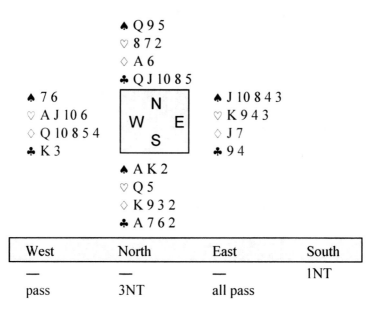

	North	
	♠ Q 9 5 ♡ 8 7 2 ◇ A 6 ♣ Q J 10 8 5	
West ♠ 7 6 ♡ A J 10 6 ◇ Q 10 8 5 4 ♣ K 3	N W E S	**East** ♠ J 10 8 4 3 ♡ K 9 4 3 ◇ J 7 ♣ 9 4
	♠ A K 2 ♡ Q 5 ◇ K 9 3 2 ♣ A 7 6 2	

West	North	East	South
—	—	—	1NT
pass	3NT	all pass	

How will you play 3NT when West leads the ◇5?

You can see how hopeless the situation would be if you won East's ◇J with the ◇K and then crossed to the ♠Q to run the ♣Q. Not only would West know that the diamonds were still stopped (by dummy's ◇A), he would also know that you held the ♠A and ♠K. It would not take a genius to switch to the ♡6 when he won with the ♣K.

It will not work every time but you should win the first trick with the ◇A and drop the ◇9 from your hand. Some of the world's West players will then persist with diamonds when they win with the ♣K. At least you give yourself a chance.

Note that you must sometimes be a bit delicate with false cards aimed at making RHO's card look like an encouraging attitude signal. Suppose this is the suit that has been led and you wish to encourage a subsequent continuation:

	♡ A 5	
♡ Q 10 6 4 2		♡ J 7
	♡ K 9 8 3	

West leads the ♡4 against 3NT and you win with the ♡A. If East chooses to play the ♡7, it would be a mistake to false-card with the ♡9. West would then ask himself: 'Who has the ♡8? If my partner held ♡K873, he would have signaled with the ♡8, not the ♡7.' He will suspect that you are up to some mischief.

You should play the lowest card that is bigger than the spot-card East has played (the ♡8 here). You might try the same play from ♡KJ83, to make the East's 7 from ♡97 look like an encouraging card.

Similar tactics may pay off in a suit contract. Look at this heart game:

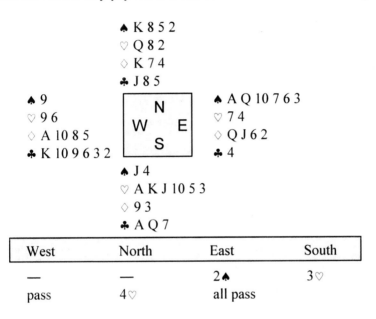

	North	
	♠ K 8 5 2 ♡ Q 8 2 ◊ K 7 4 ♣ J 8 5	
West ♠ 9 ♡ 9 6 ◊ A 10 8 5 ♣ K 10 9 6 3 2	N W E S	**East** ♠ A Q 10 7 6 3 ♡ 7 4 ◊ Q J 6 2 ♣ 4
	♠ J 4 ♡ A K J 10 5 3 ◊ 9 3 ♣ A Q 7	

West	North	East	South
—	—	2♠	3♡
pass	4♡	all pass	

West leads the ♠9. You know that this card is almost certainly a singleton. East does not and you must try to disguise the position. You play low from dummy and drop the ♠J under East's ♠A. How should East read the situation?

Even if knows that you are a slippery creature, well capable of dropping the ♠J from ♠J4, he must take into account that you may actually hold only one spade. After all, you began with many more hearts than West, so you start as favorite to hold the spade singleton.

On some deals, East will be able to reason: 'Declarer probably has a singleton spade but in that case we're unlikely to beat the contract. I'd better continue spades anyway.' That's not the case on this deal, where East's singleton ♣4 represents a promising switch. There is a fair chance that he will lead this card at Trick 2. You will rise with the ♣A, draw trumps and eventually land the contract by leading towards the ◊K.

If East persists with spades anyway, at least you did what you could. Had you followed unthinkingly with the ♠4 on the first trick, East would know for sure that West's lead was a singleton. On a spade continuation (high or low) you would lose four tricks.

Suppose you're in a suit contract and fear that a singleton has been led in this lay-out:

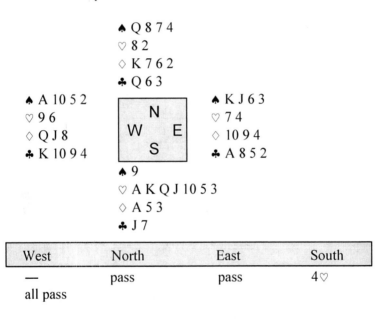

	♢ K J 6 4	
♢ 2		♢ A 10 9 7 3
	♢ Q 8 5	

To paint the illusion that West has led from ♢Q52, you should call for dummy's ♢J and drop the ♢8 from your hand. Of course this won't work every time, but it will be enjoyable when it does!

It's not just a question of remembering a few standard deceptive plays. You must be alive to the situation, constantly asking yourself how you can give the defenders a problem. Declarer missed a chance on this deal:

	♠ Q 8 7 4 ♡ 8 2 ♢ K 7 6 2 ♣ Q 6 3	
♠ A 10 5 2 ♡ 9 6 ♢ Q J 8 ♣ K 10 9 4	N W E S	♠ K J 6 3 ♡ 7 4 ♢ 10 9 4 ♣ A 8 5 2
	♠ 9 ♡ A K Q J 10 5 3 ♢ A 5 3 ♣ J 7	

West	North	East	South
—	pass	pass	4♡
all pass			

How will you play the heart game when West leads the ♢Q?

It may seem a fairly hopeless proposition. Even if the diamonds are 3-3, the defenders will surely manage to cash their three black-suit tricks when you give up a diamond.

That's true if you win the first diamond, draw trumps and duck a diamond. Suppose instead that you play a low diamond from dummy and contribute the ♢5 from your hand, hoping to make East's ♢4 look like a come-on signal from ♢A1042 or ♢A942. West will get quite a shock if he continues with the ♢J and you win with the ♢A. You can then draw trumps and discard a loser on dummy's 13th diamond.

Tips to avoid Mistake 23

(Failing to false-card)

- Many more deals than you may suspect offer a chance for declarer to disguise his hand by falsecarding.
- When you suspect that the opening lead against a suit contract is a singleton, hide a lower card in your hand to make the lead look like top of a doubleton.
- In a notrump contract when they lead a suit that you have well-guarded, look for a way to pretend you are weak there.
- Sometimes it pays to hold up when you can win the first trick, merely to encourage a continuation that will allow you to set up an extra trick in the suit.

Mistake 24

Failing to hold up in a suit contract

It is commonplace to hold up an ace in a notrump contract, aiming to break communications between the two defenders. Many declarers fail to spot that the same play can be useful in a suit contract too. Again your intention is to kill the defenders' communications in the suit that they have led.

The original declarer here was unfamiliar with the technique:

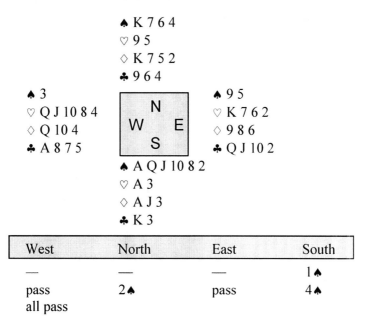

	♠ K 7 6 4 ♡ 9 5 ♢ K 7 5 2 ♣ 9 6 4	
♠ 3 ♡ Q J 10 8 4 ♢ Q 10 4 ♣ A 8 7 5	N W E S	♠ 9 5 ♡ K 7 6 2 ♢ 9 8 6 ♣ Q J 10 2
	♠ A Q J 10 8 2 ♡ A 3 ♢ A J 3 ♣ K 3	

West	North	East	South
—	—	—	1♠
pass	2♠	pass	4♠
all pass			

West led the ♡Q and declarer won with the ♡A. After drawing trumps with the ace and king, he finessed the ♢J. West won with the ♢Q and crossed to the East's ♡K. A club switch through the king then put the game one down. 'That was unlucky!' observed the declarer.

The way to side-step such misfortune is to hold up the ♡A, allowing West's ♡Q to win the first trick. You win the heart continuation, draw trumps and finesse the ♢J. Now West cannot cross to the East hand for a club switch. He will have to return a diamond and the 3-3 break in the suit will let you discard a club from your hand.

Here is another example where a hold-up will improve your chances:

	North	
	♠ K 9 7 5	
	♡ A 10 6	
	♢ 5 4	
	♣ A J 10 6	
West		**East**
♠ 10 2	N	♠ Q J 8
♡ K Q J 9 4	W E	♡ 8 5
♢ 9 8 6	S	♢ Q J 10 3 2
♣ 9 4 3		♣ K 8 5
	South	
	♠ A 6 4 3	
	♡ 7 3 2	
	♢ A K 7	
	♣ Q 7 2	

West	North	East	South
—	1♣	pass	1♠
pass	2♠	pass	3♢
pass	3♠	pass	4♠
all pass			

South marks time with 3♢, in case North has raised spades on 3-card support. How will you play the spade game when West leads the ♡K?

The original declarer was uninspired. He won the first trick and drew two rounds of trumps, everyone following. When he ran the ♣Q, East won and returned a heart. Two tricks in that suit ended declarer's prospects and the game went one down.

Since the club finesse is into the East hand, it is worth holding up the ♡A on the first round. You win the heart continuation and the 5-2 heart break means that East now has no hearts left. After two rounds of trumps, you run the ♣Q to the king. Bereft of hearts, East switches to the ♢Q. You win with the ace and play three more rounds of clubs, ditching your heart loser. Note that you would still have made the contract if West held the last trump, provided he had to follow to three rounds of clubs.

'What if West holds six hearts and East ruffs the second round?' you may be thinking. It's possible but West might have bid hearts in that case. Also if hearts are 6-1, the odds are high that East will be ruffing the second round of hearts from a natural trump trick. If he started with three trumps, you would still make the contract by discarding your last heart on dummy's clubs.

On the next deal the purpose of the hold-up is to set up an endplay:

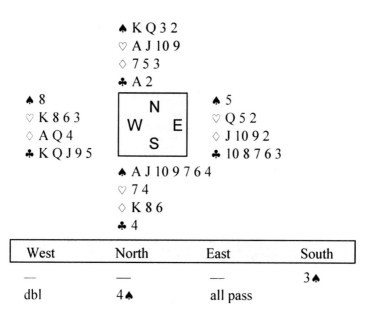

♠ K Q 3 2
♡ A J 10 9
♢ 7 5 3
♣ A 2

♠ 8	N	♠ 5
♡ K 8 6 3	W E	♡ Q 5 2
♢ A Q 4	S	♢ J 10 9 2
♣ K Q J 9 5		♣ 10 8 7 6 3

♠ A J 10 9 7 6 4
♡ 7 4
♢ K 8 6
♣ 4

West	North	East	South
—	—	—	3♠
dbl	4♠	all pass	

West leads the ♣K. If you mistakenly take the ♣A immediately, you will go down. When you subsequently finesse in hearts, East will win with the queen and a diamond switch will give the defenders three more tricks.

To keep East off lead, you must duck the first club. On this trick East will have the chance to make a suit preference signal (see Chapter 43). He may play the ♣8 to suggest a heart switch.

Let's say that West switches to a heart now (a club continuation is no better). You win with the ♡A, draw trumps with the ♠K and discard your remaining heart on the ♣A. You then run the ♡J into the safe hand if East declines to cover with the ♡Q. When West wins with the ♡K, he will have to give you a tenth trick.

Tips to avoid mistake 24

(Failing to hold up in suit contracts)

- When you hold Ax opposite xx in a side suit that has been led, it is often right to duck the first round to prevent the defenders from crossing in that suit later.
- With Axx opposite xxx, it may be right to duck the first round, to break communications when the suit breaks 5-2.
- With A10xx opposite a singleton, it may be necessary to duck the first round to a safe defender, LHO or RHO. You can then discard on the ace, setting up some other suit safely.

Mistake 25

Leading the wrong card for a finesse

With plenty of high cards in a suit, you can afford to lead a high card on the first round when you take a finesse:

	♠ A 10 9 4	
♠ K		♠ 8 7 5 3
	♠ Q J 6 2	

You lead the ♠Q, covered by the king and ace. Because you hold the jack, 10 and 9 of the suit, you can then score the remaining three spade tricks even though West's king was a singleton. Swap the ♠9 and the ♠7 and it would be a mistake to lead the ♠Q on the first round. You would score just three tricks, East claiming the fourth round. Lead a low card on the first round, intending to finesse the ♠10 and all would be well.

On the following deal, the situation is more complicated:

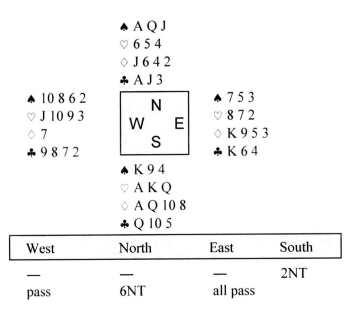

	♠ A Q J ♡ 6 5 4 ♢ J 6 4 2 ♣ A J 3	
♠ 10 8 6 2 ♡ J 10 9 3 ♢ 7 ♣ 9 8 7 2	N W E S	♠ 7 5 3 ♡ 8 7 2 ♢ K 9 5 3 ♣ K 6 4
	♠ K 9 4 ♡ A K Q ♢ A Q 10 8 ♣ Q 10 5	

West	North	East	South
—	—	—	2NT
pass	6NT	all pass	

You win the ♡J lead in your hand and run the ♣Q. East wins the trick and returns a heart. To make the slam you now need four diamond tricks. You cross to dummy with a spade and must decide whether to lead the ♢J or a low diamond. What do you think?

It would be a mistake to lead the ◇J on the first round. If East held a singleton ◇K, West would subsequently score a trick with his ◇9753. You should lead a low diamond, finessing the ◇10 successfully. You return to dummy in one of the black suits and must now make your second play in diamonds. Should you lead the ◇J or a low diamond?

It is now right to lead the ◇J. If East covers with the ◇K, you will be happy. If West follows, the suit will be breaking 3-2. If he shows out, the way will be clear for a finesse of the ◇8.

See what happens if you mistakenly lead a low diamond on the second round, finessing the ◇Q successfully. These cards will remain:

	◇ J 6	
◇ —		◇ K 9
	◇ A 8	

East will then score a trick in the suit.

The following position is similar:

	♡ J 6 3 2	
♡ 8		♡ K 9 5 4
	♡ A Q 10 7	

You cannot afford to lead the ♡J in case East holds a singleton ♡K. You lead low to the ♡10, interested to see the ♡8 fall offside. You return to dummy in a different suit and lead the jack, as on the previous deal. This is covered by the king and ace, West showing out. The way is then clear to finesse the ♡7 on the third round.

Let's look at some positions where you hold greater length in the suit:

	♡ J 8 6 5 3	
♡ —		♡ K 10 2
	♡ A Q 9 7 4	

If you lead low to the queen on the first round, East's ♡K10 will be worth a trick. Instead you should lead the ♡J because you will be 'happy if the jack is covered'. Either West follows, the suit breaking 2-1, or he will show out. In the latter case you can return to dummy for a marked finesse of the ♡9.

When entries to the weaker hand are sparse, you sometimes cannot afford to lead a low card for the first finesse, even though you would like to:

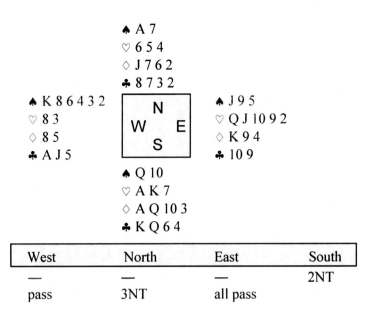

	♠ A 7 ♡ 6 5 4 ♢ J 7 6 2 ♣ 8 7 3 2	
♠ K 8 6 4 3 2 ♡ 8 3 ♢ 8 5 ♣ A J 5	N W E S	♠ J 9 5 ♡ Q J 10 9 2 ♢ K 9 4 ♣ 10 9
	♠ Q 10 ♡ A K 7 ♢ A Q 10 3 ♣ K Q 6 4	

West	North	East	South
—	—	—	2NT
pass	3NT	all pass	

West leads the ♠4. You play low from dummy and (it's your lucky day!) the ♠J appears from East. How will you continue after winning with the ♠Q?

You have five top tricks. To make 3NT, you will need a full four diamond tricks along with one club trick. You cannot afford to release the ♠A yet, so you must lead the ♣K from your hand. West wins with the ♣A and clears the spades. You now need four diamond tricks. With one more entry to dummy, you would lead low on the first round – guarding against a single ♢K onside. You cannot afford that luxury here. You lead the ♢J, so that you will remain in dummy if East holds the ♢K and declines to cover. On this occasion the diamonds break 3-2 with the king onside. The game is yours.

Tips to avoid mistake 25

(Leading the wrong card for a finesse)

- Unless there are entry considerations, do not lead a high card for a finesse unless you would be happy to see it covered.
- The more adjacent middle cards that you hold, the more likely it is that you can afford to lead a high card.
- The advantage of leading a high card is that you retain the lead in that hand if it is not covered.
- If you do not have an outside entry to the hand from which you are leading, you may have to lead a high card even if this would cost a trick against a bad break.

Mistake 26

Failing to lead through an honor

There are many situations when you can bring home a contract by leading a low card through an ace or a king held by a defender. If he rises with the card, he will promote your honors. If he declines to play the card, you will win the trick and perhaps continue in some different direction.

The technique is most useful in notrump where you need extra tricks from two different sources and have only one stopper left in the suit led:

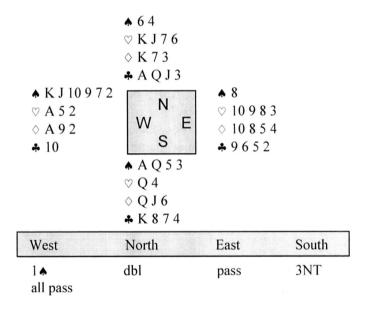

		♠ 6 4		
		♡ K J 7 6		
		◇ K 7 3		
		♣ A Q J 3		
♠ K J 10 9 7 2		N		♠ 8
♡ A 5 2	W		E	♡ 10 9 8 3
◇ A 9 2		S		◇ 10 8 5 4
♣ 10				♣ 9 6 5 2
		♠ A Q 5 3		
		♡ Q 4		
		◇ Q J 6		
		♣ K 8 7 4		

West	North	East	South
1♠	dbl	pass	3NT
all pass			

West leads the ♠J and you win with the queen. How will you continue?

You have six tricks in the black suits and need three more from hearts and diamonds. Neither red suit will provide three tricks on its own. If your next move is to lead the ♡Q or a diamond, you will go down. West will win with the ace and clear the spades before you have a chance to score a trick from the other red suit.

At Trick 2 you should lead the ♡4 through the defender's high card. If West rises with the ♡A, you will have three heart tricks and the contract. If instead he plays low, you will pocket one heart trick and bring your total to nine by turning to diamonds.

Thousands of such deals arise every day. By leading through the defender's high card (a form of 'avoidance play') you force him to pay a hefty price for the privilege of winning with that card.

On the next deal, declarer's task is again eased by information from the bidding.

	North	
	♠ K Q 6 3 ♡ K Q J 7 3 ◇ 7 4 ♣ A 2	
West ♠ 9 5 4 ♡ A 10 6 2 ◇ J 10 9 8 5 2 ♣ —	N W E S	**East** ♠ 10 7 ♡ 9 5 ◇ 6 3 ♣ K 10 8 7 6 4 3
	♠ A J 8 2 ♡ 8 4 ◇ A K Q ♣ Q J 9 5	
	South	

West	North	East	South
—	—	3♣	3NT
pass	6NT	all pass	

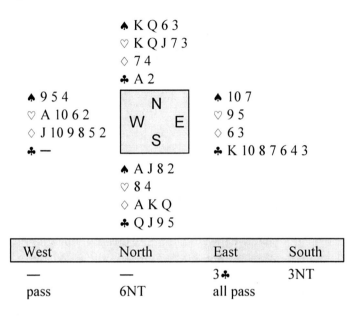

How would you play 6NT when West leads the ◇J?

The original declarer was uninspired. He led twice towards the hearts, West withholding the ace. Seeing no other chance but a 3-3 heart break, he played a third round of the suit and went one down.

To make the slam, you must score extra tricks from both hearts and clubs. You win the diamond lead and play a heart to dummy's king. You return to the ♠J and lead another heart to the ♡Q, the ♡9 appearing from East. Now you should take a second diamond trick, finding East with two cards there, followed by a spade to the queen, East again following for a second time. With East following twice to each of the suits outside clubs, you expect his initial shape to be 2=2=2=7. Rather than try for a 3-3 heart break, you play ace and another club. East plays low on the second round and you finesse the ♣9. You then run the ♣Q to East's king, setting up a third club trick. He has no heart to play and the slam is yours.

On the next deal you can again place the missing high cards, thanks to an opening bid from West.

	♠ Q 10 ♡ K J 10 6 ♢ Q J ♣ Q J 7 6 4	
♠ A K J 9 2 ♡ 9 5 ♢ K 7 4 2 ♣ A 5	N W E S	♠ 8 7 6 4 ♡ 3 2 ♢ 10 6 3 ♣ 10 9 8 2
	♠ 5 3 ♡ A Q 8 7 4 ♢ A 9 8 5 ♣ K 3	

West	North	East	South
1♠	pass	pass	2♡
pass	2♠	pass	3♢
pass	4♡	all pass	

West cashes two spades and switches to a trump. How will you play?

The original declarer drew trumps and led the ♣K to the ace. West exited with his remaining club and declarer tested the clubs for a 3-3 break. When this did not materialize, he took the diamond finesse and went one down.

After drawing trumps, you should lead the ♣3 through West. If he rises with the ♣A, you will have four club tricks and can discard all three diamond losers. If West plays low instead, you will win with the ♣Q and continue with a club to the king and ace. West will then be endplayed, forced to lead a diamond from the king or give a ruff-and-sluff. The latter option will allow you to throw a diamond from dummy and ruff in your hand. You can then ruff two diamond losers in dummy and discard the other on the ♣J.

Tips to avoid mistake 26

(Failing to lead through a high card)

- It is often effective to lead through a defender's ace or king. If he rises with the card, he will promote your honors. If he plays low, you can pocket a trick and turn elsewhere.
- Suppose you hold ♢Q85 in dummy and ♢K3 in your hand. You lead the ♢3 through LHO's ♢A. If he rises, you have two diamond tricks; if he ducks you may be able to discard the ♢K.

Mistake 27

Playing the wrong suit first

When you have two suits that may yield the extra trick(s) that you need, it is sometimes essential to play the right suit first. We start with a deal where you need only one extra trick. The original declarer is still looking for it!

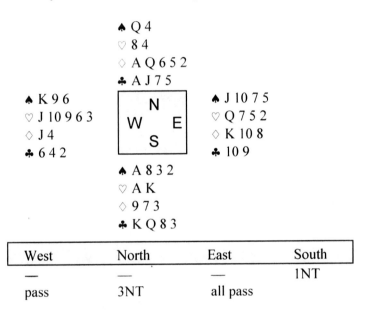

	♠ Q 4 ♡ 8 4 ♢ A Q 6 5 2 ♣ A J 7 5	
♠ K 9 6 ♡ J 10 9 6 3 ♢ J 4 ♣ 6 4 2	N W E S	♠ J 10 7 5 ♡ Q 7 5 2 ♢ K 10 8 ♣ 10 9
	♠ A 8 3 2 ♡ A K ♢ 9 7 3 ♣ K Q 8 3	

West	North	East	South
—	—	—	1NT
pass	3NT	all pass	

West leads the ♡J, East encouraging with the ♡7. How will you play?

The original declarer won with the ♡K and counted eight top tricks. Dummy's diamond suit caught his eye and he promptly finessed the ♢Q. Mistake! East won with the ♢K and cleared the heart suit. There was no way to make the contract after this start and declarer ended one down.

The spade suit offered another chance of establishing a ninth trick and declarer should have played this suit first. If West held the ♠K, a lead towards dummy's ♠Q would create a ninth trick. If instead East won with the ♠K and cleared the heart suit, declarer could still try his luck with the diamond finesse. He would get two chances instead of one.

The theme is the same on the next deal:

♠ K 6
♡ 9 6 5 2
◇ K Q 10 3
♣ 8 5 3

♠ Q J 10 8 2	N	♠ 9 7 4 3
♡ K 10 3	W E	♡ J 8 4
◇ 9 7 2	S	◇ 8 4
♣ 10 7		♣ K Q 9 6

♠ A 5
♡ A Q 7
◇ A J 6 5
♣ A J 4 2

West	North	East	South
—	—	—	2NT
pass	3NT	all pass	

West led the ♠Q and declarer won with dummy's ♠K. With eight top tricks on view, declarer tried his luck with a finesse of the ♡Q. This lost to the king and West cleared the spade suit. Declarer sat back in his chair to consider the matter, somewhat too late, but the contract could no longer be made.

There is some chance of creating an extra trick (or two) from the club suit. Not a particularly good chance because it would require East to hold both the missing club honors. However, by playing on clubs first, you can add an extra chance to that of the heart finesse. You win the first trick with the ♠K and play a club to the jack. When the cards lie as in the diagram, the jack wins and you have your ninth trick. It would make little difference if East decided to split his club honors. You would win with the ♣A and cross to a diamond to lead towards the ♣J. Again the game would be yours.

Why was it right to play clubs before hearts? Because the club chance would involve losing the lead even if the cards were well placed; the heart chance would not. If no joy comes from the clubs, you can take the heart finesse then.

Next we'll see a very common type of deal where you need to gather tricks from two different suits to bring your total to the required number.

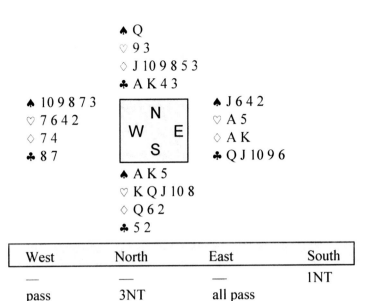

♠ Q
♡ 9 3
♢ J 10 9 8 5 3
♣ A K 4 3

West		East
♠ 10 9 8 7 3 ♡ 7 6 4 2 ♢ 7 4 ♣ 8 7	N W E S	♠ J 6 4 2 ♡ A 5 ♢ A K ♣ Q J 10 9 6

♠ A K 5
♡ K Q J 10 8
♢ Q 6 2
♣ 5 2

West	North	East	South
—	—	—	1NT
pass	3NT	all pass	

West leads the ♠10 to dummy's ♠Q. Will you play a heart or a diamond?

The original declarer played a heart to the king. This was allowed to win and only then did declarer spot a small problem. If he cashed even one more top spade before making the first play in diamonds, the defenders would clear the spade suit in time; he would lose two spades, two diamonds and a heart. Without a second spade, however, four diamond tricks would not bring his total to nine.

When declarer tried a low diamond to the jack, East won with the king and switched to the ♣Q. Declarer won in dummy and led a second diamond to East's ace. It was end of the road for declarer. He had to unblock the ♢Q in order to score four more diamond tricks in dummy after a club return. Since this would leave the ♠AK stranded, he duly went one down.

At Trick 2 you must play a diamond instead of a heart. East wins and switches to the ♣Q. Now you must play a heart! East has to duck and you take advantage by cashing one more spade. You then revert to diamonds, scoring nine tricks.

Tips to avoid mistake 27

(Playing the wrong suit first)

- When you need tricks from two suits, there will often be an element of Avoidance in your first play.
- Consider what will happen if the suit that you intend to play first does not lie favorably.

Mistake 28

Allowing a trump promotion

The defenders derive considerable enjoyment from promoting an extra trump trick. As declarer, it is your task to reduce such hilarity to a minimum. See if you can avoid the mistake that declarer made on this deal:

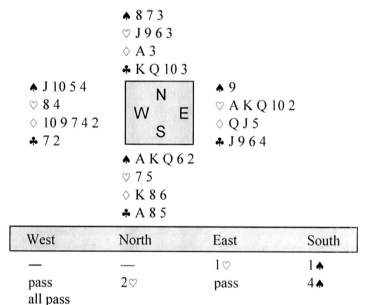

	♠ 8 7 3 ♡ J 9 6 3 ◇ A 3 ♣ K Q 10 3	
♠ J 10 5 4 ♡ 8 4 ◇ 10 9 7 4 2 ♣ 7 2	N W E S	♠ 9 ♡ A K Q 10 2 ◇ Q J 5 ♣ J 9 6 4
	♠ A K Q 6 2 ♡ 7 5 ◇ K 8 6 ♣ A 8 5	

West	North	East	South
—	—	1♡	1♠
pass	2♡	pass	4♠
all pass			

West leads the ♡8 and East wins with the ♡10, He continues with the ♡A, West following, and then the ♡K. How will you play the contract?

The original declarer ruffed with the ♠Q and played his two top trumps. If trumps had broken 3-2, he could then have ruffed his losing diamond in dummy and claimed the contract. Trumps were 4-1, as sometimes happens, and West scored two trump tricks to put the game one down.

It wasn't at all difficult to make the contract, declarer needed to ruff the third heart with a low trump. If West overruffed, this would consume his natural trump trick and declarer would make the remaining tricks.

If you held only ♠AK652, you would again ruff low and hope that West's overruff came from a 3-card trump holding. With ♠AK1052, you might ruff with the ♠10, just in case East held the ♠Q and ♠J.

On the next deal the prescribed remedial action is different.

	North	
	♠ A 7 3 ♡ J 10 3 ♢ Q 9 5 ♣ K Q J 2	
West ♠ J 9 5 ♡ K 8 7 4 ♢ 7 3 ♣ 9 8 4 3	N W E S	**East** ♠ 10 4 ♡ Q 9 2 ♢ A K J 10 6 2 ♣ 10 6
	South ♠ K Q 8 6 2 ♡ A 6 5 ♢ 8 4 ♣ A 7 5	

West	North	East	South
—	1♣	2♢	2♠
pass	3♠	pass	4♠
all pass			

West leads the ♢7 against your spade game. East wins with the ♢10 and continues with the ♢A and ♢K. What is your plan?

If you ruff the third diamond with spot-card, West will overruff and you will eventually lose a heart trick for one down. A better idea is to discard a heart loser on the third round of diamonds. If East persists with a fourth round of diamonds, giving a ruff-and-sluff, it will do no good for West to ruff with the ♠9. You will overruff with dummy's ♠A and draw the outstanding trumps with the ♠K and ♠Q.

If West had started with ♠95, the ruff-and-sluff defense on the fourth round of diamonds (with dummy overruffing the ♠9 with the ♠A) would doubtless succeed. You would have no reason to take a deep finesse of the ♠8 on the first round of trumps.

Suppose instead that West held ♠J9. You would overruff the ♠9 with the ♠A and lead to the ♠K, dropping West's ♠J. It would then be with the odds to cross to a club and finesse the ♠8 on the second round. Such a play would win against ♠J9, ♠J10 or ♠109 with West, losing only to ♠J109. It would be an example of Restricted Choice.

See what you make of this one:

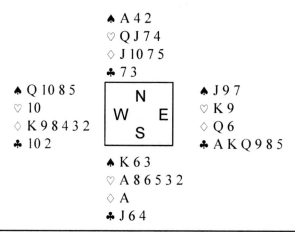

North: ♠ A 4 2 ♡ Q J 7 4 ◇ J 10 7 5 ♣ 7 3

West: ♠ Q 10 8 5 ♡ 10 ◇ K 9 8 4 3 2 ♣ 10 2

East: ♠ J 9 7 ♡ K 9 ◇ Q 6 ♣ A K Q 9 8 5

South: ♠ K 6 3 ♡ A 8 6 5 3 2 ◇ A ♣ J 6 4

West	North	East	South
—	—	1♣	1♡
dbl	2♣	3♣	4♡
all pass			

West led the ♣10, his partner claiming two tricks in the suit. When East continued with a third high club West ruffed with the ♡10, hoping to promote East's trump holding. This is exactly what happened. Declarer overruffed with the jack and led a trump to the ace, West showing out. There was no way to avoid a subsequent spade loser, as well as a trump, and that was one down.

Did you spot declarer's mistake? Instead of overruffing on the third round of clubs, he should have discarded a spade from dummy. On any return, he could have reached dummy with the ♠A to run the ♡Q successfully.

Discarding a loser rather than suffering a trump promotion is a move that happens quite often. Not as often as it should do, however!

Tips to avoid mistake 28

(Allowing a trump promotion)

- Ruffing high may promote a defender's trumps, while ruffing low may allow an overruff. You must judge which is the better action.
- Sometimes you can discard a loser instead of ruffing high. This may gain when the other hand will be able to cope with a continuation of the defenders' suit.

Mistake 29

Failing to overtake an honor

Some players go through their entire bridge career without realizing that it can be beneficial to overtake one honor with another. The purpose is to gain entry to the opposite hand. Look at this 3NT contract:

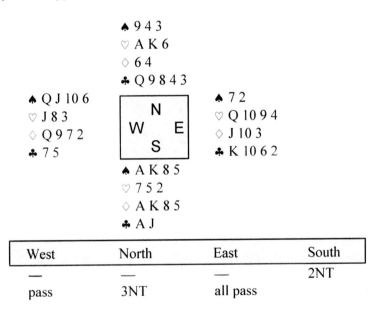

	♠ 9 4 3 ♡ A K 6 ♢ 6 4 ♣ Q 9 8 4 3	
♠ Q J 10 6 ♡ J 8 3 ♢ Q 9 7 2 ♣ 7 5	N W E S	♠ 7 2 ♡ Q 10 9 4 ♢ J 10 3 ♣ K 10 6 2
	♠ A K 8 5 ♡ 7 5 2 ♢ A K 8 5 ♣ A J	

West	North	East	South
—	—	—	2NT
pass	3NT	all pass	

In the system being played, 2NT showed 19-21 points. How would you play 3NT when West leads the ♠Q?

The original declarer won with the ♠A and continued with the ♣A and ♣J, playing low from dummy. If East were to win with the ♣K, the contract would be made. Declarer would win the spade return, cross to a heart and clear the clubs. A heart entry would remain to reach dummy's last club.

East was in no mood to assist declarer and meanly allowed the ♣J to win. It was no longer possible to make the contract. Declarer crossed to a heart and played another club, hoping for a 3-3 break. The clubs divided 4-2, as was always likely, and he ended one down.

To make the contract, declarer needed to overtake his ♣J with the ♣Q on the second round of the suit. It would then do East no good to duck. The lead would be in dummy and declarer could continue to play on clubs while the two heart entries were intact.

Declarer went down on the next contract too. You will have a slight advantage over him, recalling the present chapter title (ahem). Still, you will surely cast that from your mind and tackle the deal under normal table conditions.

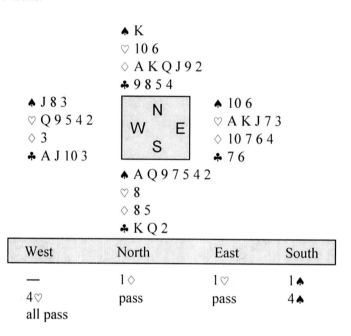

	North	
	♠ K ♡ 10 6 ♢ A K Q J 9 2 ♣ 9 8 5 4	
♠ J 8 3 ♡ Q 9 5 4 2 ♢ 3 ♣ A J 10 3	N / W E / S	♠ 10 6 ♡ A K J 7 3 ♢ 10 7 6 4 ♣ 7 6
	♠ A Q 9 7 5 4 2 ♡ 8 ♢ 8 5 ♣ K Q 2	

West	North	East	South
—	1♢	1♡	1♠
4♡	pass	pass	4♠
all pass			

How would you play 4♠ when West leads the ♢3?

'Ace, please,' said the declarer, who proceeded to cash the ♠K. He then needed to reach his hand to draw the outstanding trumps. He tried a club to the king but West won with the ace and switched to the ♡4. East won with the king and lost no time in delivering a diamond ruff. Not only was this ruff an extra trick for the defense, it also cut off declarer from the dummy. He ruffed the next heart and drew trumps. With no way to avoid an eventual second club loser, he went one down.

Declarer should have realized that the diamond lead, in dummy's first-bid suit, was heavy odds to be a singleton. At Trick 2 he should have led the ♠K and overtaken with the ♠A. He could then draw a second round of trumps with the ♠Q, finding a 3-2 break. The next move would be a trump to West's ♠J, to stop him from interrupting the run of the diamond suit. After this bright start, the defenders would score one trump and two side-suit aces. The game would be made.

On the next deal the purpose of the overtaking is different — to preserve trump control rather than avoiding an adverse ruff.

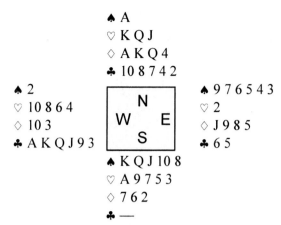

	♠ A ♡ K Q J ♢ A K Q 4 ♣ 10 8 7 4 2	
♠ 2 ♡ 10 8 6 4 ♢ 10 3 ♣ A K Q J 9 3	N W E S	♠ 9 7 6 5 4 3 ♡ 2 ♢ J 9 8 5 ♣ 6 5
	♠ K Q J 10 8 ♡ A 9 7 5 3 ♢ 7 6 2 ♣ —	

West	North	East	South
—	—	—	1♠
2♣	2♢	pass	2♡
pass	3♣	pass	3♡
pass	5♡	pass	6♡
all pass			

You ruff the ♣K lead and play the ♡K and ♡Q, East discarding a spade on the second round. How will you play from this point?

On the face of it, you have five spades, five hearts and three diamonds. However, the club lead has reduced you to four trumps. If you simply draw a third round of trumps with the jack, you will have only the bare ace of trumps in your hand and no way to reach this card to draw West's last trump.

With the chapter title floating in your mind, you will see that you can make the slam by unblocking the ♠A and overtaking the ♡J with the ♡A on the third round. This promotes West's ♡10, but you preserve trump control. You can play spade winners (and then diamond winners, if necessary) until West is forced to ruff with the ♡10. Your ♡9 will then be the twelfth trick.

Tips to avoid mistake 29

(Failure to overtake an honor)

- When establishing a suit in dummy, it may be necessary for entry reasons to overtake an honor in your hand.
- In a trump contract, the need to draw trumps may be so pressing that you benefit from overtaking an honor. By sacrificing a trump trick you save two tricks elsewhere.

Mistake 30

Missing the only chance

Sometimes you arrive in a contract that has only one (small) chance of succeeding. You must then assume that the cards lie as you need them to:

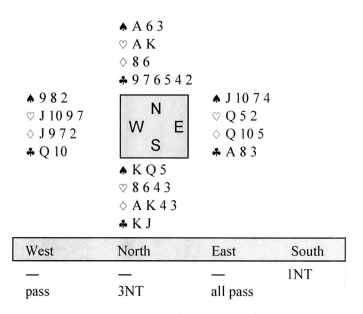

	North	
	♠ A 6 3 ♡ A K ◇ 8 6 ♣ 9 7 6 5 4 2	
West ♠ 9 8 2 ♡ J 10 9 7 ◇ J 9 7 2 ♣ Q 10	N W E S	**East** ♠ J 10 7 4 ♡ Q 5 2 ◇ Q 10 5 ♣ A 8 3
	♠ K Q 5 ♡ 8 6 4 3 ◇ A K 4 3 ♣ K J	

West	North	East	South
—	—	—	1NT
pass	3NT	all pass	

West led the ♡J, won in the dummy. Declarer played a club and tried the ♣J from his hand. This lost to West's ♣Q and the hearts were cleared. On the next club, East correctly played low again. Declarer won with the ♣K but could not make a further club trick and went one down.

To make the contract, you need one of the defenders to hold ♣Q10 doubleton. Here East will follow with the ♣3 on the first round and you must hope that West holds the ♣Q10. You rise with the ♣K and continue with the ♣J to West's ♣Q. You win the next heart in the dummy and clear the club suit. The game will be yours for the lost of just two hearts and two clubs.

Suppose East followed with the ♣10 on the first round. You would have to hope that he held ♣Q10. You would cover with the ♣J and score five clubs, whether or not West held up the ♣A. An overtrick would be yours.

(Note that if East holds ♣AQx or ♣AQ10, he can beat the contract by rising with the ♣A on the first round.)

Prospects do not look good, three tricks into the next deal. Can you spot the 'only chance'?

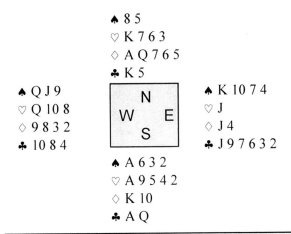

	North	
	♠ 8 5 ♡ K 7 6 3 ♢ A Q 7 6 5 ♣ K 5	
West ♠ Q J 9 ♡ Q 10 8 ♢ 9 8 3 2 ♣ 10 8 4	N W E S	**East** ♠ K 10 7 4 ♡ J ♢ J 4 ♣ J 9 7 6 3 2
	♠ A 6 3 2 ♡ A 9 5 4 2 ♢ K 10 ♣ A Q	

West	North	East	South
—	1♢	pass	1♡
pass	2♡	pass	4NT
pass	5♡	pass	6♡
all pass			

West leads the ♠Q and you win with the ace. If trumps break 3-1, you will need to avoid a spade loser. How can this be done?

You play the ♡A and ♡K, East discarding a club. You now need to throw three spades on the diamonds. A 3-3 break would not help because West would ruff the fourth diamond and cash a spade. You need West to follow four times. To score five diamond tricks, East must hold ♢Jx!

You ended in dummy after two rounds of trumps (by good luck or ice-cool calculation) and are in the right hand to play a diamond to the 10. The finesse wins and you are delighted to see the ♢J fall on the second round under your ♢K. You return to dummy by overtaking the ♣Q with the ♣K and discard your remaining spades on the ♢AQ7. West can ruff the fifth round of diamonds with his master trump if he wishes. The slam is yours for the loss of one trump trick.

You would play the same way if East had shown up with a trump trick. You would then need him to hold ♢Jxxx.

On the final deal in this chapter dummy resembles a distant, unreachable island. Can you see how the contract should be played?

	♠ 6 3 ♡ J 7 5 ♢ Q J 9 6 3 ♣ 7 6 3		
♠ Q 10 4 2 ♡ K 10 3 ♢ 10 7 2 ♣ K 8 5	N W E S	♠ K J 9 7 ♡ 9 8 4 2 ♢ 8 5 4 ♣ 10 2	
	♠ A 8 5 ♡ A Q 6 ♢ A K ♣ A Q J 9 4		

West	North	East	South
—	—	—	2♣
pass	2♢	pass	3NT
all pass			

West led the ♠2, suggesting a 4-4 break. Four club tricks would bring the total to eight. How could a ninth trick be found in time?

Declarer won the third spade and cashed the ♢AK. Playing on clubs was unlikely to work, even if they broke 3-2; the defenders would cash three spades and exit safely. Instead he played the ♡A and ♡Q, West holding up the ♡K to prevent declarer reaching dummy with the ♡J. In desperation declarer played the ace and queen of clubs. The defenders were then able to accumulate three spades, the ♣K and the ♡K for one down.

There was only one real chance of making the contract and that was to lead the ♡Q at Trick 4. West would have to let this win or declarer would be able to score five diamonds, two hearts and two black aces. With a heart trick in the bag, declarer would then set up the club suit.

Tips to avoid mistake 30

(Missing the only chance)

- When a contract appears hopeless, do not play until you're sure that no plausible lie of the cards will permit a make.
- If you can make the contract only when (say) East has a singleton ♣Q, play for that lie. It may be tiny chance, but the gain of IMPs or matchpoints will be substantial if it succeeds.

Mistake 31

Misplaying the trump suit

Suppose that you have decided to draw trumps. Let's go further and assume that it is the correct thing to do! There may still be a right and a wrong way to play the suit. Look at this example:

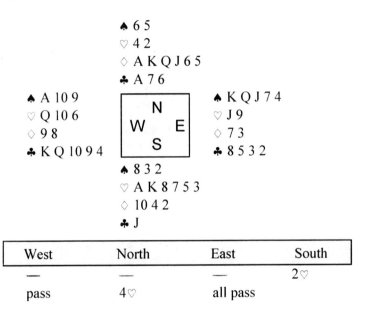

West	North	East
	♠ 6 5 ♡ 4 2 ♢ A K Q J 6 5 ♣ A 7 6	
♠ A 10 9 ♡ Q 10 6 ♢ 9 8 ♣ K Q 10 9 4	N W E S	♠ K Q J 7 4 ♡ J 9 ♢ 7 3 ♣ 8 5 3 2
	♠ 8 3 2 ♡ A K 8 7 5 3 ♢ 10 4 2 ♣ J	

West	North	East	South
—	—	—	2♡
pass	4♡	all pass	

How will you tackle this contract when West leads the ♣K?

You win with the ♣A and decide to draw trumps before taking some discards on dummy's splendid diamond suit. What will happen if you cash the ♡A and ♡K next? Nothing good. The trumps break 3-2, yes, but you will be exposed to the loss of three spade tricks now that dummy has no trumps left. You will have to hope that three rounds of diamonds emerge unruffed. No such luck on this occasion and you will lose three spades and one trump.

You need to lose a trump trick (you hope it is only one) at a time when dummy still has a trump to protect you in spades. In other words, you must duck the **first** round of trumps. There is nothing the defenders can do then. They can take two spade tricks but you will claim the remainder.

The best play in the trump suit, viewed on its own, will often vary when there has been opposition bidding. Suppose an opponent has overcalled in a suit or has opened with a pre-emptive bid. You should generally finesse against his partner for a missing queen of trumps, even if there are only four trumps out.

On the next deal, West opens with a pre-emptive bid, suggesting that he is short in the trump suit.

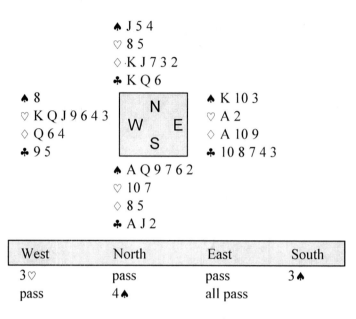

	♠ J 5 4 ♡ 8 5 ◇ K J 7 3 2 ♣ K Q 6	
♠ 8 ♡ K Q J 9 6 4 3 ◇ Q 6 4 ♣ 9 5	N W E S	♠ K 10 3 ♡ A 2 ◇ A 10 9 ♣ 10 8 7 4 3
	♠ A Q 9 7 6 2 ♡ 10 7 ◇ 8 5 ♣ A J 2	

West	North	East	South
3♡	pass	pass	3♠
pass	4♠	all pass	

West leads the ♡K against your spade game, East overtaking with the ♡A and returning the ♡2. How will you play the contract when West wins the second heart and switches to the ♣9?

You have at least one diamond loser awaiting you and will therefore need to pick up the trump suit without loss. In the absence of any opposition bidding, you would lead a low spade towards the South hand on the first round and finesse the ♠Q. If West followed with the ♠10, you could then return to dummy to pick up East's remaining ♠K8. Here, though, West has only six vacant places for non-hearts while East has eleven. You should therefore be inclined to play East for three (or four) trumps.

Since you are not worried that East will hold a singleton ♠K, you win the club switch in dummy and lead the ♠J. Let's say that this is covered by the ♠K and ♠A, West dropping the ♠8. The odds then strongly favor a finesse against the ♠10 on the second round. You cross to dummy's remaining club honor and finesse the ♠9 successfully, picking up the trump suit. It only remains to guess the diamond suit. West can hardly hold the ◇A in addition to his splendid heart suit, so it doesn't take a genius to finesse the ◇J. This duly forces the ◇A and the contract is yours.

Suppose East had started with ♠K1083 and West had shown out when the ♠J was covered by the king and ace. You would then need two further entries to dummy to pick up East's remaining ♠1082. The ♣Q would be one and you would generate another entry in diamonds by playing a diamond to the jack.

Imagine the bidding had been slightly different, with South opening 1♠ in first seat and West overcalling 2♡ or a weak 3♡. Again this would be sufficient to tilt your play in the trump suit to the one just described.

The next deal, from the 2014 Australian Interstate Teams final, illustrates a common error when playing the trump suit against a forcing defense:

N-S Vul. Dealer East

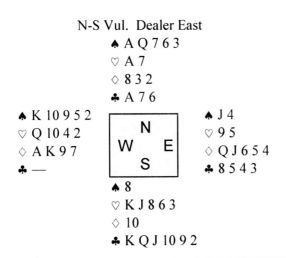

	North	
	♠ A Q 7 6 3 ♡ A 7 ♢ 8 3 2 ♣ A 7 6	
West ♠ K 10 9 5 2 ♡ Q 10 4 2 ♢ A K 9 7 ♣ —	N W E S	**East** ♠ J 4 ♡ 9 5 ♢ Q J 6 5 4 ♣ 8 5 4 3
	South ♠ 8 ♡ K J 8 6 3 ♢ 10 ♣ K Q J 10 9 2	

West	North	East	South
—	—	pass	2♡
2♠	dbl	pass	4♣
pass	4♡	all pass	

South's 2♡ showed hearts and an unspecified minor suit. How would you play the eventual contract of 4♡ when West starts with the ace and king of diamonds?

Declarer ruffed the second diamond, crossed to the ♡A and finessed the ♡J. Mistake! West won with the ♡Q and was quick to force South again in diamonds. Declarer ruffed and played the ♡K, praying for a 3-3 break. This last-minute request for assistance went unanswered and the contract failed by two tricks. The defenders scored two trumps and three diamonds.

To make the contract, declarer needed to rise with the ♡K on the second round and then play club winners. The defenders would be welcome to score two trump tricks, even if the trumps divided 3-3. Declarer would lose just two trumps and one diamond.

We will see one more deal where the choice of play in the trump suit is affected by the need to repel a forcing defense:

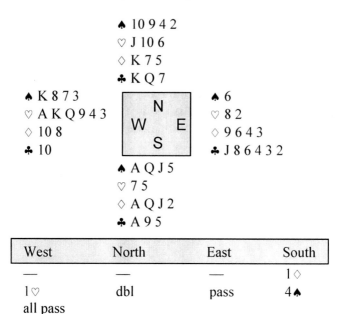

	North	
	♠ 10 9 4 2 ♡ J 10 6 ♢ K 7 5 ♣ K Q 7	
West ♠ K 8 7 3 ♡ A K Q 9 4 3 ♢ 10 8 ♣ 10	N W E S	**East** ♠ 6 ♡ 8 2 ♢ 9 6 4 3 ♣ J 8 6 4 3 2
	♠ A Q J 5 ♡ 7 5 ♢ A Q J 2 ♣ A 9 5	
	South	

West	North	East	South
—	—	—	1♢
1♡	dbl	pass	4♠
all pass			

How will you play when West leads the ♡AKQ, East ruffing with the ♠6?

The original declarer overruffed with the ♠J and continued with the ♠A and ♠Q. West had played the game before and refused to win with the king. Had he done so, declarer would have been able to ruff a fourth round of hearts with the last trump in the South hand.

It was the end of the road for the contract. If declarer played a third round of trumps, West would win and force dummy's last trump with another heart. Trump control would be lost. If instead declarer abandoned the trump suit, West would score two trump tricks.

The winning line of play is to give up a trump trick while you still have protection against hearts in the already shortened South hand. At Trick 4, you lead the ♠Q from your hand. If West wins this, he cannot damage you. Let's say that he ducks. You continue with a low trump from the South hand, retaining the ♠A. If West goes in with the ♠K, you can ruff a further heart with the ♠A and cross to dummy to draw the outstanding trumps with the ♠109. If instead West ducks again, you will simply cash the ♠A and play winners until West ruffs. Dummy still has a trump to protect you in hearts and you will make the contract.

Many players would go wrong on this deal:

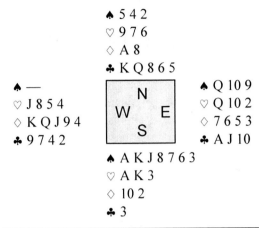

	North	
	♠ 5 4 2 ♡ 9 7 6 ◇ A 8 ♣ K Q 8 6 5	
♠ — ♡ J 8 5 4 ◇ K Q J 9 4 ♣ 9 7 4 2	N W E S	♠ Q 10 9 ♡ Q 10 2 ◇ 7 6 5 3 ♣ A J 10
	♠ A K J 8 7 6 3 ♡ A K 3 ◇ 10 2 ♣ 3	

West	North	East	South
—	—	—	1♠
pass	2♠	pass	4♠
all pass			

How would you play the spade game when West leads the ◇K?

If you win the first (or second) diamond and make the apparently natural play of a trump to the ace, West will show out and you will have a loser in each of the four suits. The winning play, which more or less guarantees the contract, is to finesse the ♠J once East has followed on the first round.

If this loses to the queen, the trumps are 2-1. You can win West's heart switch, draw the last trump and play a club to the king and ace. You will lead the ♠3 to the ♠5 to reach the established ♣Q for a heart discard. When the cards lie as in the diagram, your finesse of the ♠J will win. You will then score seven trump tricks and the three top cards in the red suits.

Tips to avoid mistake 31

(Misplaying the trump suit)

- It is sometimes right to spurn a trump finesse because you cannot afford to lose the lead. (The defenders may score a ruff or be able to force the long trump holding.)
- When you can afford to lose a trump trick, consider ducking an early round. This may secure your control of the hand.
- When you are missing four trumps to the queen, you may choose to finesse to keep the danger hand off lead.

Mistake 32

Allowing an honor to be ruffed

Sometimes there is no way to prevent the defenders from scoring a ruff, but you can prevent them from ruffing a winner. This is a common scenario.

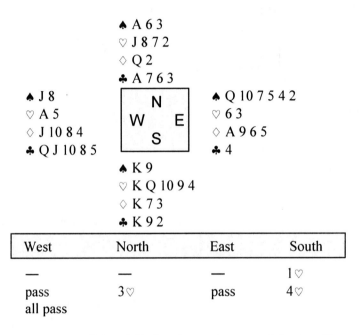

West		East
	♠ A 6 3 ♡ J 8 7 2 ◊ Q 2 ♣ A 7 6 3	
♠ J 8 ♡ A 5 ◊ J 10 8 4 ♣ Q J 10 8 5	N W E S	♠ Q 10 7 5 4 2 ♡ 6 3 ◊ A 9 6 5 ♣ 4
	♠ K 9 ♡ K Q 10 9 4 ◊ K 7 3 ♣ K 9 2	

West	North	East	South
—	—	—	1♡
pass	3♡	pass	4♡
all pass			

North makes a traditional limit raise and you end in 4♡. How would you play this when West leads the ♣Q?

You start with three potential losers – one in trumps, one in diamonds and another in clubs. Only an adverse ruff can defeat the contract. Which of the defenders, if any, is more likely to hold a singleton club? It is possible that the ♣Q opening lead is a singleton, but it's much more likely that West is leading from an honor sequence and that East holds a singleton club.

Look what will happen if you win the first trick in your hand, with the ♣K. When you play a trump, West will rise with the ace and play the ♣J. Disaster! Not only will East score a ruff, he will be able to ruff dummy's ♣A. With a club trick still to be lost, you will go one down.

To prevent East from ruffing a top honor in clubs, you must win the first trick with the ♣A. When West wins the first round of trumps and continues with the ♣J, it will not help East to ruff this card. You would follow with the

♣9 from your hand and score ten tricks. You would not lose a club trick in addition to the ruff.

Note that the same play would be necessary if the position of the red aces was switched. If you mistakenly won the first trick with the ♣K, East could win the first trump and cross to partner's ♢A for a club continuation through dummy's ♣A.

There is another way in which some players allow an honor to be ruffed unnecessarily. Would you have made the next contract?

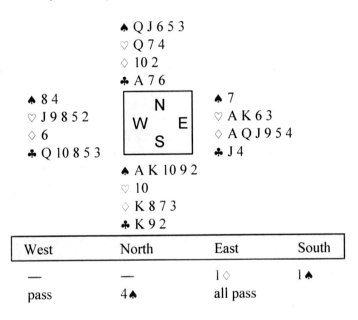

North: ♠ Q J 6 5 3 ♡ Q 7 4 ♢ 10 2 ♣ A 7 6

West: ♠ 8 4 ♡ J 9 8 5 2 ♢ 6 ♣ Q 10 8 5 3

East: ♠ 7 ♡ A K 6 3 ♢ A Q J 9 5 4 ♣ J 4

South: ♠ A K 10 9 2 ♡ 10 ♢ K 8 7 3 ♣ K 9 2

West	North	East	South
—	—	1♢	1♠
pass	4♠	all pass	

West leads the ♢6, East winning with the ♢A and returning the ♢Q. There's no particular reason to suspect that the opening lead is a singleton and many players would try to win the trick with the ♢K. Mistake! West would ruff and further losers in hearts and clubs would sink the contract.

Think for a few moments and you will see that the contract is a certainty if you play low at Trick 2, allowing East's ♢Q to win. If he continues with the ♢J, you will play low again and ruff in the dummy. After drawing trumps, you will be able to play your carefully preserved ♢K and discard a club from dummy. You can then ruff the third round of clubs and make the contract for the loss of two diamonds and one heart.

You should make this play even in a duplicate pairs (where an overtrick can be very valuable). That's because you would gain nothing by winning the second diamond if West held more than one card in the suit. You would still have to lose a heart, a diamond and a club.

See if you can save a precious honor from decapitation on this deal:

	♠ K 8 5 ♡ Q 10 6 4 ◇ 10 5 ♣ A K 7 2	
♠ 10 7 4 ♡ A 2 ◇ J 9 7 3 ♣ Q J 10 8	N W E S	♠ Q J 9 3 2 ♡ 8 3 ◇ Q 8 6 4 2 ♣ 6
	♠ A 6 ♡ K J 9 7 5 ◇ A K ♣ 9 5 4 3	

West	North	East	South
—	1♣	pass	1♡
pass	2♡	pass	4♡
all pass			

There would have been an easy ten tricks in 3NT, but this contract was difficult to reach. Dismissing that thought from your mind, how would you tackle 4♡ when West leads the ♣Q?

You win with dummy's ace and play a trump to the king and West's ace. When he continues with the ♣J, you must be careful. If you commit dummy's ♣K to this trick, East will ruff and you will have two subsequent club losers for one down. Instead you must play a low card from dummy. If West plays another club, from his ♣108, you can run this to your ♣9. East is welcome to ruff because he will be ruffing a loser. You will make the contract for the loss of one trump, one club and one club ruff.

It's not at all likely but suppose West leads a tricky ♣8 at Trick 3. Again you will go down if you rise with the ♣K. Play low from dummy and the worst that can happen is that East wins with the ♣10 from an original ♣J106 and gives his partner a club ruff. You will still make the contract for the loss of one trump, one club and a club ruff. If the cards lie as in the diagram and East ruffs a loser on the second round, you will make ten tricks easily.

Would you have spotted the danger on this slam hand?

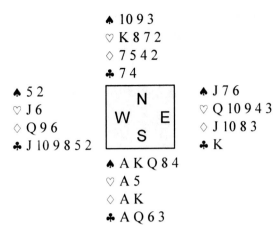

	North	
	♠ 10 9 3 ♡ K 8 7 2 ◊ 7 5 4 2 ♣ 7 4	
West ♠ 5 2 ♡ J 6 ◊ Q 9 6 ♣ J 10 9 8 5 2	N W E S	**East** ♠ J 7 6 ♡ Q 10 9 4 3 ◊ J 10 8 3 ♣ K
	♠ A K Q 8 4 ♡ A 5 ◊ A K ♣ A Q 6 3	

West	North	East	South
—	—	—	2♣
pass	2◊	pass	2♠
pass	4♠	pass	6♠
all pass			

West leads the ♣J to the king and ace. You are left with two club losers in your hand. How can you reduce them to just one? It seems easy. After cashing the ♣Q, you will ruff a club with the ♠10. If East overruffs with the ♠J, you will ruff the fourth round with the ♠9.

Happy with this analysis, the original declarer continued with the ♣Q. Mistake! East ruffed and was able to overruff with the ♠J subsequently.

To make the slam you must cross to dummy's ♡K and lead **towards** the ♣Q. If East discards, you will win and ruff the third club with the ♠10. East overruffs but you can ruff the fourth club with the ♠9.

If instead East ruffs air on the second round of clubs, your ♣Q will survive. You will draw two rounds of trumps before ruffing your remaining club loser. You make the slam unless East holds ♠Jxxx or ♠Jxxxx.

Tips to avoid mistake 32

(Allowing an honor to be ruffed)

- By leading towards side-suit honors, you can reduce the chance of them being ruffed by a defender.
- An honor lead is more likely to be from a sequence than to be a singleton. Choose where to win the trick accordingly.
- Even when you have no loser in a suit, it can be right to duck an early round to avoid an honor being ruffed.

Mistake 33

Running into Entry Problems

Making a good plan for the contract often involves considering the entries required. Sometimes you will encounter problems only if one or more suits break badly. That's the case on the first deal:

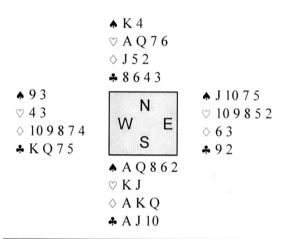

West		East
	♠ K 4 ♡ A Q 7 6 ◇ J 5 2 ♣ 8 6 4 3	
♠ 9 3 ♡ 4 3 ◇ 10 9 8 7 4 ♣ K Q 7 5	N W E S	♠ J 10 7 5 ♡ 10 9 8 5 2 ◇ 6 3 ♣ 9 2
	♠ A Q 8 6 2 ♡ K J ◇ A K Q ♣ A J 10	

West	North	East	South
—	—	—	2♣
pass	2◇	pass	3NT
pass	6NT	all pass	

The original declarer won the diamond lead and unblocked the two heart honors in his hand. He then played the ace and king of spades, both defenders following suit. With spades known to be 4-2 at worst, it seemed for a moment that declarer was guaranteed to make four hearts, three diamonds, the ♣A and at least four spades.

Declarer cashed the ♡A and ♡Q, discarding two clubs and noting that the hearts had broken 5-2. When he returned to his hand with a diamond and played the ♠Q, bad news arrived. The same defender held the spade stopper and a good heart! An extra trick in spades could not be safely established and the slam went one down.

After unblocking his two heart honors, declarer needed to duck the first round of spades. East would gain the lead when he could do no damage (his fifth heart was not established). Declarer would win the club switch with the ace and cross to the ♠K to score dummy's two heart winners, discarding clubs. A diamond back to hand would allow him to cash the remaining tricks.

The next deal arose in the 2006 European Championships. Both declarers in the Ireland-Netherlands match played the deal faultlessly, but you can guess that some performers in a club game would run into entry trouble. See how you fare.

	♠ K Q ♡ K Q J 7 4 ♢ A Q 8 7 4 ♣ 3	
♠ 9 6 5 4 3 ♡ 8 ♢ K 10 9 5 ♣ K 5 4	N W E S	♠ J 10 ♡ 10 9 6 5 2 ♢ J 2 ♣ A J 10 9
	♠ A 8 7 2 ♡ A 3 ♢ 6 3 ♣ Q 8 7 6 2	

West	North	East	South
—	1♡	pass	1♠
pass	2♢	pass	3NT
all pass			

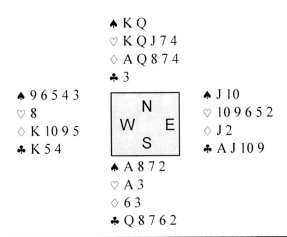

How would you play 3NT when West leads the ♠4, won in the dummy?

Three spades, five hearts and the ♢A will bring the total to nine. How easy it would be to cash dummy's other spade honor and cross to the South hand with the ♡A. After scoring the ♠A, you would return to dummy with a heart and… disaster! Hearts break 5-1. With no entry to the South hand, to rescue the ship with a diamond finesse, you will go one down.

Correct technique is to test the hearts while you still have an entry to your hand. After unblocking dummy's second spade honor, you play the ♡K and ♡A. When West shows out, you know that you have only four heart tricks and will therefore need a successful diamond finesse to bring your total to nine. You cash the ♠A and lead a diamond to the queen. Justice is done when the finesse wins (the opponents won't agree) and you claim nine tricks.

We'll end the chapter with a deal where many would play carelessly:

	♠ 4 ♡ K Q 9 4 3 ◇ A Q 8 4 ♣ Q J 10	
♠ K 7 3 ♡ J 7 ◇ J 9 7 5 ♣ 7 6 4 2	N W E S	♠ 9 8 6 2 ♡ A 10 8 6 ◇ K 10 2 ♣ K 3
	♠ A Q J 10 5 ♡ 5 2 ◇ 6 3 ♣ A 9 8 5	

West	North	East	South
—	1♡	pass	1♠
pass	2◇	pass	2NT
pass	3NT	all pass	

West leads the ♣2 to dummy's ♣Q and East's ♣K. How will you play?

If you win with the ♣A, you will have no entry to your spade winners. To ensure that the ♣A remains as an entry to your hand, you should allow East's ♣K to win. You take the club continuation in the dummy and lead a spade, finessing the queen. When West wins with the ♠K, he may switch to a low diamond. What then?

The one card you must not play from dummy is the ◇Q. If you do, East will win and continue diamonds. You will then lose two diamonds and one trick in each of the other suits. It's best to play low on the diamond switch. East wins with the ◇10 but cannot effectively continue the suit. You will make four spades, three clubs, the ◇A and a heart trick, for a total of nine.

Tips to avoid mistake 33

(Running into entry problems)

- The time to plan your entries is at Trick 1, before playing from dummy.
- By conceding an early round of a suit, you can preserve the high cards as entries.
- Do not waste potential entries in the trump suit.

Mistake 34

Going Wrong at Trick 2

They say that you should always make a plan right at the start because many a contract is lost on the very first trick. This is true, but the same applies to Trick 2! In this chapter we will look at some errors that arise when declarer wins the first trick in the dummy and must consider how best to use this entry.

Several declarers went down on this deal from a club game:

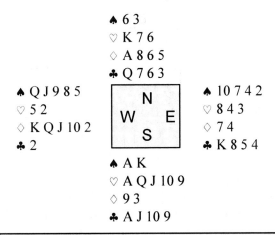

	North	
	♠ 6 3 ♡ K 7 6 ♢ A 8 6 5 ♣ Q 7 6 3	
♠ Q J 9 8 5 ♡ 5 2 ♢ K Q J 10 2 ♣ 2	N W E S	♠ 10 7 4 2 ♡ 8 4 3 ♢ 7 4 ♣ K 8 5 4
	♠ A K ♡ A Q J 10 9 ♢ 9 3 ♣ A J 10 9	

West	North	East	South
—	—	—	1♡
2♡	3♡	pass	3♠
pass	4♢	pass	4NT
pass	5♡	pass	6♡
all pass			

West's 2♡ is a Michaels cuebid, showing spades and an undisclosed minor. You win the ♢K lead with dummy's ♢A. Suppose you then draw trumps with the ace, queen and king. You lead the ♣Q, winning the trick when East declines to cover. So far so good, but West shows out when you lead a second round of clubs to the jack. You have no further entry to dummy for a third club finesse and the slam tumbles to defeat.

The error occurred at Trick 2. When in dummy with the ♢A, declarer should have led a low club to the jack. He could then draw trumps in three rounds, ending in the dummy, and lead the ♣Q. Whether or not East decides to cover, the club suit is brought in and twelve tricks are made.

What move would you make at Trick 2 on this deal:

	North	
	♠ A ♡ K Q 10 7 5 4 ◇ 6 4 ♣ Q 5 4 3	
West ♠ 10 9 7 4 3 2 ♡ — ◇ 8 7 5 3 ♣ 9 6 2	N W E S	**East** ♠ 8 ♡ J 9 8 3 2 ◇ J 10 9 2 ♣ A J 10
	♠ K Q J 6 5 ♡ A 6 ◇ A K Q ♣ K 8 7	

West	North	East	South
—	1♡	pass	1♠
pass	2♡	pass	4NT
pass	5♠	pass	6NT
all pass			

What is your plan for 6NT when West leads the ♠10?

You win with dummy's bare ace and count ten top tricks with an easy eleventh coming in clubs. If spades break 4-3, all will be easy. If hearts divide 3-2, East is void or the ♡J is singleton, again you will have a straightforward twelfth trick. West is likely to hold the spade length if that suit is breaking badly, in which case East will have the heart length. Since you have a tenace position in the heart suit and can survive bad breaks in the majors when East holds the ♣A, you should lead a club through East at Trick 2. He will have to hold up the ace and will be open to an endplay later.

When you do this, the ♣10 appears from East and your ♣K wins the trick. You play the ♠K and East discards a heart. When you play the ♡A, West discards a spade. Two horrible breaks, yes, but because you made the right play at Trick 2, you will bring home the slam. You continue with two more spade winners and three diamond winners, reducing the dummy to ♡KQ10 and ♣Q. East has to come down to ♡J98 and ♣A and you then throw him in with a club, forcing a lead back into dummy's heart tenace.

If you had made any play at Trick 2 other than a low club from dummy, there would have been no safe way to lead through East's ♣A. The slam would have gone down.

Now that you're in the habit of concentrating hard before playing the second trick, you will have a good chance of solving this problem:

	♠ K 8 6 3 ♡ J 10 9 6 ◇ A 9 7 4 ♣ 7		
♠ J ♡ 8 5 4 ◇ K Q J 6 5 ♣ A 6 5 4	N W E S	♠ Q 10 9 7 ♡ 7 2 ◇ 10 8 2 ♣ K Q 9 8	
	♠ A 5 4 2 ♡ A K Q 3 ◇ 3 ♣ J 10 3 2		

West	North	East	South
—	—	—	1♣
1◇	dbl	pass	1♡
pass	3♡	pass	4♡
all pass			

West leads the ◇K and you win with dummy's ◇A. How will you continue?

In addition to the three top tricks in the side suits you will need seven ruffing tricks. When you surrender a club trick, preparing for club ruffs in the dummy, the defenders will doubtless play a trump. That's OK. You can still aim for one round of trumps and six more trumps scored separately.

Only one action is good enough at Trick 2. You must take advantage of being in the dummy by ruffing a diamond in your hand. Not only that, you must ruff with a trump honor! Next you surrender a club trick, East winning and switching to a trump. After your high-ruff unblock, you can win this trick in the dummy. You ruff another diamond in your hand, ruff a club and then ruff dummy's last diamond. Finally you cross to the ♠K and draw the outstanding trumps with the ♡J10. The ♠A will be your tenth trick.

Tips to avoid mistake 34

(Going wrong at Trick 2)

- 'Many a contract is lost at Trick 1,' they say. Yes, but a similar number are lost at Trick 2. Always plan the contract at the start.
- When you have to win the first trick in dummy and dummy is short of entries, think carefully how to use this entry.

Mistake 35

Taking an Unnecessary Finesse

Some players rather enjoy taking finesses. My mother used to think that she was conjuring an extra trick out of thin air. Nevertheless, you should be wary of taking an unnecessary finesse. Test yourself on this deal:

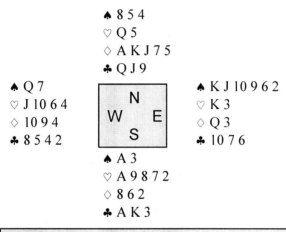

	North	
	♠ 8 5 4 ♡ Q 5 ◇ A K J 7 5 ♣ Q J 9	
West ♠ Q 7 ♡ J 10 6 4 ◇ 10 9 4 ♣ 8 5 4 2	N / W E / S	**East** ♠ K J 10 9 6 2 ♡ K 3 ◇ Q 3 ♣ 10 7 6
	South ♠ A 3 ♡ A 9 8 7 2 ◇ 8 6 2 ♣ A K 3	

West	North	East	South
–	–	2♠	dbl
pass	3♠	pass	3NT
all pass			

This was a neat auction to a worthwhile contract. How would you play 3NT when West leads the ♠Q and East overtakes with the king?

The spades are surely breaking 2-6. Since you are not fearful of any switch, you should duck the first trick to break the link between the two defenders. You win the next spade and cross to the ◇A, just in case the ◇Q drops singleton. What next?

The original declarer returned to the ♣K and led a second round of diamonds, the ◇9 appearing from West. Since East had begun with six spades to West's two, there was a good chance that West held the ◇Q. Declarer duly finessed the ◇J and didn't think much of his luck when East won with the ◇Q and cashed four spade tricks to put the contract two down.

What did you make of that? Declarer held five tricks outside diamonds and therefore needed only four more from the diamond suit. Since he could not afford a diamond finesse to lose to the dangerous East hand, he should have played the ♢A and ♢K. As it happens, the ♢Q would have fallen and declarer would have ended with an overtrick. Suppose instead that East had followed with a low card on the second round, or even shown out. Declarer would still make the contract when West held the ♢Q. In the 4-1 case, he would return to his hand with a club and lead towards the ♢J.

On the next deal you face a potential ace-queen finessing chance on the first trick. Would you take the finesse or not?

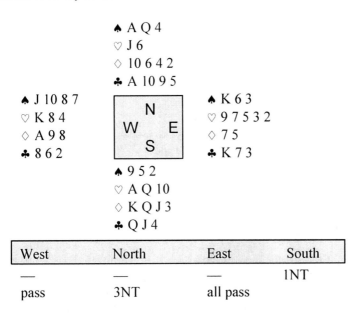

	♠ A Q 4 ♡ J 6 ♢ 10 6 4 2 ♣ A 10 9 5	
♠ J 10 8 7 ♡ K 8 4 ♢ A 9 8 ♣ 8 6 2	N W E S	♠ K 6 3 ♡ 9 7 5 3 2 ♢ 7 5 ♣ K 7 3
	♠ 9 5 2 ♡ A Q 10 ♢ K Q J 3 ♣ Q J 4	

West	North	East	South
—	—	—	1NT
pass	3NT	all pass	

West leads the ♠J and you can expect him to hold the ♠10. Playing standard leads, he may or may not hold the ♠K as well. If you commit the ♠Q to the first trick, you will go down. East will win and the defenders will clear three spade tricks, shortly to be joined by the ♢A and the ♣K.

You don't need to take the spade finesse! If you rise with the ♠A at Trick 1 the remaining cards in the spade suit will be 'frozen'. Neither defender can continue the suit without giving you an extra trick.

You win with the ♠A and play a diamond to the king and ace. If West fails to continue spades now, you will have time to run the ♣Q. The finesse will lose but you will then have eight top tricks. Since the defenders cannot play spades effectively, you will establish a ninth trick from the heart suit.

Suppose instead that West does persist with spades, leading the ♠7. You will run this to your ♠9, forcing East's ♠K. East is welcome to clear the spades because you can cross to a diamond to run the ♣Q into the safe hand.

Even if you held only ♠652 and the spades would not be frozen, it would rarely by right to play the ♠Q on the first trick. By retaining that card, you would be able to block the suit when East had started with a doubleton ♠K.

On the next deal taking an 'unnecessary finesse' surrendered a tempo.

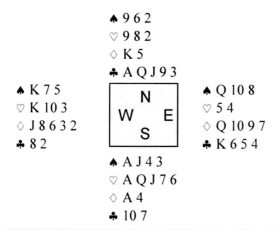

	North	
	♠ 9 6 2 ♡ 9 8 2 ◇ K 5 ♣ A Q J 9 3	
West ♠ K 7 5 ♡ K 10 3 ◇ J 8 6 3 2 ♣ 8 2	N / W E / S	**East** ♠ Q 10 8 ♡ 5 4 ◇ Q 10 9 7 ♣ K 6 5 4
	South ♠ A J 4 3 ♡ A Q J 7 6 ◇ A 4 ♣ 10 7	

West	North	East	South
—	—	—	1♡
pass	2♣	pass	2♠
pass	3♡	pass	4♡
all pass			

West led the ♣8 and declarer played low from dummy. East won with the ♣K and switched to the ♠10. This was a 'surround play', with his ♠108 surrounding dummy's ♠9. Declarer was doomed. He played the ♠J, West winning and returning the ♠7. Dummy's ♠9 was covered by the queen and ace. Declarer lost a heart trick and a further spade trick for one down.

Declarer should have risen with the ♣A and taken the trump finesse. West would win and play a second club to East's king. A third round of clubs would promote West's ♡10, yes, but declarer would simply discard a spade from his hand and allow West to enjoy a ruff. His two remaining spade losers would disappear on dummy's established clubs.

Tips to avoid mistake 35

(Taking an unnecessary finesse)

- Taking a finesse at Trick 1 can be a mistake in various ways. If it loses, your RHO may deliver or receive a ruff. He may also make a damaging switch.
- When the opening lead comes through AQx in the dummy, it is rarely right to play the queen on that trick.

Mistake 36

Missing an extra chance

It is nearly always better to have two chances of making a contract rather than one. Many a contract fails because declarer didn't even spot the extra chance. Even if you do see a second possible way home, you may need to arrange the play in a particular way to benefit from both chances.

Test yourself on this deal:

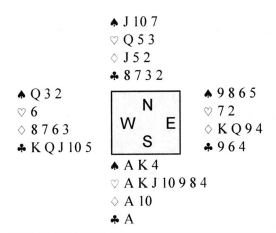

	North	
	♠ J 10 7 ♡ Q 5 3 ♢ J 5 2 ♣ 8 7 3 2	
West ♠ Q 3 2 ♡ 6 ♢ 8 7 6 3 ♣ K Q J 10 5	N / W E / S	**East** ♠ 9 8 6 5 ♡ 7 2 ♢ K Q 9 4 ♣ 9 6 4
	♠ A K 4 ♡ A K J 10 9 8 4 ♢ A 10 ♣ A	

West	North	East	South
—	—	—	2♣
pass	2♢	pass	2♡
pass	4♡	pass	6♡
all pass			

How would you play 6♡ when West leads the ♣K to your ace?

The original declarer was pleased to see that dummy's ♠J10 gave him the chance of a successful finesse in the suit. He drew trumps with the ace and queen, crossed his fingers and called for the ♠J. Despite the thoughtful digital manipulation, the spade finesse lost and the slam went one down.

The diamond suit offers a second chance of making the contract. If East holds the ♢KQ (or one of the honors doubleton), a single diamond finesse will allow a discard to be set up. Two dummy entries will be required for this line of play. Everyone follows to the ♡A and you continue with the ♡8 to dummy's ♡Q. Next you lead a low diamond towards your hand, intending to finesse the 10. With both honors onside, you cannot go wrong. If East splits his top cards, you will win with the ♢A and lead the ♢10 to clear a diamond trick in dummy. Since you retained the ♡4, you will be able to overtake that card with the ♡5 to reach the established ♢J.

If your venture in diamonds proves unsuccessful, nothing is lost. You can return to dummy with the ♡5 to run the ♠J.

There are several plays in bridge that can become 'automatic'. On the next deal, making one such automatic play cost declarer the contract. It prevented him from taking an extra chance in a different suit.

	♠ Q 2 ♡ J 5 2 ♢ A 4 ♣ A K 7 5 3 2	
♠ J 10 9 5 3 ♡ K 8 7 4 ♢ 8 6 5 ♣ 9	N W E S	♠ 8 7 6 4 ♡ Q 6 ♢ 9 7 2 ♣ Q J 10 6
	♠ A K ♡ A 10 9 3 ♢ K Q J 10 3 ♣ 8 4	

West	North	East	South
—	—	—	1♢
pass	2♣	pass	2♡
pass	2♠	pass	2NT
pass	6NT	all pass	

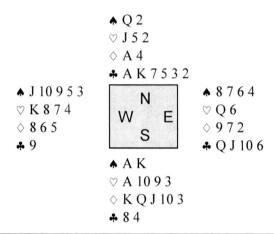

Declarer won the spade lead and saw that a 3-2 club break would give him enough tricks. Playing in notrump with such a club combination, one play was automatic… you duck the first round to retain a second-round entry to the long cards.

Looking no further into the matter, declarer promptly ducked a round of clubs. He won the spade return and led a second round of clubs. Oh no, West showed out! There was no way to recover and the slam went down.

How should declarer have done better? If clubs were 3-2, there was no need to duck the first round of clubs since dummy still had the ♢A as an entry. He should have tested the clubs by playing the ace and king. If a 3-2 break came to light, he would concede a round of clubs and claim the remaining tricks. When instead West showed out on the second club, the contract would still be alive. Declarer could seek three tricks from the heart suit to bring his total to twelve.

A heart to the nine would lose to the king (in the safe hand) and West would clear the spades. A diamond to the ace would allow a second round of hearts to be led towards the South hand. When the ♡Q appeared from East, declarer would win with the ♡A and cross to the ♡J. He could then return to his hand with a diamond and score the ♡9, bringing the total to twelve.

Sometimes the missed extra chance lies within the confines of a single suit. Many declarers went down when this deal arose in a club duplicate:

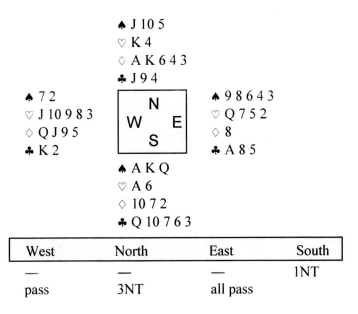

West	North	East
	♠ J 10 5 ♡ K 4 ◇ A K 6 4 3 ♣ J 9 4	
♠ 7 2 ♡ J 10 9 8 3 ◇ Q J 9 5 ♣ K 2	N W E S	♠ 9 8 6 4 3 ♡ Q 7 5 2 ◇ 8 ♣ A 8 5
	♠ A K Q ♡ A 6 ◇ 10 7 2 ♣ Q 10 7 6 3	

West	North	East	South
—	—	—	1NT
pass	3NT	all pass	

How will you give yourself the best chance in 3NT when West leads the ♡J?

You have seven tricks on top. Where can you find two more tricks? The answer does not lie in the club suit; the defenders will have scored three hearts and the ♣AK before you can enjoy any extra club tricks. Instead you must hope to score four diamond tricks. This will be easy if the diamonds divide 3-2, of course. You must see if you can cope with any of the possible 4-1 breaks. What do you think?

Suppose you win with the ♡A and play the ◇A, perhaps thinking this will give you a chance when West began with a singleton ◇Q or ◇J. It won't when East is a good player! If he holds ◇Q985 or ◇J985, he will rise with his honor on the second round, leaving the diamond suit blocked. He will then revert to hearts, removing the last side entry to dummy, and you will score only two diamond tricks.

Think about it for a moment and you will see that the only possibility of surviving a 4-1 diamond break is to find East with a singleton ◇8 or ◇9. You should win the heart lead with the ace and lead the ◇10 from your hand, aiming to pin the 8 or 9 in the East hand. If West declines to cover, your 10 will win the trick. You can then play ace, king and another diamond, using the ♡K as a subsequent entry to the thirteenth diamond.

What if West covers the ♢10 with the queen or jack? You win with dummy's ace, noting the fall of the ♢8 on your right, and continue with a low diamond to the 7. If West wins, you will be able to finesse with dummy's ♢K6, sitting over his ♢Q5. If instead West allows the ♢7 to win, you will continue with king and another diamond. It may seem a small extra chance (in fact it's around 6%) but looking for such edges is the hallmark of an expert player.

This chapter has been quite hard work, I dare say, but perhaps you're the sort of player who is very happy to work at their game. No? Oh well…

There's only one more deal. Charge up the brain cells and give it your best shot.

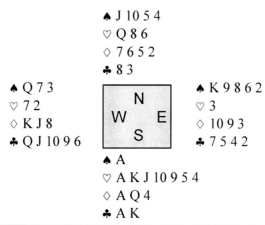

	♠ J 10 5 4 ♡ Q 8 6 ♢ 7 6 5 2 ♣ 8 3	
♠ Q 7 3 ♡ 7 2 ♢ K J 8 ♣ Q J 10 9 6	N W E S	♠ K 9 8 6 2 ♡ 3 ♢ 10 9 3 ♣ 7 5 4 2
	♠ A ♡ A K J 10 9 5 4 ♢ A Q 4 ♣ A K	

West	North	East	South
—	—	—	2♣
pass	2♢	pass	2♡
pass	4♡	pass	4♠
pass	5♡	pass	6♡
all pass			

How would you play the slam when West leads the ♣Q?

The main chance is a diamond finesse. If you use the three potential entries in dummy's trump suit, however, you can benefit from a possible extra chance. You win the club lead, cash the ♠A and lead the ♡J to dummy's ♡Q. You then ruff a spade with the ♡9. If a spade honor falls doubleton (or singleton), you can re-enter dummy with the ♡4 to the ♡8 and lead the ♠J, discarding a diamond loser. The ♠10 will then be established for a further diamond discard and the ♡6 will be your entry to dummy.

When the cards lie as in the diagram, no spade honor will fall on the second round. You cash the remaining club honor, eliminating that suit. You then lead the ♡4 to the ♡8 and run the ♠J to West's queen, discarding a diamond from your hand. By good fortune, West began with only three spades and is endplayed; he will have to return a diamond or give you a ruff-and-sluff. If the spade lie was not so favorable, you would have used dummy's third entry (the ♡5 to the ♡6) for a last-ditch finesse of the ◇Q.

Poor West will curse the day that he was dealt such a handsome club sequence! Had his clubs been less enticing, he might have led a 'safe' trump and beaten the slam!

Tips to avoid mistake 36

(Missing an extra chance)

- Even when you spot a promising line of play, spend a while looking for an additional chance.
- A common extra chance is that an honor can be ruffed out. (With ◇Qxxx opposite the ◇A, perhaps a defender holds ◇Kxx.)
- Suppose you need four tricks from a side suit of ♣AQxx in your hand and ♣Kxx in the dummy. A commonly missed extra chance is that you can draw only two rounds of trumps (leaving a trump out). You can then ruff the fourth round of clubs when the club length lies with the outstanding trump.

Mistake 37

Failing to Count the Hand

One of the most important techniques available to declarer is that of 'counting the hand'. What does that mean? It means that you keep track of the shape of the defenders' hands, using information from the bidding and noting every time someone shows out of a suit. Another source of information comes from the defenders' signals. In this regard, do not become over suspicious, worrying that the defenders may be false-carding. This is rarely the case.

The declarer on this hand thought that he had a guess to make:

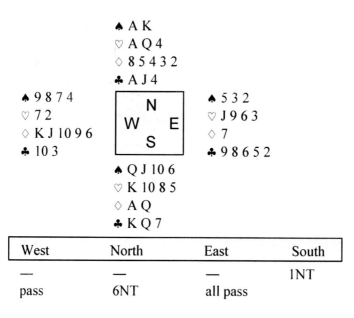

	North	
	♠ A K ♡ A Q 4 ♢ 8 5 4 3 2 ♣ A J 4	
West ♠ 9 8 7 4 ♡ 7 2 ♢ K J 10 9 6 ♣ 10 3	N W E S	**East** ♠ 5 3 2 ♡ J 9 6 3 ♢ 7 ♣ 9 8 6 5 2
	♠ Q J 10 6 ♡ K 10 8 5 ♢ A Q ♣ K Q 7	

West	North	East	South
—	—	—	1NT
pass	6NT	all pass	

Declarer won the ♠9 lead in dummy and saw that he had eleven top tricks. He needed to make one extra trick from the red suits. A finesse of the ♢Q lost to the ♢K and West returned the ♢J, East discarding a club. Declarer turned his attention to the heart suit. Perhaps the ♡J would appear at some stage, saving him from an awkward guess on the third round. When the ace and queen were played, spot-cards appeared from both defenders. A third round of hearts was led from dummy and declarer was not pleased to see East follow with the last spot-card, the ♡9. He then had to guess whether to play for the drop or to finesse the ♡10. What do you think is the best chance after this start to the play?

The correct answer is: 'I have absolutely no idea – it's a complete guess – but I wouldn't have played it that way!' The original declarer thought for a few moments and then misguessed, rising with the ♡K. West showed out and the slam was one down.

Seek a 'complete count of the hand', and there is no need to guess in hearts. You finesse the ◇Q at Trick 2, as before, win the return and play all your winners outside hearts. West will show up with four spades, five diamonds and two clubs. His shape is therefore 4=2=5=2. He has only two hearts! You play the ♡A and ♡Q and then finesse the ♡10, absolutely certain that the finesse will win. It does, of course, and the slam is yours.

Suppose West had shown up with only three spades. His shape would be 3=3=2=5 and you would play for the drop in hearts, again making the slam.

The theme is similar on the next deal. You have a suit that may require a good guess and can spare yourself this guess by seeking a complete count. The original declarer fell short in this respect.

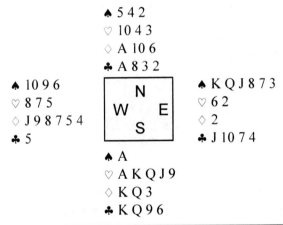

	North	
	♠ 5 4 2 ♡ 10 4 3 ◇ A 10 6 ♣ A 8 3 2	
West ♠ 10 9 6 ♡ 8 7 5 ◇ J 9 8 7 5 4 ♣ 5	N W E S	**East** ♠ K Q J 8 7 3 ♡ 6 2 ◇ 2 ♣ J 10 7 4
	South ♠ A ♡ A K Q J 9 ◇ K Q 3 ♣ K Q 9 6	

West	North	East	South
—	—	2♠	dbl
pass	3♣	pass	3♡
pass	4♡	pass	4NT
pass	5♡	pass	7♡
all pass			

North would have bid 2NT (Lebensohl) if his hand was weak. His actual 3♣ suggested around 8-10 points and South's 3♡ was then forcing. How would you play 7♡ when West leads the ♠10?

The original declarer won the spade lead and drew trumps. He then turned his attention to the club suit, where four tricks would give him the grand. The best play, it seemed to him, was to play the ♣K first. If the ♣J or ♣10 fell from West, he would cross to the ♣A next, picking up ♣10xxx or ♣Jxxx with East. If instead the ♣J or ♣10 fell from East, he could continue with the ♣Q from his hand. This was the best play, looking at the club suit in isolation, but he went down when East turned up with ♣J10xx.

Before tackling the club suit, nothing can be lost by cashing the king and queen of diamonds. You can catch ♣J10xx only when it is East who has that holding. He is already known to be 6-2 in the major suits and will have a singleton diamond when he holds four clubs. East does indeed show out on the second round of diamonds! You cross to the ♣A to see West's singleton in the suit. It is the six-spot. You then lead a low club from dummy and finesse the ♣9. It will not help East to split his ♣J10 because you have kept the ♢A to re-enter dummy for a third-round club finesse.

We will end the chapter with a deal where you cannot obtain a complete count of the defenders' hands. However, a partial count is good enough to determine the winning line of play.

	♠ 5 3 ♡ K Q 10 ♢ A Q 7 4 ♣ Q 10 6 2	
♠ 10 9 8 4 ♡ J 4 3 2 ♢ J 8 6 3 ♣ 9	N W E S	♠ A J 7 6 2 ♡ 9 7 6 ♢ 2 ♣ 8 7 5 3
	♠ K Q ♡ A 8 5 ♢ K 10 9 5 ♣ A K J 4	

West	North	East	South
—	—	—	2NT
pass	6NT	all pass	

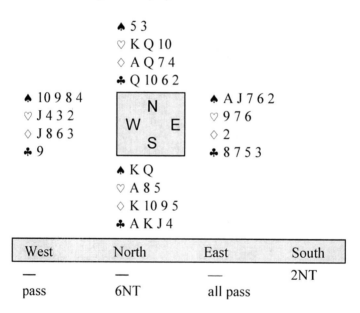

West leads the ♠10 to East's ♠A and the ♠6 is returned. The original declarer counted 11 top tricks and made the mistake of turning immediately to the diamond suit. All followed to the ♢A but East showed out when the ♢Q was played. 'Typical of my luck!' exclaimed the declarer.

Since South held the ♢10 and the ♢9, he began with a two-way guess in diamonds. He should therefore have made some attempt to read the lie of the other three suits before deciding which way to finesse in diamonds. Four rounds of clubs and three of hearts will place East with four clubs and at least three hearts. West's ♠10 opening lead means that East must have started with at least ♠AJx. This leaves him with at most three cards in diamonds! You will never need to finesse him for ◊Jxxx. After playing the ◊A, you should cross to the ◊K. East shows out on this trick and you then know that running the ◊10 will give you the slam.

It's a bit of an effort to keep a track of the cards but the rewards are astronomical. You can become the best guesser in the universe! Well, first equal with everyone else who takes the trouble to count the hand.

Tips to avoid mistake 37

(Failing to count the hand)

- When you need to make a critical guess in one suit, try to obtain a complete count on the defenders' hands.
- In the absence of informative bidding by the opponents, the defender with the greater number of cards in a suit will be the favorite to hold any missing honor.
- Even a partial count of the defenders' hands may allow you to tilt the odds in your favor.
- Keep track of the count right from the start. It is much harder if you have to recall, later in the play, exactly when a defender showed out of a particular suit.

Mistake 38

Allowing a defensive ruff

The defenders score a ruff and beat your contract. It has happened to us all, on countless occasions. Sometimes declarer could have prevented it, as on this example:

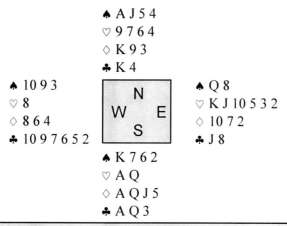

	North	
	♠ A J 5 4 ♡ 9 7 6 4 ♢ K 9 3 ♣ K 4	
West ♠ 10 9 3 ♡ 8 ♢ 8 6 4 ♣ 10 9 7 6 5 2	N W E S	**East** ♠ Q 8 ♡ K J 10 5 3 2 ♢ 10 7 2 ♣ J 8
	♠ K 7 6 2 ♡ A Q ♢ A Q J 5 ♣ A Q 3	

West	North	East	South
—	—	2♡	dbl
pass	3♡	pass	3♠
pass	4♠	pass	6♠
all pass			

How would you play 6♠ when West leads the ♡8 to East's king and your ace?

The original declarer recalled the maxim 'Eight ever, nine never', he played the king of trumps and then finessed dummy's jack. This was the best chance of avoiding a trump loser, yes, but it did not give him the best chance of making the slam! East won with the ♠Q and promptly gave his partner a heart ruff for one down.

After East's 2♡ opening, it could hardly be more obvious that the opening lead was a singleton. Declarer could afford to lose one trump trick but not two. He should have played the king and ace of trumps. As it happens, the queen would drop and he would score an overtrick. This was not the purpose of the play. Declarer would still have made the slam even if

West had started with ♠Qxx or ♠Qxxx. He would simply return to his hand with a club and lead towards dummy's remaining ♠J5.

A different technique is needed on the next deal:

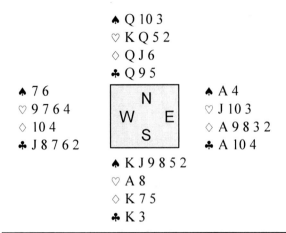

	♠ Q 10 3 ♡ K Q 5 2 ◇ Q J 6 ♣ Q 9 5	
♠ 7 6 ♡ 9 7 6 4 ◇ 10 4 ♣ J 8 7 6 2	N W E S	♠ A 4 ♡ J 10 3 ◇ A 9 8 3 2 ♣ A 10 4
	♠ K J 9 8 5 2 ♡ A 8 ◇ K 7 5 ♣ K 3	

West	North	East	South
—	—	1◇	1♠
pass	2◇	pass	4♠
all pass			

West leads the ◇10, East winning with the ◇A and returning a diamond. How will you play the contract?

The deal arose in a club game and declarer gave the matter little thought. He won the diamond return in the dummy and led a trump. East rose promptly with the ♠A and gave his partner a diamond ruff. A subsequent club trick put the game one down.

This outcome was entirely predictable from declarer's point of view. Instead of playing a trump, declarer should have taken the three top hearts, discarding the ◇K on the third round. Only then should he play a trump. If East rose with the ♠A and played a third diamond now, it would cause no problem. Declarer would ruff high in his hand.

The winning move may be harder to spot on the next deal because the risk of an adverse ruff is not clearly sign-posted.

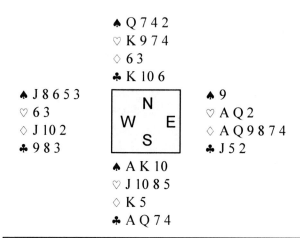

	♠ Q 7 4 2 ♡ K 9 7 4 ◇ 6 3 ♣ K 10 6		
♠ J 8 6 5 3 ♡ 6 3 ◇ J 10 2 ♣ 9 8 3	N W E S	♠ 9 ♡ A Q 2 ◇ A Q 9 8 7 4 ♣ J 5 2	
	♠ A K 10 ♡ J 10 8 5 ◇ K 5 ♣ A Q 7 4		

West	North	East	South
—	—	—	1NT
pass	2♣	2◇	2♡
pass	4♡	all pass	

West leads the ◇J against the heart game and East lets this pass to your ◇K in the South seat. What is your plan as declarer?

How easy it would be to run the ♡J at Trick 2. Mistake! East would win with the ♡Q and return his singleton spade. When he won the next round of trumps, he would be able to cross to West's ◇10 to receive a spade ruff.

The deal was originally played by USA world champion Alan Sontag in the late 1980s. At Trick 2 he returned his remaining diamond, cutting the link to the West hand. The defenders could no longer score a ruff and he soon had ten tricks before him.

What was the thought process behind this line of play? With one loser in the side suits, the only way to go down was to lose three trump tricks. By playing a second diamond, Sontag greatly reduced the chance of this happening. It was a form of the play known as the Scissors Coup.

On the next deal the bidding and early play allow you to reconstruct the East-West hands with some accuracy. Not that the original declarer took advantage of this.

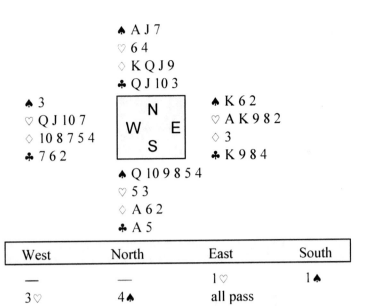

	♠ A J 7 ♡ 6 4 ◇ K Q J 9 ♣ Q J 10 3	
♠ 3 ♡ Q J 10 7 ◇ 10 8 7 5 4 ♣ 7 6 2	N W E S	♠ K 6 2 ♡ A K 9 8 2 ◇ 3 ♣ K 9 8 4
	♠ Q 10 9 8 5 4 ♡ 5 3 ◇ A 6 2 ♣ A 5	

West	North	East	South
—	—	1♡	1♠
3♡	4♠	all pass	

West's 3♡ was pre-emptive; he would have bid 2♠ with a sound double raise in hearts. When West leads the ♡Q, East overtakes with the ♡K and returns the ◇3. It's fairly clear that East's ◇3 is a singleton and that he is hoping to cross to partner's ♡J to receive a diamond ruff. How can you prevent this?

The original declarer played ace and another trump. East won and returned a low heart to receive his diamond ruff. That was one down.

The bidding and early play indicated that East was 5-1 in the red suits and a 3=5=1=4 shape was more likely than 2=5=1=5. As on the previous deal, you need to cut the link to the dangerous West hand. You win the diamond shift in dummy and run the ♣Q. After a second round of clubs to the ace, you return to dummy with the ♠A and lead the ♣J. East covers with the ♣K and you discard your remaining heart. This loser-on-loser play kills the entry to the West hand. If East returns a fourth club, you will ruff high. West cannot overruff and you will draw trumps, claiming the contract.

Tips to avoid mistake 38

(Allowing a defensive ruff)

- Finessing in the trump suit can be a bad idea when the defenders are threatening a ruff.
- You can sometimes avoid a ruff by discarding that suit, even if this means discarding winners.
- Another preventative measure is to cut the link between the two defenders.

PART III

Mistakes in defense

Board	Contract	By	Tricks	Score	IMPs
26	6♣X	S	12	1540	17

Mistake 39

Conceding a trick by playing high

'Play high in the third seat' is a reasonable guideline for beginners. The general aim is to attempt to win the trick or at least force out a higher card from declarer. The more you play the game, the more you realize that general guidelines on cardplay cannot compete with 'common sense'. Many a contract is given away on the first trick because the defender in third seat mistakenly plays a high card.

Let's see some examples. Take the East cards here:

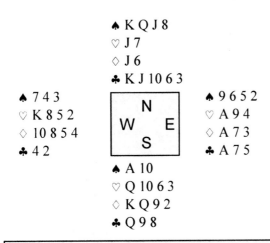

	North	
	♠ K Q J 8	
	♡ J 7	
	◇ J 6	
	♣ K J 10 6 3	
♠ 7 4 3	N	♠ 9 6 5 2
♡ K 8 5 2	W E	♡ A 9 4
◇ 10 8 5 4	S	◇ A 7 3
♣ 4 2		♣ A 7 5
	♠ A 10	
	♡ Q 10 6 3	
	◇ K Q 9 2	
	♣ Q 9 8	

West	North	East	South
—	—	—	1◇
pass	1♠	pass	1NT
pass	3NT	all pass	

West, your partner, leads the ♡2 and the ♡7 is played from dummy. What is your plan to defeat the contract?

West's ♡2 lead suggests that he holds an honor in the suit. This marks the ♠A in the South hand, to make up his opening bid. Apart from your three glittering aces, you will need two extra tricks in the red suits to beat 3NT.

The original East won with the ♡A and returned the ♡9. In fact it didn't matter what he returned. Once he had played the ace on the first trick, catching a miserly ♡7 and ♡3 in the net, declarer's three top heart cards would be worth two tricks and would guarantee the contract.

See the difference if you retain the ♡A to deal with dummy's jack and play your ♡9 at Trick 1. Declarer wins with the ♡10 and clears the clubs. You win with the ♣A and cash the ♡A, picking up dummy's jack. You can then lead the ♡4 through South's ♡Q6 to West's awaiting ♡K8. One down!

The original defense would have worked if West's hearts were ♡KQ52, which was possible if South had opened on an 11-count. The recommended defense would have won in that case too, so it was clearly much better.

The situation on the next deal arises frequently, with many defenders going wrong.

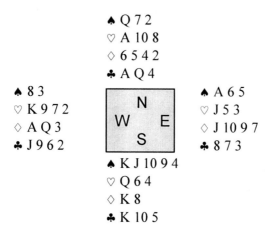

	North	
	♠ Q 7 2 ♡ A 10 8 ♢ 6 5 4 2 ♣ A Q 4	
West ♠ 8 3 ♡ K 9 7 2 ♢ A Q 3 ♣ J 9 6 2	N W E S	**East** ♠ A 6 5 ♡ J 5 3 ♢ J 10 9 7 ♣ 8 7 3
	♠ K J 10 9 4 ♡ Q 6 4 ♢ K 8 ♣ K 10 5	
	South	

West	North	East	South
—	1♢	pass	1♠
pass	1NT	pass	2♣
pass	2♠	pass	4♠
all pass			

South used a check-back 2♣ to locate the 5-3 spade fit. Sitting East, you see your partner lead the ♡2. The ♡8 is played from dummy and you must plan your defense.

The original East player saw no reason to allow dummy's ♡8 to win the trick. 'How can it be wrong to play my jack?' he thought to himself.

Declarer soon showed him the answer to this question. He won with the ♡Q, drew trumps and finessed the ♡10 successfully to make three heart tricks. The contract was his, even though two diamond tricks had to be lost.

Look back to Trick 1, where West led the ♡2 and the ♡8 was played from dummy. West would not have led the ♡2 from something like ♡KQ72. Against a suit contract he would have led the ♡K, making sure that his honors participated in the first two rounds of the suit. West's ♡2 lead suggested that his hearts were headed by the king or the queen. If West held the ♡Q, declarer would score three heart tricks however East defended. If instead West held the ♡K, it would cost a trick for East to put in the ♡J. If he played low instead, allowing dummy's ♡8 to win, the declarer would score only two heart tricks and go one down.

Let's see another deal where the defender in the East seat made a mistake on the first trick:

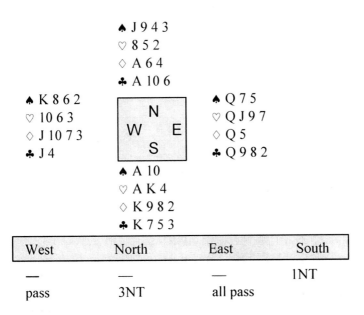

	North	
	♠ J 9 4 3 ♡ 8 5 2 ◇ A 6 4 ♣ A 10 6	
♠ K 8 6 2 ♡ 10 6 3 ◇ J 10 7 3 ♣ J 4	N W E S	♠ Q 7 5 ♡ Q J 9 7 ◇ Q 5 ♣ Q 9 8 2
	♠ A 10 ♡ A K 4 ◇ K 9 8 2 ♣ K 7 5 3	

West	North	East	South
—	—	—	1NT
pass	3NT	all pass	

With 4-3-3-3 shape North quite rightly declined to bid Stayman. Take the East cards now and consider your defense when West leads the ♠2 and dummy plays low.

The original East gave the matter little thought and played 'third hand high', contributing the ♠Q. Declarer won with the ♠A and counted seven top tricks. He soon established two more spade tricks and the game was made.

It was barely possible that playing the ♠Q would assist the defense. If East plays low instead, declarer wins with the ♠10. The ♠A will give him a second trick in the suit but he will end with just two spade tricks instead of three, going one down.

There are other situations where rising with the queen will cost. If West has led from ♠10862, with declarer holding ♠AK, rising with the queen gives South three quick spade tricks. If instead declarer holds ♠K8, let him win the first trick with the 8. The ♠A and ♠Q will score the next two rounds for the defenders. So, beware of 'third hand high' when dummy has a respectable holding in the suit led.

It is remarkable how many defenders go wrong in the situation featured in the next deal. Take the East cards and see how you fare:

	North	
	♠ 9 8 5 ♡ 5 ♢ K J 8 4 ♣ A 10 8 6 4	
West ♠ K J 10 3 ♡ 8 6 3 ♢ 10 6 3 ♣ K Q 3	N W E S	**East** ♠ Q 6 4 ♡ K 10 9 7 4 2 ♢ 9 7 ♣ J 9
	♠ A 7 2 ♡ A Q J ♢ A Q 5 2 ♣ 7 5 2	

West	North	East	South
—	—	2♡	2NT
pass	3NT	all pass	

West leads the ♡8. What is your plan for the defense?

Partner's lead tells you that declarer holds ♡AQJ(x). If you make the mistake of playing your ♡K, he will enjoy three heart tricks to go with four diamonds and the two black aces. He will be able to claim the contract!

You should play a discouraging ♡2 on the first trick. Declarer will win with the ♡Q and lead a club. West plays the ♣3, covered with dummy's ♣8, and you win. Persevering with hearts is no good and you switch to spades. Declarer holds up the ♠A until the third round, exhausting your spades, and then plays another club. He cannot establish the clubs without West gaining the lead with his ♣KQ and the thirteenth spade will be the setting trick.

As you see, West could not afford to split his club honors on the first round (nor if he had been dealt ♣QJx in the suit). Declarer could then have played low from dummy, won the third round of spades, and ducked a club into the safe East hand.

Tips to avoid mistake 39

(Conceding a trick by playing high)

- Do not 'play high in third seat' without considering what effect this may have. When such a play would set up a finesse in the dummy, it will often be wrong.
- Playing high may also be wrong when it will leave you unable to beat dummy's top card in the suit.
- When partner's opening lead denies an honor, you will often assist declarer if you play your top card.

Mistake 40

Not keeping the right cards

An important part of defending accurately is to keep the right cards for the endgame. Occasionally this will involve a bit of guesswork. More often your partner's signals and a careful analysis of the situation will allow you to judge the right cards to retain.

East was put under pressure on this deal and did not come up with the winning answer. Take the East cards and see if you do better.

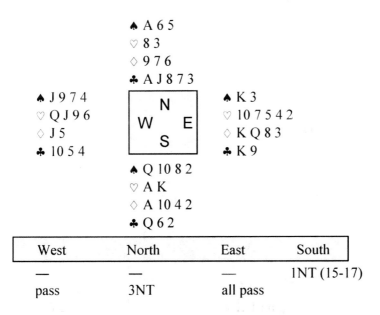

	♠ A 6 5 ♡ 8 3 ♢ 9 7 6 ♣ A J 8 7 3	
♠ J 9 7 4 ♡ Q J 9 6 ♢ J 5 ♣ 10 5 4	N W E S	♠ K 3 ♡ 10 7 5 4 2 ♢ K Q 8 3 ♣ K 9
	♠ Q 10 8 2 ♡ A K ♢ A 10 4 2 ♣ Q 6 2	

West	North	East	South
—	—	—	1NT (15-17)
pass	3NT	all pass	

Declarer wins the ♡Q lead with the king and plays a club to the jack and your king. When you return the ♡4, declarer wins with the ace and your partner plays the ♡J. Declarer now leads queen and another club, running four tricks in the suit. You can afford to throw the ♢3 and ♢8. Your remaining cards are: ♠K3 ♡1052 ♢KQ. What will your final discard be?

The original East was unwilling to bare the ♠K. Nor did he like the idea of parting with a diamond honor. He decided to throw a heart. Declarer continued with ace and another spade and then had nine tricks. With only two heart tricks to take after East's discard in the suit, the defenders could not beat him to the tape.

When it was pointed out to East that he could have beaten the contract by discarding a diamond honor, he replied: 'Easy to say that now but declarer might have held the ◇AJ.' Indeed, but in that case the chosen heart discard would not have beaten the contact. With the king and queen of diamonds both onside, declarer would have had time to set up his ninth trick in diamonds.

The next type of deal arises very frequently. Both declarer and the defenders need to understand the position. Here we will concentrate on the defense, viewing proceedings from the West seat.

	♠ 7 6 3	
	♡ K 6 4	
	◇ Q J 7	
	♣ K Q J 7	
♠ K Q J 9 5 2	N	♠ 4
♡ J 9 5	W E	♡ Q 10 8 7
◇ K 8 5		◇ 10 6 4
♣ 8	S	♣ 10 9 5 4 3
	♠ A 10 8	
	♡ A 3 2	
	◇ A 9 3 2	
	♣ A 6 2	

West	North	East	South
2♠	pass	pass	2NT
pass	3NT	all pass	

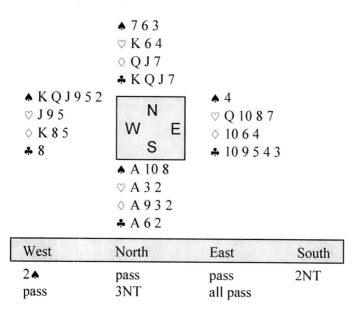

You lead the ♠K, which wins. Declarer takes the next spade, East throwing a club, and plays four club winners. What will you discard in the West seat?

Declarer surely holds the four aces and that gives him a total of eight tricks. You must assume that your partner has the ♡Q. How many discards will you need to find? Declarer can play six winners in clubs and hearts, putting you to three discards. You can afford one heart and one diamond. You cannot afford a spade as your third discard or declarer will be able to throw you in with a spade, forcing you to lead a diamond. Your fifth discard must therefore be another diamond. If you bare the ◇K, retaining enough spades to beat the contract, declarer will have to guess who has the ◇K. If you have it, the card will drop under the ace; if partner has it, a finesse will be necessary.

Provided you bare the ◇K smoothly, it will be a tricky decision for the declarer. He may well elect to run the ◇Q since many defenders are not up to the task of baring the ◇K. In that case the contract will go two down.

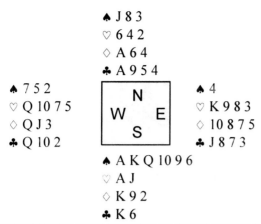

	♠ J 8 3 ♡ 6 4 2 ◇ A 6 4 ♣ A 9 5 4		
♠ 7 5 2 ♡ Q 10 7 5 ◇ Q J 3 ♣ Q 10 2	N W E S	♠ 4 ♡ K 9 8 3 ◇ 10 8 7 5 ♣ J 8 7 3	
	♠ A K Q 10 9 6 ♡ A J ◇ K 9 2 ♣ K 6		

West	North	East	South
–	–	–	2♣
pass	2◇	pass	2♠
pass	3♠	pass	4♠
pass	6♠	all pass	

You are East. Your partner leads a trump and declarer plays five rounds of the suit, your partner following twice more. What will you discard?

Your clubs are potentially valuable. You can see dummy's ♣A954. If declarer holds ♣KQx, your ♣J873 guards the suit. If instead declarer has ♣Kx, a club discard from you will allow him establish an extra club trick with a ruff. So, you plan to keep all four clubs. The next important point is that your hearts may well be worthless. If declarer has ♡AQx he has two (and only two) heart tricks, however many hearts you throw.

So, discard all four hearts. If declarer were to continue with the ♡A, you would release a diamond. You can see the 4-card club threat but declarer may not have a 4-card diamond threat.

Tips to avoid mistake 40

(Not keeping the right cards)

- It is often right to 'match the length' with a 4-card suit in the dummy.
- Similarly, you may choose to match length with a 4-card suit that declarer holds (or you suspect he holds).
- Honor cards lying under declarer's holding may be valueless, since he can finesse against them.

Mistake 41

Not thinking straight

One of the most common mistakes in defense is failing to think clearly. Players sometimes refer to such aberrations as 'having a blind spot'. What they really mean is that they didn't stop to make a clear plan.

In this chapter, we will look at some deals where the defender in question should have beaten the contract but never even considered the winning action. Take the West cards here:

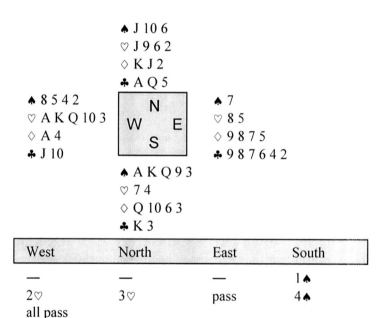

	♠ J 10 6 ♡ J 9 6 2 ◇ K J 2 ♣ A Q 5	
♠ 8 5 4 2 ♡ A K Q 10 3 ◇ A 4 ♣ J 10	N W E S	♠ 7 ♡ 8 5 ◇ 9 8 7 5 ♣ 9 8 7 6 4 2
	♠ A K Q 9 3 ♡ 7 4 ◇ Q 10 6 3 ♣ K 3	

West	North	East	South
—	—	—	1♠
2♡	3♡	pass	4♠
all pass			

West scored two top hearts, everyone following. To play a third top heart would make little sense, since it would set up dummy's ♡J. He eventually switched to the ♣J, hoping to find East with the ♣K. This shot failed and the players moved to the next board without comment.

Do you see the mistake that West made? It wasn't particularly likely that East held the ♣K when South had accepted the game-try and only 14 points were missing. In any case, all that West needed to beat the contract was to find East with a trump! At Trick 3, West should continue with a low heart. East ruffs whichever card is played from dummy and declarer has to overruff. He now holds four trumps, the same number as West. When he plays a round of trumps, East shows out. Declarer is doomed! If he draws all of West's trumps, he will have none left himself. As soon as he plays a diamond, West will win with the ace and score the ♡Q and another heart. If instead declarer plays diamonds before drawing trumps, West will win and force declarer to ruff again by playing the ♡Q, West will then have more trumps than declarer and again the game will go down. Any time you hold four trumps, consider playing a 'forcing defense', leading a strong suit in the hope that you can force declarer to ruff.

Try this one from the East seat. For a change, let's see only two hands this time:

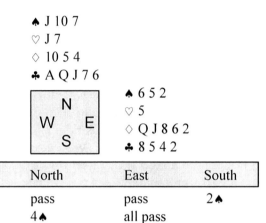

♠ J 10 7
♡ J 7
◇ 10 5 4
♣ A Q J 7 6

N / W E / S

♠ 6 5 2
♡ 5
◇ Q J 8 6 2
♣ 8 5 4 2

West	North	East	South
1♡	pass	pass	2♠
pass	4♠	all pass	

You are playing standard attitude and count signals. West leads the ♡K and continues with the ♡A. What card will you play on the second trick?

The deal arose in a duplicate match, the same situation arising at both tables. The first East player played the ◇6, intending the card to show mild interest in diamonds. The other East preferred to discard the ♣2, showing no interest in that suit. Did you choose one of these options?

Partner's hand was ♠3 ♡AKQ1093 ◇A73 ♣1093. The only way to defeat the contract was to ruff partner's ♡A and return the ◇Q through declarer's ◇K. The question to ask yourself is: which card does partner need to beat this contract? The answer is the ◇A. Diamonds can only be played successfully from your side of the table, so you need to ruff at Trick 2.

It seemed to work well, presenting only two hands. Let's try it again on a deal from the final of the women's world championship, with England facing China. One defender solved the problem and one did not. You'll be in good company either way!

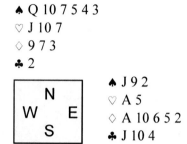

♠ Q 10 7 5 4 3
♡ J 10 7
◇ 9 7 3
♣ 2

N	
W E	♠ J 9 2
S	♡ A 5
	◇ A 10 6 5 2
	♣ J 10 4

West	North	East	South
—	pass	pass	2NT
pass	4♡	pass	4♠
all pass			

North's 4♡ was a transfer to spades. How will you defend when your partner leads the ◇Q to your ◇A, declarer following with the ◇4?

Nevena Senior, East for England, was thinking straight. It was unlikely that the opening lead was from ◇Qx. West might have led from ◇QJ doubleton, in which case a second diamond trick could be set up. But that would give the defense only three tricks (including the ♡A); a fourth trick would still be needed. It was more likely that the lead was from ◇QJx, in which case only one diamond trick was available.

By far the most likely way to defeat the contract was to find partner with the ♡K. Senior duly switched to the ♡A, on which partner gave an encouraging signal. A heart to West's king and a heart ruff put the game one down. At other table, The Chinese East returned a diamond and the contract was made. The USA East in the Seniors' final also let the game through by returning a diamond. (The West hand was ♠6 ♡K986 ◇QJ8 ♣98765.)

We will end with a deal from an international match between Belgium and France. Take the East cards and see if you would have out-defended the two original East players.

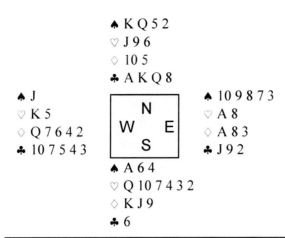

	North	
	♠ K Q 5 2 ♡ J 9 6 ♢ 10 5 ♣ A K Q 8	
♠ J ♡ K 5 ♢ Q 7 6 4 2 ♣ 10 7 5 4 3	N W E S	♠ 10 9 8 7 3 ♡ A 8 ♢ A 8 3 ♣ J 9 2
	♠ A 6 4 ♡ Q 10 7 4 3 2 ♢ K J 9 ♣ 6	

West	North	East	South
—	1♣	pass	1♡
pass	1NT	pass	4♡
all pass			

Your partner leads the ♠J, a likely singleton, since you hold the ♠10. Declarer wins with dummy's king and cashes three clubs, discarding the ♢9 and ♢J. He then leads a low trump from dummy. How will you defend?

Both Easts made the same mistake. They rose with the ♡A to give their partner a spade ruff. West ruffed all right but the ruff was with the ♡K and the defenders scored only three tricks, allowing the game to make.

As East, you should count the available defensive tricks. You will score the trump ace, a spade ruff and (you hope) the ♢A. A fourth trick will be possible only if your partner can win the first trump and cross in diamonds for a spade ruff. So, you should play low on the first trump.

(Declarer should have played a fourth club, throwing the ♢K. This would break the link between the defenders and allow him to make the game.)

Tips to avoid mistake 41

(Not thinking straight)

- Think clearly how you can score the tricks necessary to defeat the contract. Do not follow glib defensive maxims.
- Look for the most likely card(s) in partner's hand that will yield the tricks that you need.
- Do not return partner's suit when you can see that this will not defeat the contract. Look for a chance to score tricks elsewhere.

Mistake 42

Taking a high card too soon

An ace is a precious card, whether you're defending or playing the dummy. Defenders who make the mistake of always taking their aces at the first opportunity give away many a contract. Take the West cards on this deal.

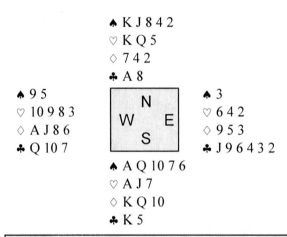

	♠ K J 8 4 2 ♡ K Q 5 ♢ 7 4 2 ♣ A 8	
♠ 9 5 ♡ 10 9 8 3 ♢ A J 8 6 ♣ Q 10 7	N W E S	♠ 3 ♡ 6 4 2 ♢ 9 5 3 ♣ J 9 6 4 3 2
	♠ A Q 10 7 6 ♡ A J 7 ♢ K Q 10 ♣ K 5	

West	North	East	South
—	—	—	1♠
pass	2NT	pass	3♠
pass	4♣	pass	4NT
pass	5♡	pass	6♠
all pass			

You lead the ♡10 and declarer wins with the ace. He draws trumps in two rounds, East discarding a low club, and cashes the ace and king of clubs. He continues with two more heart winners, East following all the time. Declarer plays a diamond to the king, East contributing the ♢3. What is your reaction in the West seat?

The original West player won with the ♢A and, since it was a slam, sat back in his chair to consider the next move carefully. Too late! A diamond return would be into declarer's ♢Q10; a heart or club return would concede a ruff-and-sluff. When it was pointed out to West that he should have ducked the first round of diamonds, retaining his ♢AJ to score two tricks subsequently, he claimed that declarer might have started with ♢Kx; a duck would then have given away the slam.

Why did this justification for his defense cut no ice? On the first round of diamonds, East played the ◇3. This was a count signal, showing an odd number of diamonds (three). If declarer held only two diamonds, East would have four and would have signaled with a higher spot-card.

Sometimes you must not release a king too early. East went wrong here:

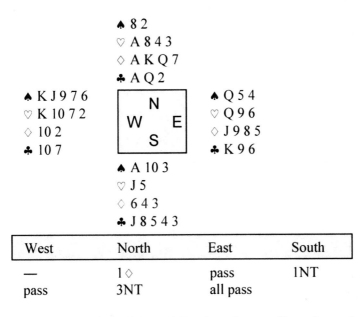

	♠ 8 2 ♡ A 8 4 3 ◇ A K Q 7 ♣ A Q 2	
♠ K J 9 7 6 ♡ K 10 7 2 ◇ 10 2 ♣ 10 7	N W E S	♠ Q 5 4 ♡ Q 9 6 ◇ J 9 8 5 ♣ K 9 6
	♠ A 10 3 ♡ J 5 ◇ 6 4 3 ♣ J 8 5 4 3	

West	North	East	South
—	1◇	pass	1NT
pass	3NT	all pass	

West led the ♠7 against 3NT and East's ♠Q was allowed to win. Declarer ducked the spade return too, West winning and clearing the suit. Declarer's next move was a club to West's ♣10 and dummy's queen. East won with the king and paused to consider his continuation.

Too late! Whatever East did next, declarer would score one spade, one heart, three diamonds and four clubs. It was careless play by East. His partner had played a high club, the ♣10, to show him an even number of cards in the suit. Since he would have played the ♣J from ♣J10, declarer almost certainly held ♣Jxxxx. By holding up the ♣K, he could have restricted declarer to two club tricks instead of four. (Declarer had even illustrated the necessary hold-up technique for him, in the spade suit!)

Entries were at the heart of declarer's problems on the next deal too:

♠ 6 4 2
♡ 7 5 4 2
♢ 10 6 3
♣ 7 6 3

♠ 10 8 5	N	♠ 9 3
♡ K Q J 8 6	W E	♡ 10 9 3
♢ 8 4	S	♢ A 7 5 2
♣ 10 9 4		♣ A K 8 2

♠ A K Q J 7
♡ A
♢ K Q J 9
♣ Q J 5

West	North	East	South
—	—	—	2♣
pass	2♢	pass	2♠
pass	2NT	pass	3♢
pass	3♠	pass	4♠
all pass			

Take the East cards on this one. You partner leads the ♡K and declarer wins with the ace, proceeding to draw trumps in three rounds. What is your plan for the defense when declarer's next move is to lead the ♢K, West following with the ♢8?

Suppose you win with the ace. Declarer will ruff the heart return and cross to the ♢10 to lead a club. If you play low, hoping that South holds ♣QJ9 and will finesse the 9, you will be disappointed. He will win with the ♣Q and claim the contract. If instead you rise with a club honor and force South's last trump with a heart, the contract will again survive. When you win with your second club honor, you will have no heart to play.

To beat the contract, you must keep declarer out of the dummy, preventing him from leading towards his club honors. You let the diamond king win and South continues with the diamond queen, West completing a high-low. You duck again and win the third round of diamonds. Declarer ruffs the heart return with his penultimate trump, cashes the established ♢9 and plays the ♣Q to your ace. You exit safely with your last heart, ruffed by declarer. He then has to play a second round of clubs himself, allowing your side to score the ♣10 and the ♣K for one down.

If a job's worth doing, it's worth doing properly. West botched the defense on the next deal because he didn't think the job was worth doing at all.

♠ 7 6 5
♡ 5 2
♢ 10 9 6 4
♣ K 7 5 3

West		East
♠ A 8 2	N	♠ J 10 9 4
♡ J 10 9 7	W E	♡ Q 8 4
♢ A 8 7 3	S	♢ 2
♣ 9 6		♣ J 10 8 4 2

♠ K Q 3
♡ A K 6 3
♢ K Q J 5
♣ A Q

West	North	East	South
—	—	—	2♣
pass	2♢	pass	2NT
pass	3NT	all pass	

West led the ♡J, his partner playing the ♡8. Declarer won immediately, and continued with the ♢K, West won with the ♢A and played another heart. Seeing that a hold-up could serve no purpose, declarer won with his remaining heart honor and led the ♠K. West scored the ♠A and two good hearts, but that was the end of the defense. Declarer used the ♢10 as the entry to reach the blocked ♣K and had nine tricks.

'Nothing we could do,' declared West.

Oh, no? West should have ducked the first round of diamonds. This was the 'job worth doing' on the deal. To 'do it properly', West also needed to duck the second and the third round of diamonds. By preventing declarer from reaching dummy with the ♢10, West would restrict him to only two club tricks, beating the contract.

Tips to avoid mistake 42

(Taking a high card too soon)

- Winning a trick in an elimination position may leave you endplayed. With such as AJx over KQ10, you need to duck.
- Releasing a high card too early can set up a vital extra entry for declarer.

Mistake 43

Conceding an entry by playing high

We saw in Chapter 39 how defenders can give a trick away by mistakenly playing high in the third seat. Now we will inspect some deals where playing high will establish a critical extra entry for the declarer.

Take the East cards here:

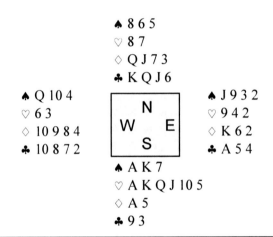

	North	
	♠ 8 6 5 ♡ 8 7 ♢ Q J 7 3 ♣ K Q J 6	
West ♠ Q 10 4 ♡ 6 3 ♢ 10 9 8 4 ♣ 10 8 7 2	N / W E / S	**East** ♠ J 9 3 2 ♡ 9 4 2 ♢ K 6 2 ♣ A 5 4
	♠ A K 7 ♡ A K Q J 10 5 ♢ A 5 ♣ 9 3	

West	North	East	South
—	—	—	2♣
pass	2♢	pass	2♡
pass	3♣	pass	4♡
pass	5♡	pass	6♡
all pass			

The opponents reach a poor slam and your partner leads the ♢10, covered by dummy's ♢Q. What is your plan for the defense in the East seat?

Many a player will make the mistake of covering the ♢Q with the ♢K. Declarer wins with the ♢A, draws trumps in three rounds and leads a club to the king. Holding up the ♣A for one round will not assist the defense after the mishap at Trick 1, because the ♢J has been set up as an extra entry to dummy. Declarer will score six trumps and two tricks in each side suit.

You must play low at Trick 1, allowing dummy's ♢Q to win. When declarer draws trumps and plays a club, your partner will follow with the ♣8 to tell you that he has an even number of clubs. Placing West with four clubs and declarer with two, you hold up the ♣A for one round, beating the slam.

We can extract extra mileage from the deal. Look back at the diagram and suppose that West has led the ♡6 (or ♡3), dummy playing the ♡7. You will give away the slam if you play the ♡9 in third seat! Declarer will win and clear the clubs, using the ♡8 as an entry. He will then discard the spade loser and take the diamond finesse. Play low at Trick 1, giving declarer an entry to dummy when it's of no use, and you beat the slam.

East made a similar mistake on this deal:

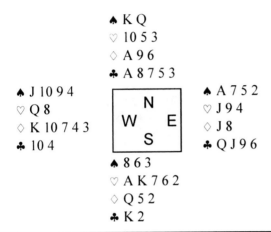

North:
♠ K Q
♡ 10 5 3
◇ A 9 6
♣ A 8 7 5 3

West:
♠ J 10 9 4
♡ Q 8
◇ K 10 7 4 3
♣ 10 4

N
W E
S

East:
♠ A 7 5 2
♡ J 9 4
◇ J 8
♣ Q J 9 6

South:
♠ 8 6 3
♡ A K 7 6 2
◇ Q 5 2
♣ K 2

West	North	East	South
—	1♣	pass	1♡
pass	2♡	pass	4♡

West led the ♠J and the ♠K was played from dummy. East won with the ♠A and paused to consider the best defense.

Too late! Declarer won the trump return and drew a second round of trumps. He then played the king and ace of clubs and ruffed a club, West showing out. A spade to the queen was followed by a second club ruff. Declarer then ruffed a spade and led the established thirteenth club to discard a diamond loser, not caring whether East ruffed with his master ♡J.

To beat the game, East must play low at Trick 1, killing the later spade entry to dummy. Declarer cannot start on the clubs immediately, or West will score an overruff. If instead he draws two rounds of trumps and then plays on clubs, East can draw dummy's last trump when he wins with the ♠A. (It's not good enough for East to win with the ♠A and return a spade at Trick 2. Declarer will still have enough entries to enjoy a long club.)

East didn't know exactly what would happen on that deal, without sight of declarer's hand. He could see that declarer might need to set up the clubs and it was sound defense to kill one of dummy's entries at Trick 1.

You are East on the last deal of the chapter. How will you plan the defense against the heart game when partner leads the ♣9?

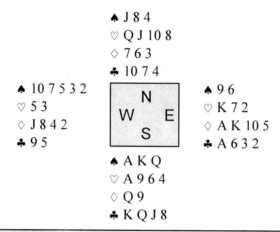

	North	
	♠ J 8 4 ♡ Q J 10 8 ♢ 7 6 3 ♣ 10 7 4	
West ♠ 10 7 5 3 2 ♡ 5 3 ♢ J 8 4 2 ♣ 9 5	N W E S	**East** ♠ 9 6 ♡ K 7 2 ♢ A K 10 5 ♣ A 6 3 2
	♠ A K Q ♡ A 9 6 4 ♢ Q 9 ♣ K Q J 8	
	South	

West	North	East	South
—	—	—	2NT (20-21)
pass	3♣	pass	3♡
pass	4♡	all pass	

You can see three certain tricks in the minors and need to score a fourth trick with the ♡K. This will be possible if you can keep declarer out of dummy.

Playing your ♣A at Trick 1 is all too likely to establish the ♣10 as an entry to the dummy! The ♣9 lead marks declarer with the ♣KQJ. If partner is leading from a doubleton, declarer will be able to unblock a club honor under your ace and lead his remaining spot-card to the ♣10 to take a trump finesse. Once you refuse to play the ♣A on the first trick, declarer is doomed. If he wins with the ♣K and continues with the ♣Q, you can either duck again or win and give your partner a club ruff.

Tips to avoid Mistake 43

(Conceding an entry by playing high)

- When dummy is short of entries, beware of releasing a high card that lies over a potential entry there.
- If your partner leads a high spot-card, suggesting that he holds no honor, you can often see that playing your own honor can serve no purpose and may be costly.
- When dummy holds two honors of equal value, lower than your own honor (for example, QJ or Q10 under your king) it is often wrong to play high at Trick 1.

Mistake 44

Failure to kill dummy's winners

One of the most common lines of play, both at notrump and in a suit contract, is for declarer to establish a long suit in dummy. This is annoying enough for the defenders when there was nothing they could do about it. It is doubly annoying if there was a way to prevent such an outcome.

The winning defense on the first deal was not particularly difficult but many players would go wrong. Take the East cards here:

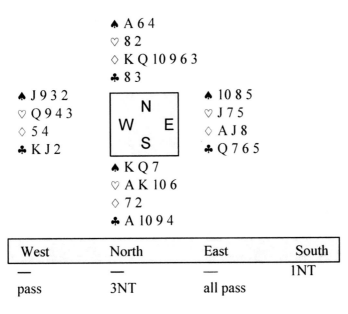

West		East
	♠ A 6 4 ♡ 8 2 ♢ K Q 10 9 6 3 ♣ 8 3	
♠ J 9 3 2 ♡ Q 9 4 3 ♢ 5 4 ♣ K J 2	N W E S	♠ 10 8 5 ♡ J 7 5 ♢ A J 8 ♣ Q 7 6 5
	♠ K Q 7 ♡ A K 10 6 ♢ 7 2 ♣ A 10 9 4	

West	North	East	South
—	—	—	1NT
pass	3NT	all pass	

Your partner leads the ♡3 to your jack and South's ace. Declarer then leads the ♢2 to West's ♢5 and dummy's ♢10. How will you defend?

Suppose you win with the ♢J and pause to consider the best return. The contract will be made! If you switch to a club, declarer can play low from hand and your partner will have no constructive continuation. If instead you return a heart, declarer can win and clear the diamonds, losing just two hearts and two diamonds. It is essential that you duck the first round of diamonds, allowing the ♢10 to win. Declarer may then choose to return to his hand with a spade and finesse the ♢9, going one down.

I simplified the East-West cards slightly on the deal we have just seen. France's Michel Lebel sat East on the original deal and his hand was:

♠ 10 8 5 2
♡ J 7 5
◇ J 8
♣ Q 7 6 5

When declarer won the heart lead and played a diamond to the 10, Lebel held up the jack! Declarer returned to the ♠K and led to the ◇9, losing to the ◇J. After this brilliant defense the contract had to go down. How did Lebel judge that his partner held ◇Axx? He reasoned that if declarer had started with three low diamonds, rather than two, he might well have played a diamond to the king on the first round.

East was kicking himself when he missed the winning defense here:

	North	
	♠ A ♡ 9 8 3 ◇ K Q 10 7 5 4 ♣ 8 6 2	
West ♠ 10 7 6 4 ♡ Q 10 7 2 ◇ 9 3 ♣ Q 9 7	N W E S	**East** ♠ J 8 5 2 ♡ A 6 4 ◇ A 6 2 ♣ J 10 3
	♠ K Q 9 3 ♡ K J 5 ◇ J 8 ♣ A K 5 4	

West	North	East	South
—	—	—	1NT
pass	3NT	all pass	

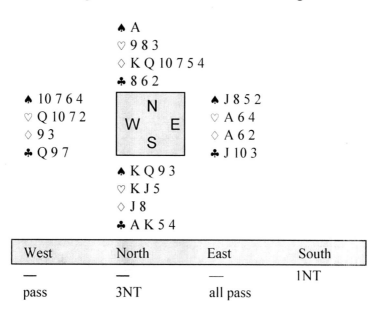

When West led the ♡2, East won with the ace and returned the ♡6. Declarer rose gratefully with the ♡K and led the ◇J. Any hold-up by East was useless now because the ♠A was still in dummy as an entry. The defenders scored three hearts and the ◇A but declarer had the remaining tricks.

'Didn't you notice the ♠A in dummy?' asked West helpfully.

It wasn't difficult to kill dummy's diamond suit. East needed to switch to a spade at Trick 2. Declarer would lead the ◇4 next and East would duck. The diamond position would be clear when West followed to the second round. East would win with the ◇A and dummy would be dead.

Many players would have duplicated West's mistake on the next deal, but the clues were available for those willing to seek them.

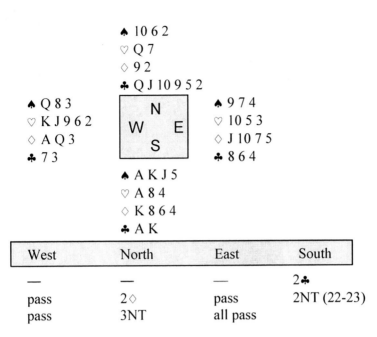

♠ 10 6 2
♡ Q 7
◇ 9 2
♣ Q J 10 9 5 2

West		East
♠ Q 8 3 ♡ K J 9 6 2 ◇ A Q 3 ♣ 7 3	N W E S	♠ 9 7 4 ♡ 10 5 3 ◇ J 10 7 5 ♣ 8 6 4

♠ A K J 5
♡ A 8 4
◇ K 8 6 4
♣ A K

West	North	East	South
—	—	—	2♣
pass	2◇	pass	2NT (22-23)
pass	3NT	all pass	

Sitting West, you lead the ♡6, won by dummy's ♡Q. The ♠2 is led from dummy, to the ♠4 from partner and the ♠J from declarer. What is your plan for the defense?

At the table West won with the ♠Q and persisted with the ♡K. Declarer won with the ♡A and unblocked the ♣AK. He could then cross to the ♠10 and score the rest of the clubs, for eleven tricks. The lie of the spades was clear. Partner could have at most one jack in his hand. His ♠4 was a count signal, proclaiming three spades, so declarer must have started with ♠AKJx. If he has six club tricks ready to run, the contract is his. So, you must assume that he has ♣AK doubleton and the suit is blocked.

To beat the contract, you must allow South's ♠J to win! With no entry to dummy he has only eight top tricks. No doubt he will cash his black-suit winners and exit with a third round of hearts, hoping to endplay you. No, partner can win with the ♡10 and play a diamond through the king. That's one down.

Let's see an entirely different defensive technique that can allow you to kill potential winners in the dummy:

	North	
	♠ Q J 6 4 ♡ A Q J 3 ♢ 6 5 ♣ 9 5 2	
♠ 9 7 ♡ 10 8 7 4 2 ♢ 8 3 ♣ Q J 10 4	N W E S	♠ K 10 5 3 ♡ 9 6 ♢ A 7 ♣ A 8 7 6 3
	♠ A 8 2 ♡ K 5 ♢ K Q J 10 9 4 2 ♣ K	

West	North	East	South
—	—	—	1♢
pass	1♡	pass	3♢
pass	3♠	pass	5♢
all pass			

Take the East cards. How will you defend when partner leads the ♣Q and declarer's ♣K falls under your ace?

If you return another club, declarer will ruff, draw trumps and score four heart tricks, discarding his spade losers. How can you prevent this?

If South held three hearts, he would surely have bid 4♡ at his third turn. He is very likely to hold ♡Kx and you can break his link with the dummy. You return a heart and he wins with the king. When he plays a trump, you take your ♢A on the first round and return another heart. Declarer is in dummy for the last time. If he tries to cash another heart, you will ruff and subsequently make a spade trick. If instead he leads the ♠Q, you will refuse to cover and your ♠K10 will subsequently guarantee you a spade trick.

Tips to avoid mistake 44

(Failure to kill dummy's winners)

- The most important technique to kill a suit in dummy is the hold-up. Use partner's count signals to assist you.
- Another way to prevent declarer from enjoying dummy's long suit is to attack the side entry to it.
- When there is a running suit in dummy, aim to remove declarer's cards in the suit before he can draw trumps.

Mistake 45

Not helping your partner

When your partner makes a wrong move in defense, there is not much point in glaring across the table (tempting as this can be). You should check whether there was some way in which you could have helped him to beat the contract.

By far the most important way to help partner is by issuing accurate signals. Most of the world's defenders use the general method of signaling attitude on partner's leads and count on declarer's leads. That's absolutely fine but there are situations where a defender should realize that the normal (primary) signal will be of no value to partner whereas a secondary signal may be. Look at this deal:

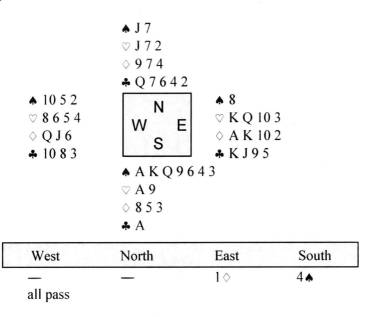

	North	
	♠ J 7 ♡ J 7 2 ◇ 9 7 4 ♣ Q 7 6 4 2	
West ♠ 10 5 2 ♡ 8 6 5 4 ◇ Q J 6 ♣ 10 8 3	N / W E / S	**East** ♠ 8 ♡ K Q 10 3 ◇ A K 10 2 ♣ K J 9 5
	♠ A K Q 9 6 4 3 ♡ A 9 ◇ 8 5 3 ♣ A	
	South	

West	North	East	South
—	—	1◇	4♠
all pass			

Sitting West, you lead the ◇Q against South's spade game. You continue with ◇J, East overtaking with the king and cashing a third round of the suit. How will you signal on the West cards when East continues with the ♡K, won by South's ace?

Even if your normal method on partner's lead is to signal attitude, this cannot be of any interest to partner on the present deal. He can see the ♡J in dummy and knows that you cannot have any meaningful attitude signal to give. What he may need to know is your **count** in the heart suit. You should therefore switch to the secondary signal on partner's leads – a count signal. With four cards you signal with your second-highest card, the ♡6.

Your signal tells partner that declarer has another heart left. When seven rounds of trumps are run, East will have to find one more discard from ♡Q ♣KJ. He will retain the ♡Q and discard the ♣J, knowing that declarer's presumed ♣A must be bare.

Had you signaled with your lowest heart, the ♡4, East would have placed declarer with one heart and two clubs. In that case he would discard the ♡Q and score the setting trick in clubs.

Would you have helped your partner, sitting East here?

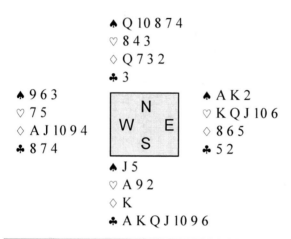

	North	
	♠ Q 10 8 7 4 ♡ 8 4 3 ◇ Q 7 3 2 ♣ 3	
West ♠ 9 6 3 ♡ 7 5 ◇ A J 10 9 4 ♣ 8 7 4	N W E S	**East** ♠ A K 2 ♡ K Q J 10 6 ◇ 8 6 5 ♣ 5 2
	♠ J 5 ♡ A 9 2 ◇ K ♣ A K Q J 10 9 6	

West	North	East	South
—	—	1♡	dbl
pass	1♠	pass	3NT
all pass			

Your partner leads the ♡7 to your ♡10 and South's ♡2. How will you continue?

The original East returned the ♡K. Declarer won with the ace and led the ◇K. West won immediately with his ace and returned the ◇J. Trying not to look too happy, declarer won with dummy's ◇Q and claimed the contract, displaying his seven club tricks. Meanwhile, the defenders could have taken two spades and four hearts for two down. Who do you blame?

East was first on to the attack. 'Did you not see my ♡K?' he demanded. 'It was my highest heart honor, a suit preference signal for a spade return. Surely you could tell from your hand that declarer must have a long string of clubs?'

The players moved to the next deal without further comment. However, it was East who should have taken the lion's share of the blame. At Trick 2 he should have cashed the ♠K, making it clear that the held the ♠A too. Only then should he clear the heart suit by leading the ♡K. When declarer played a diamond at some stage it would be obvious for West to win immediately and return a spade.

To ring the changes, let's present the next defensive problem in two-hand format.

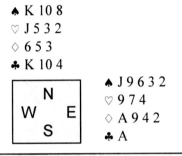

♠ K 10 8
♡ J 5 3 2
♢ 6 5 3
♣ K 10 4

N	
W E	♠ J 9 6 3 2 ♡ 9 7 4 ♢ A 9 4 2 ♣ A
S	

West	North	East	South
—	—	—	1♡
pass	2♡	pass	4♡
all pass			

West leads the ♢K against the heart game. You would rather like him to switch to a club, which might result in an eventual club ruff for the setting trick. Playing standard signals, how will you defend?

The original East player discouraged in diamonds, following with the ♢2. 'I also meant it as suit preference,' he explained learnedly afterwards.

West, who held ♠Q754 ♡6 ♢KQJ8 ♣8632, continued with another diamond honor and the contract was easily made.

The right way to 'help partner' on this deal is to give him no chance to go wrong. You should overtake with the ♢A at Trick 2, cash the ♣A and return a diamond to receive your club ruff.

The defense went astray on the next deal tool. Who would you blame?

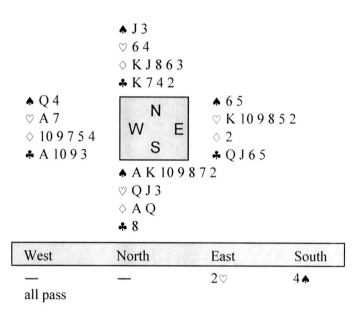

♠ J 3
♡ 6 4
◊ K J 8 6 3
♣ K 7 4 2

West		East
♠ Q 4	N	♠ 6 5
♡ A 7	W E	♡ K 10 9 8 5 2
◊ 10 9 7 5 4	S	◊ 2
♣ A 10 9 3		♣ Q J 6 5

♠ A K 10 9 8 7 2
♡ Q J 3
◊ A Q
♣ 8

West	North	East	South
—	—	2♡	4♠
all pass			

West led the ♡A, his partner signaling encouragement with the ♡10. East won the second round of hearts with the king. Since West held a higher trump than dummy's jack, a heart return would now have promoted a trump trick and beaten the contract. This was not at all clear to East. After a few moments he concluded that the best chance was to find West with the ◊A. When he returned the ◊2, declarer won with the ace and drew trumps in two rounds. He discarded his club loser on the diamonds and claimed an overtrick.

West knew that a heart return would beat the game. To assist his partner he should have cashed the ♣A at Trick 2, before playing his remaining heart. It would then be clear to East that West could not also hold the ◊A. The only remaining chance of beating the contract would be to lead a third heart.

Tips to avoid mistake 45

(Not helping partner)

- Accurate signaling is the best way to help partner. When you do not have to 'play high' in third seat, it is normal to signal 'attitude' (high to encourage). When your attitude is obvious, because of dummy's holding, switch to 'count'.
- In situations where neither attitude nor count can be of any interest (perhaps because dummy has a singleton the suit led) switch to 'suit preference'.

Mistake 46

Failing to Count Declarer's Tricks

One of your tasks, when defending, is to count declarer's tricks. If the defense that you're currently considering will result in declarer scoring enough tricks for the contract, you must look elsewhere. This may seem obvious but countless contracts are let through because one of the defenders does not perform this step.

Take the East cards on this deal and see if you can avoid the mistake made by the original defender.

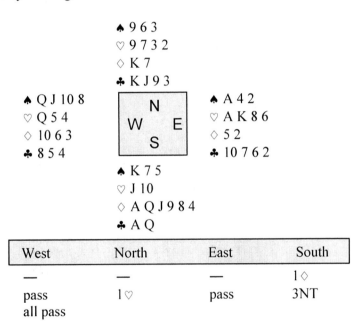

	♠ 9 6 3 ♡ 9 7 3 2 ◇ K 7 ♣ K J 9 3	
♠ Q J 10 8 ♡ Q 5 4 ◇ 10 6 3 ♣ 8 5 4	N W E S	♠ A 4 2 ♡ A K 8 6 ◇ 5 2 ♣ 10 7 6 2
	♠ K 7 5 ♡ J 10 ◇ A Q J 9 8 4 ♣ A Q	

West	North	East	South
—	—	—	1◇
pass	1♡	pass	3NT
all pass			

With a balanced hand of 18-19 points, you would rebid 2NT. A rebid of 3NT is used to show a strong hand with long diamonds. West leads the ♠Q and down goes the dummy. What is your plan for the defense in the East seat?

At least half of the world's defenders would win with the ♠A and return a spade, not even considering any alternative. Suppose instead that you take the trouble to count declarer's tricks. He surely holds the ♣A, so he has three available tricks in that suit. It is also a near certainty that dummy's king will solidify the long diamond suit that South has advertised. So, if you return a spade to declarer's king, he will surely run at least nine tricks.

The only real chance of beating the contract is to score four heart tricks and this can be done when partner holds ♡Qxx. You must cash the ♡K at Trick 2, the ♡10 falling from South, and continue with a low heart to West's queen. He can then lead a third round of hearts through dummy's 97 to your awaiting A8. (If West holds ♡Q10x, he must unblock the ♡10 on the first round.)

East faced a similar decision on the next deal. Take his cards and see how you assess the situation. Again it is possible to work out what to do by counting declarer's likely tricks.

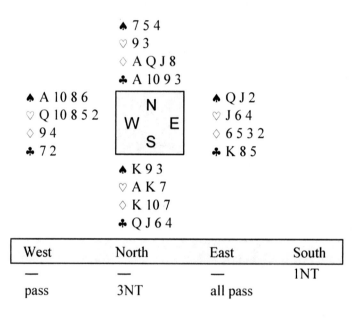

	North	
	♠ 7 5 4 ♡ 9 3 ♢ A Q J 8 ♣ A 10 9 3	
West ♠ A 10 8 6 ♡ Q 10 8 5 2 ♢ 9 4 ♣ 7 2	N / W E / S	**East** ♠ Q J 2 ♡ J 6 4 ♢ 6 5 3 2 ♣ K 8 5
	♠ K 9 3 ♡ A K 7 ♢ K 10 7 ♣ Q J 6 4	
	South	

West	North	East	South
—	—	—	1NT
pass	3NT	all pass	

West leads the ♡5 against 3NT. You play the ♡J and declarer wins with the ♡A. How will you defend when he runs the ♣Q to your ♣K, West playing the ♣7?

Defenders who tend to play on auto-pilot will return a heart without thinking. The contract will then easily be made. Instead you should pause for a moment to decide what to do next. Is it possible that your partner led from ♡KQxxx and that the heart suit is now ready to run? No, because if declarer had started with ♡Axx, he would have held up the ♡A for two rounds to exhaust your holding.

So, declarer began with three or four hearts to the ace-king. (He should have won the first trick with the king, to make this less obvious to you, but not all declarers know that.) Before knocking out declarer's remaining heart stopper, you should count the tricks that will then be at his disposal. He will have three club tricks, two hearts and almost certainly four diamond tricks.

That is a total of nine, so you cannot afford to persevere with partner's hearts.

You must hope to score four quick tricks elsewhere and this can be achieved only in spades. Switch to the ♠Q in the hope that partner holds ♠A10xx in the suit. When the cards lie as in the diagram you will beat the contract.

A defensive decision that you will face time and again is whether you need to cash out (perhaps hoping that partner has a particular high card) or whether you can afford to defend passively. Take the West cards on the next deal and see how you cope with the problem that comes your way after a few tricks.

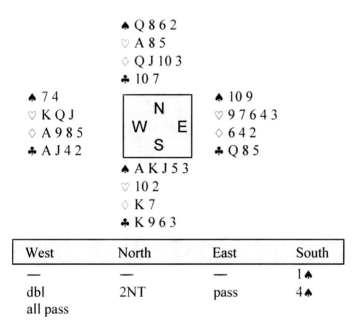

	North	
	♠ Q 8 6 2 ♡ A 8 5 ♢ Q J 10 3 ♣ 10 7	
West ♠ 7 4 ♡ K Q J ♢ A 9 8 5 ♣ A J 4 2	N / W E / S	**East** ♠ 10 9 ♡ 9 7 6 4 3 ♢ 6 4 2 ♣ Q 8 5
	♠ A K J 5 3 ♡ 10 2 ♢ K 7 ♣ K 9 6 3	

West	North	East	South
—	—	—	1♠
dbl	2NT	pass	4♠
all pass			

You lead the ♡K and dummy wins with the ace, your partner playing the ♡3 to show an odd number of cards in the suit. Declarer draws trumps in two rounds, partner following with the 9 and 10. He then leads the ♢K. How will you defend?

When you take the ♢A, either on the first or the second round, it will be clear that dummy's remaining diamonds will provide a discard or two. You mark time by playing the ♡Q, East playing the 4 and South the 10. It seems that East began with five hearts and declarer is now out of the suit. Ask yourself: 'Do I need to play on clubs, hoping that East holds the ♣K and we can score two club tricks before declarer takes discards on the diamonds?'

You need to do some counting to determine the answer. Suppose you count declarer's tricks. He has five trumps, one heart and three diamonds. That is only nine tricks. You cannot afford to play the ♣A (or a low club) because this might set up his ♣K as a tenth trick. So, you should exit passively with the ♡J. Declarer is welcome to ruff this and discard two clubs on the ◇QJ. You will score two club tricks subsequently, putting the contract one down.

You can reach the same conclusion on the last deal by counting shape. After seeing the second round of hearts, you place declarer with five spades and two hearts. On the ◇K, your partner will have given you an odd count signal with the ◇2. If East holds three diamonds, declarer will have two diamonds and four clubs. In that case you don't need to seek two quick club tricks. If instead East holds only a singleton diamond (you could wait a round to find this out, in fact), declarer would have four diamonds and two clubs. With no discard coming on the diamonds, you would again have no need to play aggressively in clubs.

The final deal in this chapter comes from actual play, a 2005 tournament held in Brighton. Goran Mattson from Cologne was able to land his slam after a defensive mistake by East. This is how the cards lay:

N-S Vul. Dealer South

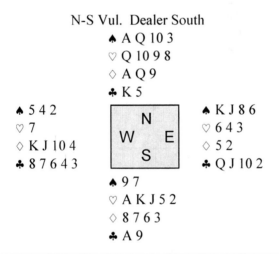

North:
♠ A Q 10 3
♡ Q 10 9 8
◇ A Q 9
♣ K 5

West:
♠ 5 4 2
♡ 7
◇ K J 10 4
♣ 8 7 6 4 3

East:
♠ K J 8 6
♡ 6 4 3
◇ 5 2
♣ Q J 10 2

South:
♠ 9 7
♡ A K J 5 2
◇ 8 7 6 3
♣ A 9

West	North	East	South
—	—	—	1♡
pass	2NT	pass	4♡
pass	4NT	pass	5♣
pass	6♡	all pass	

West led the ◇J and declarer finessed the ◇Q successfully. He drew two rounds of trumps and led a second diamond towards dummy. West inserted the ◇10 and the trick was won with dummy's ace. Mattson drew the last trump and continued with the king and ace of clubs. He then ran the ♠9 to East's ♠J, West contributing the ♠2 to the trick. This was the key moment of the deal. What card would you have returned from the East hand? You are left with ♠K86 and the ♣J10.

Unwilling to lead into dummy's ♠AQ10, East played back a club. Mattson ruffed in the South hand and discarded the last diamond from dummy. He was then able to lead the ◇8 for a ruffing finesse against West's remaining ◇K. When West covered, declarer ruffed with dummy's last trump and returned to his hand with a spade ruff to score the ◇7 as his twelfth trick.

Had East taken the trouble to count declarer's tricks at the key moment, he would have known that he had five heart tricks, one spade, two diamonds and two clubs. That is a total of only ten tricks. So, a spade return into dummy's tenace would not give declarer the slam. He would end one trick short.

Tips to avoid mistake 46

(Failing to count declarer's tricks)

- By counting declarer's tricks, you can decide whether to defend passively (giving nothing away) or actively (trying to cash or establish the setting tricks quickly).
- Do not automatically 'return partner's suit'. Make a plan for the defense – one that has a chance of beating the contract.
- Counting declarer's tricks can assist you in the endgame. You can calculate that one defense cannot give him enough tricks; another one may do.

Mistake 47

Saving declarer a guess

One of the most important aspects of defense is to give declarer a chance to go wrong. Many defenders are easy to play against. They take their high cards as soon as they can and rarely spot an opportunity to give declarer an awkward ride. Let's see some deals where you can make life unpleasant for the declarer.

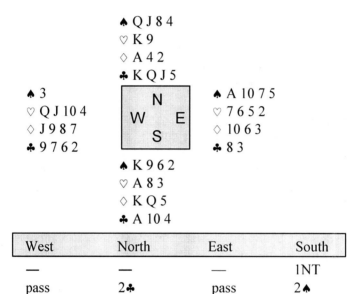

	North	
	♠ Q J 8 4 ♡ K 9 ♢ A 4 2 ♣ K Q J 5	
West ♠ 3 ♡ Q J 10 4 ♢ J 9 8 7 ♣ 9 7 6 2	N / W E / S	**East** ♠ A 10 7 5 ♡ 7 6 5 2 ♢ 10 6 3 ♣ 8 3
	South ♠ K 9 6 2 ♡ A 8 3 ♢ K Q 5 ♣ A 10 4	

West	North	East	South
—	—	—	1NT
pass	2♣	pass	2♠
pass	6♠	all pass	

West leads the ♡Q and declarer wins with the ace, continuing with a trump to dummy's queen. Sitting East, you should follow smoothly with the ♠5. What will declarer do next? He is likely to conclude that West holds the ♠A. Since the contract is at risk only if trumps are 4-1, declarer may well lead low to the ♠K next. When West shows out, it will be a sweet moment for you.

What would have happened if you had won the ♠Q with the ♠A? Declarer would still have to decide which spade honor to play next, it's true. However, since few defenders are good enough to duck in this situation, he may well assume that the ace is more likely to be in the 4-card holding than the 1-card holding. He will play the ♠J next and pick up your ♠10.

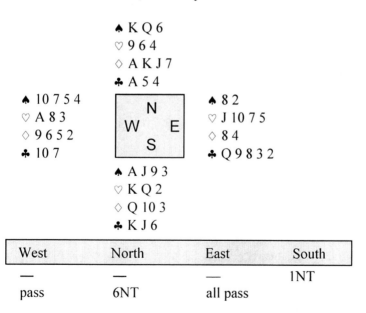

This is a similar position. Imagine declarer has this trump suit:

	♡ A J 9 6	
♡3		♡ K 10 7 4
	♡ Q 8 5 2	

He leads low to the ♡J and East drops the ♡7. If declarer can afford one trump loser, the safety play is to lead a low card towards the ♡Q next. However, he may not know at an early stage of the deal whether he can afford a trump loser. Also, he may be tempted (particularly at matchpoints) to try for an overtrick. In that case he will return to his hand to lead the ♡Q, hoping to pin an original ♡107 in the East hand. How he will wince when West shows out on the ♡Q and he has to lose two trump tricks!

If instead East wins the first round of hearts with the ♡K, declarer will surely play the ♡A on the second round and pick up the ♡10. That's because ♡K10xx is much more likely that a singleton ♡K

When declarer leads towards a KQ10 combination in dummy, it is usually right to hold up the ace in fourth seat to give declarer a guess on the next round. Many defenders handle these positions correctly but fail to realize that the same tactic may apply when declarer leads towards his own hand. It's more difficult then, because you can't see what cards he holds:

	♠ K Q 6 ♡ 9 6 4 ◇ A K J 7 ♣ A 5 4	
♠ 10 7 5 4 ♡ A 8 3 ◇ 9 6 5 2 ♣ 10 7	N W E S	♠ 8 2 ♡ J 10 7 5 ◇ 8 4 ♣ Q 9 8 3 2
	♠ A J 9 3 ♡ K Q 2 ◇ Q 10 3 ♣ K J 6	

West	North	East	South
—	—	—	1NT
pass	6NT	all pass	

Sitting West, you lead the ◇2. Declarer wins with dummy's ◇A and plays a heart to the king. If you win with the ace, or give away the position of the ace by thinking about it, the slam will be made. Knowing that he has only one heart trick, declarer will eventually finesse the ♣J. Not what you want!

What will happen if you hold up the ♡A smoothly on the first round of diamonds? Declarer will have to guess whether to seek his twelfth trick by leading towards the ♡Q or by finessing the ♣J. Since his ♡K won on the first round, he may conclude that a second round of hearts is the better bet.

'How do I know he has the ♡Q alongside his ♡K?' you may be thinking. The answer is that declarers very rarely make an early lead towards a king when failure of this move will lead to immediate defeat. Nearly always the king is accompanied by the queen. A hold-up can gain in various ways:

- You may give him a guess in that suit (if he holds KQ10)
- He may have to guess which suit to rely on for the contract
- By refusing to rectify the count, you may prevent a squeeze.

Let's see a slightly more complicated defense where the aim is the same: to persuade declarer that one finesse has worked, hoping to persuade him to repeat that finesse rather than try a different (winning) finesse:

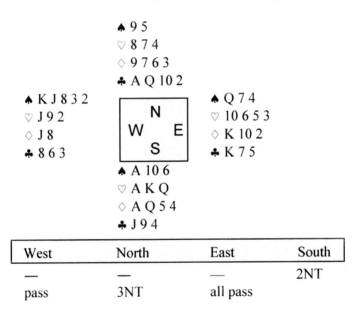

	♠ 9 5 ♡ 8 7 4 ◇ 9 7 6 3 ♣ A Q 10 2	
♠ K J 8 3 2 ♡ J 9 2 ◇ J 8 ♣ 8 6 3	N W E S	♠ Q 7 4 ♡ 10 6 5 3 ◇ K 10 2 ♣ K 7 5
	♠ A 10 6 ♡ A K Q ◇ A Q 5 4 ♣ J 9 4	

West	North	East	South
—	—	—	2NT
pass	3NT	all pass	

West leads the ♠3 against 3NT and declarer holds up the ♠A until the third round. What is your plan for the defense in the East seat when declarer runs the ♣J, West following with the ♣3?

It is clear to hold up the ♣K on the first round, because you know that declarer has at least two clubs. Declarer plays another a club to dummy's 10, West following with the 6. What now? If you win with the ♣K, as most players would, declarer will make the contract. He will count three clubs, three hearts and two aces, adding up to only eight tricks. He will therefore finesse the ♢Q and make the game. You must steel yourself to duck smoothly on the second round of clubs as well. Declarer will then return to a heart and finesse the ♣Q on the third round. Imagine his surprise as you win with the ♣K. When you exit with a heart to South's king, his only chance will be to play ace and another diamond, hoping that you started with a doubleton ♢K. Not today, you are pleased to inform him. West will win with the ♢J and cash two spades for two down.

There are many single-suit positions where you can give declarer an awkward guess if you are awake. Suppose this is the trump position:

	♡ 4	
♡ A 6 2		♡ J 10
	♡ K Q 9 8 7 5 3	

Declarer leads low from dummy. East plays the ♡J (let's say) and declarer covers with the ♡K. If you win with the ♡A in the West seat, declarer will be forced to drop the ♡10 on the next round and lose only one trump trick. Duck smoothly and declarer is likely to play East for the ♡AJ. He will duck the second round and lose two trump tricks.

Tips to avoid mistake 47

(Saving declarer a guess)

- When declarer leads towards KJx or Q10x, it can be essential to play low smoothly in the second seat.
- Thinking for a moment and then playing low can be just as expensive as rising with a high card in second seat.
- By holding up an ace (or king), you may give declarer a guess on the second round of a suit.

Mistake 48

Failing to use suit preference signals

Most defenders use suit preference signals when delivering a ruff. By leading a high card, you ask partner to return the higher of the remaining side suits. A low card would ask him to play back the lower suit. There are many more situations where you can use suit preference to help partner with his defense. Take the East cards here:

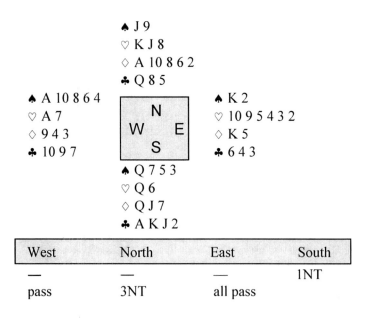

	North	
	♠ J 9 ♡ K J 8 ◇ A 10 8 6 2 ♣ Q 8 5	
West ♠ A 10 8 6 4 ♡ A 7 ◇ 9 4 3 ♣ 10 9 7	N W E S	**East** ♠ K 2 ♡ 10 9 5 4 3 2 ◇ K 5 ♣ 6 4 3
	♠ Q 7 5 3 ♡ Q 6 ◇ Q J 7 ♣ A K J 2	

West	North	East	South
—	—	—	1NT
pass	3NT	all pass	

Your partner leads the ♠6 against 3NT. You win with the ♠K and return the ♠2 to declarer's ♠5 and partner's ace. When partner continues with the ♠10, declarer wins with the ♠Q and runs the ◇Q. You win with the ◇K and must decide whether to return a heart or a club. How can you tell what to do?

Your partner should give you a suit preference signal as he clears the spade suit. He has returned the ♠10 from ♠108x and the higher of the two equal cards means that his entry is in hearts rather than clubs. You duly return a heart and the contract goes two down. Suppose you did not play suit preference signals in this situation and had to guess where partner's entry was. A club return would allow the contract to make.

Let's look at another common situation where a suit preference signal can make a big difference. Take the East cards once again:

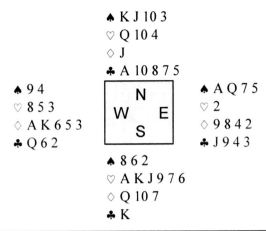

	North	
	♠ K J 10 3 ♡ Q 10 4 ◇ J ♣ A 10 8 7 5	
West ♠ 9 4 ♡ 8 5 3 ◇ A K 6 5 3 ♣ Q 6 2	N / W E / S	East ♠ A Q 7 5 ♡ 2 ◇ 9 8 4 2 ♣ J 9 4 3
	South ♠ 8 6 2 ♡ A K J 9 7 6 ◇ Q 10 7 ♣ K	

West	North	East	South
—	—	—	1♡
pass	2♣	pass	2♡
pass	4♡	all pass	

West, your partner, leads the ◇A and you must consider which card to play from your ◇9842. Will partner be interested in an attitude signal? No! Dummy is now out of diamonds and you have no further prospects in the suit. Will partner be intrigued to know your count in diamonds? No! What he would like to know is whether to switch to spades or clubs. You can tell him by following with the ◇9. This is a high suit preference signal for spades, the higher of the remaining side suits.

West duly switches to the ♠9 and you claim two spade tricks followed by a spade ruff in partner's hand. There's no point debating whether he would have switched to spades anyway. You can see that this is the right switch and you have an easy way to let partner know too.

Many players fail to spare their partner an awkward guess on this type of deal too:

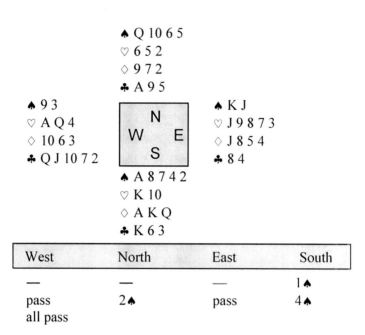

	North	
	♠ Q 10 6 5 ♡ 6 5 2 ◇ 9 7 2 ♣ A 9 5	
West ♠ 9 3 ♡ A Q 4 ◇ 10 6 3 ♣ Q J 10 7 2	N / W E / S	**East** ♠ K J ♡ J 9 8 7 3 ◇ J 8 5 4 ♣ 8 4
	♠ A 8 7 4 2 ♡ K 10 ◇ A K Q ♣ K 6 3	

West	North	East	South
—	—	—	1♠
pass	2♠	pass	4♠
all pass			

South wins the club lead with the king. What is your defensive plan when declarer continues with ace and another trump?

The original West saw no need for special action. He followed with the ♠3 and the ♠9, East winning the second round of trumps with the king. East could see that there was little reason to return a club, since if declarer had a third-round club loser it was unlikely that he could discard it. East still faced a guess as to which red suit to play. He guessed to play a diamond. Not the best! Declarer won and cashed two more diamond winners. He then played the ♣A and ♣9, throwing West on lead. West had to lead a heart, allowing declarer to score the ♡K, or give a ruff-and-sluff. The contract was made.

West needed to signal for a heart switch. He could do that with a **suit preference signal in trumps.** By playing the ♠9 followed by the ♠3, he could direct his partner's attention to hearts. A heart switch would allow West to score the ace and queen of hearts, followed later by a club trick.

The defenders often use count signals when following to one of declarer's suits. In situations where giving count would not assist your partner, it may be appropriate to switch to a secondary signal (suit preference). This happens when you expect partner to win the trick and he will need to find the right return. Take the West cards on the next deal:

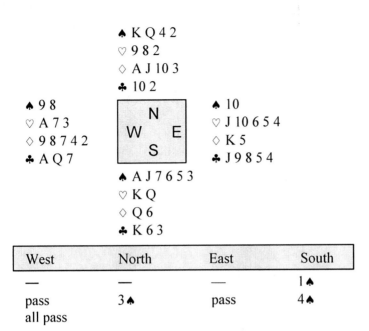

♠ K Q 4 2
♡ 9 8 2
◇ A J 10 3
♣ 10 2

♠ 9 8	N / W E / S	♠ 10
♡ A 7 3		♡ J 10 6 5 4
◇ 9 8 7 4 2		◇ K 5
♣ A Q 7		♣ J 9 8 5 4

♠ A J 7 6 5 3
♡ K Q
◇ Q 6
♣ K 6 3

West	North	East	South
—	—	—	1♠
pass	3♠	pass	4♠
all pass			

You lead the ♠9 against the spade game. Declarer wins with the ♠A and runs the ◇Q to the ◇K. Your partner must guess now whether to return a heart or a club. You can see that a club return is almost certain to defeat the contract. On the first round of diamonds, it is clear that a count signal will be worthless. When East wins with his presumed ◇K, he will need to know which suit to play back. Don't make him guess! Follow with the ◇2 on the first round of diamonds and your partner will then return a club. You quickly add three more tricks to the defensive pile and that will be one down.

Tips to avoid Mistake 48

(Failing to use suit preference signals)

- When you are dislodging declarer's last stopper in your suit, you can choose the card you lead to pass a suit preference message.
- You can sometimes pass a suit preference message when following to one of declarer's suits. (This applies when a count signal will have no purpose.)
- You can give a suit-preference signal in trumps, when following to declarer's leads.

Mistake 49

Missing the only chance

Sometimes there is only one chance to beat the contract. If you fail to spot it and the cards were helpfully disposed, it is aggravating indeed. West lay awake for several hours soon after misdefending on this deal:

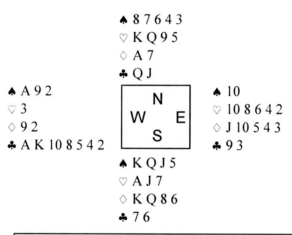

	North	
	♠ 8 7 6 4 3 ♡ K Q 9 5 ♢ A 7 ♣ Q J	
West ♠ A 9 2 ♡ 3 ♢ 9 2 ♣ A K 10 8 5 4 2	N / W E / S	**East** ♠ 10 ♡ 10 8 6 4 2 ♢ J 10 5 4 3 ♣ 9 3
	South ♠ K Q J 5 ♡ A J 7 ♢ K Q 8 6 ♣ 7 6	

West	North	East	South
—	—	—	1NT
3♣	dbl	pass	3♠
pass	4♠	all pass	

North's double is for takeout and the spade game is reached. Sitting West, you lead the ♣A and ♣K, everyone following. What next?

The original West player decided that the only chance was to find his partner with the ♢K. He switched to the ♢9, won with dummy's ♢A and a few moments later declarer had drawn trumps and claimed the contract.

'Is it any use if you play a third round of clubs?' asked East. 'I can ruff with the ten.'

West sat back in his chair. Of course! The ♠10 would force the ♠J from declarer and West's ♠A92 would then be worth two tricks.

'I couldn't have the ♢K, could I?' persisted East, in the helpful way that partners do. 'You had 11 points and there were 12 in the dummy. That only left a possible queen or two jacks for me.'

How true that was! A third round of clubs would give a ruff-and-sluff, yes, but if East happened to hold a singleton ♠Q, ♠J or ♠10, it would promote an extra trump trick for West.

Right, see if you can find the winning defense missed by East here:

	♠ 10 6 5 2 ♡ J 9 4 ♢ Q J 3 ♣ A Q J	
♠ 8 7 4 ♡ 10 8 7 3 2 ♢ K 6 ♣ 7 4 3	N W E S	♠ A Q 9 3 ♡ A 5 ♢ 8 5 2 ♣ 9 8 5 2
	♠ K J ♡ K Q 6 ♢ A 10 9 7 4 ♣ K 10 6	

West	North	East	South
—	—	—	1NT (15-17)
pass	3NT	all pass	

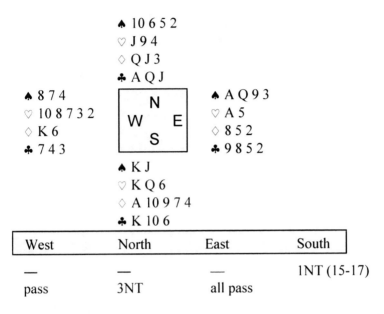

How will you defend on the East cards when your partner leads the ♡3, declarer playing low from dummy?

At the table East won with the ♡A and returned the ♡5. Declarer won with the ♡K, crossed to dummy with a club and ran the ♢Q. The finesse lost but the game was secure with four diamonds, three clubs and two hearts.

East should have paused to calculate what card(s) his partner could hold. He could see 21 points between his own hand and the dummy. Give declarer a minimum of 15 and this left no more than 4 for West. So, he could hold the ♡K but not the ♡Q as well. What's more, if West held the ♢A or ♢K, he would not hold either missing heart honor alongside it. In short, the only chance to beat the contract lay in the spade suit!

East should play the ♠A at Trick 2. When the ♠J falls from South, he continues with a low spade to declarer's king. Declarer reaches dummy with a club to finesse in diamonds. West wins with the ♢K and returns a spade through dummy's ♠106 to give you two further tricks with the ♠Q9 in the suit. That's one down.

(Note that if West began with ♠J84, he would have to unblock the ♠J under declarer's ♠K on the second round, to avoid blocking the suit.)

Few East players would find the necessary defense on the next deal. When they looked back at it, perhaps during a post-mortem in some vibrant local bar, they would realize that all the clues had been there. It was really just a question of putting some effort into planning the defense. How would you have managed the East cards here?

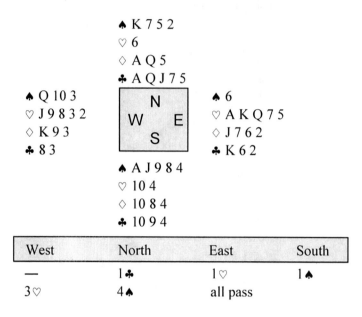

	North	
	♠ K 7 5 2 ♡ 6 ♢ A Q 5 ♣ A Q J 7 5	
West ♠ Q 10 3 ♡ J 9 8 3 2 ♢ K 9 3 ♣ 8 3	N W E S	**East** ♠ 6 ♡ A K Q 7 5 ♢ J 7 6 2 ♣ K 6 2
	♠ A J 9 8 4 ♡ 10 4 ♢ 10 8 4 ♣ 10 9 4	

West	North	East	South
—	1♣	1♡	1♠
3♡	4♠	all pass	

Your partner leads the ♡3 to your ♡Q. How can you beat the spade game?

You have one heart and one club trick coming your way. Where can you find two more tricks? You must hope that West has a trump trick and that a fourth defensive trick can be manufactured from the diamond suit. Since dummy's ♢AQ represents a double stopper in diamonds, you must switch to a diamond at Trick 2. This will remove one of declarer's stoppers in the suit.

Declarer will probably insert the ♢8, hoping that this will force an honor from West. (The diamonds would then be protected against a continuation from one or other side of the table.) No luck comes his way when West covers with the ♢9. Declarer wins with the ♢Q and now either defender will be able to persist with the diamond attack.

Declarer plays the king and ace of trumps, finding that he has a loser in the suit. A subsequent club finesse fails and East clears a diamond trick for the defense. When declarer plays more clubs, hoping to discard his diamond loser, West ruffs the third round and leads a diamond to your jack for one down. Steeling yourself to lead into dummy's ♢AQ wasn't easy but… hey, the game goes one down!

Many players would fail to find the winning defense on the next deal. After it was over, they would all agree that they should have done better. Let's go mad again and present it in two-deal format.

♠ K Q 9 3 2
♡ Q J
♢ 9 3
♣ K J 7 5

♠ 7 6 5 4
♡ K
♢ J 10 7 6
♣ A 9 8 2

N / W E / S

West	North	East	South
—	—	—	1NT (15-17)
pass	2♡	dbl	2♠
pass	3NT	pass	4♠
all pass			

Your partner's double of 2♡ shows good hearts and you lead the ♡K. Partner follows with the ♡6 and declarer produces the ♡4. What now?

Normally East's card in hearts would be a suit preference signal, in case your king is a singleton. What do you make of this middle signal of the ♡6?

One possibility is to switch to a low club, hoping that East might hold the ♣Q. It's true that your partner would not give a strong signal for clubs if he held that card, but there is no need to interpret partner's ♡6 signal! The opening bid promised 15-17 points, leaving East with at most 5 points. He has already shown the ♡A. The only chance of beating the contract is to switch to ace and another club, hoping that East has a singleton in the suit. This duly comes to pass and the game goes one down. Well defended!

Tips to avoid mistake 49

(Missing the only chance)

- When you can see that pursuing the initial line of defense is certain to allow the contract to be made, search for any chance (however unlikely) that may result in success.
- Suppose you need partner to hold the ♢A to beat the contract and declarer is 90% certain to have that card. Assume that partner holds it!

Mistake 50

Failing to avoid an endplay

Many contracts are made with an endplay and much of the time there is nothing the defenders can do about it. Sometimes it's the result of a defensive mistake. Would you have avoided the endplay, sitting East here?

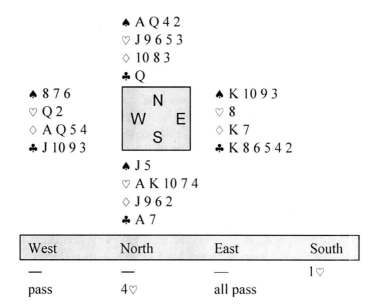

	North	
	♠ A Q 4 2 ♡ J 9 6 5 3 ♢ 10 8 3 ♣ Q	
West ♠ 8 7 6 ♡ Q 2 ♢ A Q 5 4 ♣ J 10 9 3	N W E S	**East** ♠ K 10 9 3 ♡ 8 ♢ K 7 ♣ K 8 6 5 4 2
	♠ J 5 ♡ A K 10 7 4 ♢ J 9 6 2 ♣ A 7	

West	North	East	South
—	—	—	1♡
pass	4♡	all pass	

Your partner leads the ♣J, covered the queen, king and ace. Declarer draws trumps in two rounds and ruffs the ♣7 in dummy. He then leads the ♢3 from the table. What is your plan for the defense?

Let's see what will happen if you play 'second hand low', contributing the ♢7 on the first round. Your partner will capture South's ♢J with the queen. West cannot afford to continue with the ♢A, since this will crash your ♢K. If instead he returns a low diamond to your king, you will be endplayed — forced to lead a spade into dummy's tenace or to give a ruff-and-sluff in clubs. In practice, West would probably switch to a spade. Declarer would play low from dummy, allowing you to win with the king. After cashing the ♢K, you would have to surrender the remaining tricks. Declarer would throw his last two diamonds on dummy's spades.

Let's see how sweetly everything will go if you rise smartly with the ♢K on the first round. You return the ♢7 and partner scores the queen and ace. Declarer is forced to take the spade finesse and goes one down.

The technique of unblocking a doubleton honor is so important that we will look at another example.

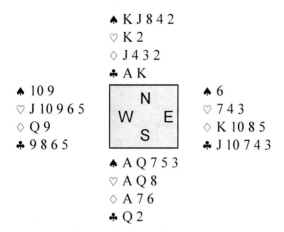

	North	
	♠ K J 8 4 2 ♡ K 2 ◇ J 4 3 2 ♣ A K	
West ♠ 10 9 ♡ J 10 9 6 5 ◇ Q 9 ♣ 9 8 6 5	N W E S	**East** ♠ 6 ♡ 7 4 3 ◇ K 10 8 5 ♣ J 10 7 4 3
	♠ A Q 7 5 3 ♡ A Q 8 ◇ A 7 6 ♣ Q 2	

West	North	East	South
—	—	—	1♠
pass	2NT	pass	3♠
pass	4♣	pass	4◇
pass	4♡	pass	4NT
pass	5♡	pass	6♠
all pass			

North's Jacoby 2NT is followed by three cue bids and Roman Key-card Blackwood, South arriving in 6♠. This time you are sitting West. You lead the ♡J and declarer wins with dummy's king. He draws trumps with the ace and queen, your partner discarding a low club.

You must be alert when declarer now cashes the ◇A. Suppose you follow with the ◇9. He will play his top cards in hearts and clubs before leading a second round of diamonds. After winning with the ◇Q, you will be stuck. (Partner cannot overtake with the ◇K, of course, since this would set up dummy's ◇J.) With only hearts and clubs in your hand, you will have to give a ruff-and-sluff. Declarer will ruff in the dummy and discard his remaining diamond loser, making the slam.

To beat the contract, you must ditch your ◇Q under declarer's ◇A. Do not think 'That's too difficult for me'. You know that declarer has plenty of trumps in both hands, always a warning sign for an elimination ending. You know also that he has no losers in trumps, hearts or clubs. The only chance of beating the contract is for the defenders to score two diamond tricks. This cannot be done if you keep the bare ◇Q. Your only chance is to ditch that card and hope that your partner holds the ♢K10 and will then score two diamond tricks for one down.

West was half asleep when he defended the next deal. How about you? Fully alert at this time of day, surely? Let's hope so.

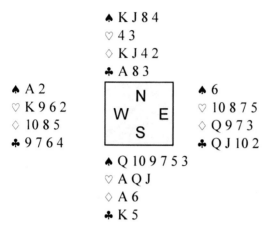

	♠ K J 8 4 ♡ 4 3 ♢ K J 4 2 ♣ A 8 3	
♠ A 2 ♡ K 9 6 2 ♢ 10 8 5 ♣ 9 7 6 4	N W E S	♠ 6 ♡ 10 8 7 5 ♢ Q 9 7 3 ♣ Q J 10 2
	♠ Q 10 9 7 5 3 ♡ A Q J ♢ A 6 ♣ K 5	

West	North	East	South
—	1♢	pass	1♠
pass	2♠	pass	4NT
pass	5♡	pass	6♠
all pass			

Awake enough to realize that it was his lead, West placed the ♣7 on the table. East played the ♣10 and declarer won with the ♣K. He then led a low trump towards dummy.

Thinking that declarer might have a guess in the trump suit, West followed smoothly with the ♠2. His hopes were raised briefly when declarer called for dummy's ♠J. No, East followed with a spot-card. Declarer continued with the ♣A and ruffed dummy's last club in his hand. After the ♢A, ♢K and a diamond ruff, West found himself staring at ♠A ♡K962. He was thrown in with the ♠A and had to lead a heart into South's heart tenace. The slam was made.

It is often right to play low when declarer leads towards a king-jack combination in dummy but not on this deal. How could West have worked that out? Firstly, declarer was almost certain to hold the ♠Q when he headed for a slam. In fact his 4NT was Roman Key-card Blackwood and North's 5♡ denied the ♠Q. If South was missing one key-card and the queen of trumps, not to mention the ♡K, he would probably not have bid the slam. Secondly, West could see the risk of an elimination ending if he left himself with the bare ♠A. By rising with that card on the first round and exiting safely, he would give himself a solid chance of eventually making the ♡K as the setting trick.

Declarer has plenty of trumps in both hands on the next deal too. Take the East cards and see if you would have prevented declarer's successful endgame.

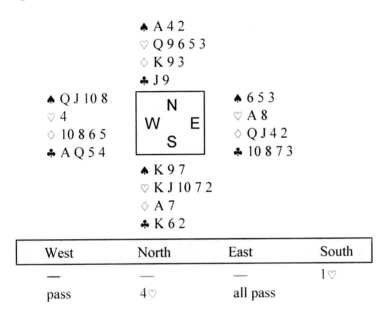

♠ A 4 2
♡ Q 9 6 5 3
◇ K 9 3
♣ J 9

♠ Q J 10 8	N	♠ 6 5 3
♡ 4	W E	♡ A 8
◇ 10 8 6 5	S	◇ Q J 4 2
♣ A Q 5 4		♣ 10 8 7 3

♠ K 9 7
♡ K J 10 7 2
◇ A 7
♣ K 6 2

West	North	East	South
—	—	—	1♡
pass	4♡	all pass	

West leads the ♠Q and declarer wins with the ♠K. He continues with a trump to the queen. Sitting East, how would you plan the defense?

The original East lost no time in 'returning partner's suit', playing a spade to knock out dummy's ace. Declarer then drew the last trump and eliminated diamonds – playing the ◇A and ◇K, followed by a diamond ruff in his hand. When he exited with a spade, West won and had no good return. If he played a club, declarer would make the ♣K. If instead he played a spade or a diamond, this would give a ruff-and-sluff allowing declarer to discard one of dummy's clubs. Either way, declarer would lose only one club trick and make the game.

The risk of West being endplayed in spades was foreseeable from the East seat. One spade and one heart would leave the defenders needing two more tricks to beat the game. Although East did not know how the minor suits lay, he should have returned the ♣8 at Trick 3. West could then win with the ♣Q and clear his spade trick before declarer could set up a discard on the third round of clubs. That would be one down.

When this was pointed out to East, he replied: 'Well, yes, as the cards lie. Suppose declarer held ♣KQx, though, and was missing the ◇A. Switching to a club would allow him to discard a spade from dummy.' Do you see the flaw in this argument?

If declarer's hand was ♠K97 ♡KJ1072 ◇87 ♣KQ2, he would have won the spade lead with the ace and led the ♣J to set up a spade discard.

Tips to avoid mistake 50

(Failing to avoid an endplay)

- Always suspect an elimination play when declarer has long trumps in both hands.
- It is dangerous to leave yourself with a bare honor in a side-suit. Consider unblocking it at the first opportunity.
- To prevent your partner from being endplayed to lead away from a side-suit king, you may need to establish his king by switching to that suit.

Mistake 51

Mistiming a defensive ruff

One of the most enjoyable parts of defending is to give partner a ruff – an extra defensive trick out of thin air! Yes, but sometimes it can be a mistake to deliver this ruff at the first opportunity. You must always keep your eye on the main target: beating the contract. Take the East cards here:

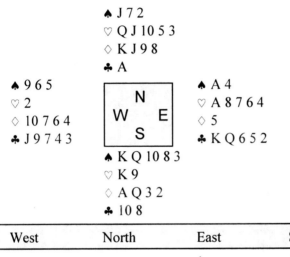

	♠ J 7 2 ♡ Q J 10 5 3 ◇ K J 9 8 ♣ A	
♠ 9 6 5 ♡ 2 ◇ 10 7 6 4 ♣ J 9 7 4 3	N W E S	♠ A 4 ♡ A 8 7 6 4 ◇ 5 ♣ K Q 6 5 2
	♠ K Q 10 8 3 ♡ K 9 ◇ A Q 3 2 ♣ 10 8	

West	North	East	South
—	—	1♡	1♠
pass	2♡	pass	4♠
all pass			

Your partner leads the ♡2 and you win with the ♡A, declarer dropping the ♡K. Partner would not have led the ♡2 from ♡92, so you know that you can give him a ruff. Is that what you should do next?

A heart ruff and two aces will not be enough to beat the contract. You need to find a fourth trick from somewhere. The setting trick will be a diamond ruff in your hand! You switch to the ◇5 at Trick 2 and declarer has to draw trumps. You win the first round with the ♠A and only then cross to partner's hand with a heart ruff. He gives you a diamond ruff and the contract tumbles to defeat.

Take the East cards again now, on a deal from the 2006 National Open Teams in Australia.

Both Vul. Dealer North

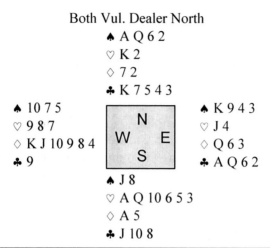

	North	
	♠ A Q 6 2	
	♡ K 2	
	◇ 7 2	
	♣ K 7 5 4 3	
West		**East**
♠ 10 7 5		♠ K 9 4 3
♡ 9 8 7		♡ J 4
◇ K J 10 9 8 4		◇ Q 6 3
♣ 9		♣ A Q 6 2
	South	
	♠ J 8	
	♡ A Q 10 6 5 3	
	◇ A 5	
	♣ J 10 8	

West	North	East	South
—	1♣	pass	1♡
pass	1♠	pass	2◇
pass	2♡	pass	4♡
all pass			

West, your partner, leads the ♣9 and a low card is played from dummy. You win with the ♣Q and declarer follows with the ♣8. What is your defensive plan?

By contributing the ♣8 to this trick, declarer has helped you to read the lie of the club suit. Your partner would not have led the 9 from J9, 109 or J109, so the opening lead must be a singleton. (Declarer should have followed with the ♣10 instead.)

One possibility now is to continue with the ♣A and give partner a ruff on the third round of the suit. It will not beat the contract! The ♣K7 will be established for discards in spades and diamonds and declarer will make ten tricks. What can you do instead?

Since declarer has generously advised you of the club position, you should take advantage and give partner his ruff immediately, retaining the ♣A in your hand. You will lead the ♣6 for the ruff, a suit preference signal for a spade return. West duly ruffs and switches to spades. Since the clubs have not yet been set up, you are certain to score the ♠K in addition to the ♣A. That will be one down.

Take the West cards on the next deal and see if you would have timed the defensive ruff correctly:

	♠ Q J 10 ♡ A K Q ♢ K 6 5 ♣ Q 8 6 4		
♠ 9 6 5 ♡ 5 4 ♢ A 10 9 ♣ A K J 7 5	N W E S	♠ 8 4 2 ♡ J 7 ♢ J 8 7 4 3 2 ♣ 9 2	
	♠ A K 7 3 ♡ 10 9 8 6 3 2 ♢ Q ♣ 10 3		

West	North	East	South
—	1NT	pass	2♣
pass	2♢	pass	4♡
all pass			

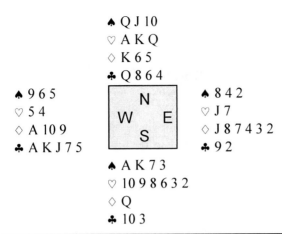

You lead the ♣K and partner produces the ♣9. When you continue with the ♣A, the closed hands follow suit. How can this contract be beaten?

By bidding Stayman and leaping to 4♡, South has shown a likely 4-6 shape in the majors. You know he began with two clubs, so a 4=6=1=2 distribution comes into focus. There is no point in leading the ♢10, hoping that declarer holds ♢Jx and will misguess; you expect him to hold only one diamond. Perhaps partner holds the ♡J and this can be promoted by leading a third round of clubs. Yes, that's a good idea!

East does hold the ♡J but see what happens if you make the mistake of leading a third club immediately. East ruffs with the ♡J but declarer will then discard his singleton diamond! The contract will survive. To beat the heart game, you must cash the ♢A and only then lead a third club for one down. After two tricks, you were almost able to write down declarer's hand.

Tips to avoid mistake 51

(Mistiming a defensive ruff)

- Giving partner a ruff may be a useful entry to his hand. If you hold an early trump entry, consider establishing tricks elsewhere and use the ruffing entry later.
- When aiming for a trump promotion, it is often right to cash side-suit tricks first.

Mistake 52

Following signals blindly

What is the purpose of the various signals that you make in defense? Many players think they will tell partner what to do next but that's not the right answer. How can you possibly know what he should do next when you can't see the cards in his hand?

The signals that you make merely tell partner something about your hand. He must combine that information with the other clues at his disposal, including his own cards. Then he decides what to do next.

Let's see some deals where a defender followed partner's signal as if it were a royal command and ended up conceding the contract.

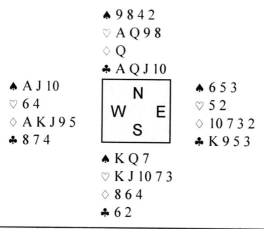

	North	
	♠ 9 8 4 2 ♡ A Q 9 8 ♢ Q ♣ A Q J 10	
West ♠ A J 10 ♡ 6 4 ♢ A K J 9 5 ♣ 8 7 4	N W E S	**East** ♠ 6 5 3 ♡ 5 2 ♢ 10 7 3 2 ♣ K 9 5 3
	♠ K Q 7 ♡ K J 10 7 3 ♢ 8 6 4 ♣ 6 2	

West	North	East	South
—	1♣	pass	1♡
2♢	3♡	pass	4♡
all pass			

West led the ♢K and dummy went down with a singleton in the suit. In such a situation, it is common practice for East to give a suit preference signal.

On the present deal East played the ♢2, since his only card of value was the ♣K. Rather than thinking about the deal as a whole, West followed partner's suggestion and switched to the ♣8. Declarer finessed, losing to East's ♣K, but the contract could no longer be beaten. East returned a spade to the king and ace and declarer won the spade return. He then drew trumps and claimed the remaining tricks, discarding the ♠7 on the clubs.

From West's point of view it seemed that the defenders needed two spade tricks. If East held the ♠Q, a spade switch would be good enough when East won with the ♣K. It was more likely that South held ♠KQx, in which case some preparatory work in spades was required. West must switch to ♠J at Trick 2! Declarer wins, draws trumps and takes a losing club finesse. East's spade return gives the defenders two more tricks and that is one down.

The main principle is clear. East's suit-preference signal was not a command to switch to a club. It merely suggested to his partner that he held the ♣K. Armed with this information, West could see that a switch to the ♠J would give the defenders a fair chance of beating the contract.

Here's another deal where West must keep his eye on the tricks needed:

	♠ 7 4 ♡ A K 8 4 3 2 ♢ A Q ♣ 10 9 5	
♠ 9 5 ♡ Q 10 9 ♢ 7 5 3 ♣ A K J 7 3	N W E S	♠ 8 3 2 ♡ J 5 ♢ K J 10 8 6 4 ♣ 8 2
	♠ A K Q J 10 6 ♡ 7 6 ♢ 9 2 ♣ Q 6 4	

West	North	East	South
—	1♡	pass	1♠
pass	2♡	pass	4♠
all pass			

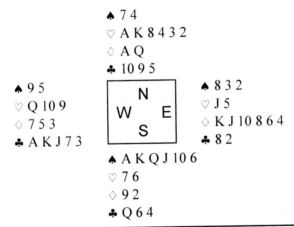

West leads the ♣K and East shows an even number of clubs, playing the ♣8. Beating the contract will be a hopeless task if East holds four clubs, so West must assume that he has two. Some players would give the matter no further thought, giving partner his ruff. On any return, declarer would be able to draw trumps, establish the hearts with a ruff and discard his diamond loser.

At Trick 2 West should consider how a fourth defensive trick can be found. When declarer has a singleton or doubleton heart, he can establish the suit for discards. West must hope that East holds the ♢K. and shift to a diamond. If declarer finesses the ♢Q, East will win and cross to the ♣A for a club ruff. If instead declarer rises with the ♢A and draws trumps, dummy's hearts will be dead. Note that West cannot afford to cash a second club before switching to diamonds. With the ♣Q established, declarer would rise with the ♢A and draw trumps.

We will end with another deal where a defender has to keep his eye on the number of tricks needed to defeat the contact:

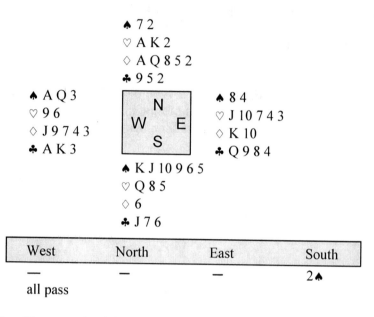

	North	
	♠ 7 2 ♡ A K 2 ♢ A Q 8 5 2 ♣ 9 5 2	
West ♠ A Q 3 ♡ 9 6 ♢ J 9 7 4 3 ♣ A K 3	N / W E / S	**East** ♠ 8 4 ♡ J 10 7 4 3 ♢ K 10 ♣ Q 9 8 4
	♠ K J 10 9 6 5 ♡ Q 8 5 ♢ 6 ♣ J 7 6	

West	North	East	South
—	–	–	2♠
all pass			

Sitting West, you lead the ♣A to ask for an attitude signal. East duly obliges with the ♣9. How will you defend from this point?

Three clubs and two trumps will not defeat the contract. At Trick 2 you put partner's encouraging signal in clubs temporarily to one side and switch to the ♡9, won in dummy. After a trump to the jack and queen, you play the ♡6. Declarer wins and plays a second trump to your ace. Only then do you continue with the ♣K and a club to partner's queen. A hard-earned heart ruff is the setting trick.

Tips to avoid mistake 52

(Following signals blindly)

- A signal is not an instruction to tell partner what to do next. It merely describes something about the signaler's hand, to assist partner with his defense.
- One of the saddest cries in bridge is: 'But you asked for a club, partner!' Your partner cannot be certain what you should do next when he cannot see your hand.

CPSIA information can be obtained
at www.ICGtesting.com
Printed in the USA
FFOW01n1103231215
19930FF

9 781771 401517